ELECTRIC DREAMS

ELECTRIC
DREAMS

One Unlikely Team of Kids and
the Race to Build the Car of the Future

Caroline
Kettlewell

CARROLL & GRAF PUBLISHERS
NEW YORK

ELECTRIC DREAMS

Carroll & Graf Publishers
An Imprint of Avalon Publishing Group Inc.
245 West 17th Street
New York, NY 10011

Library of Congress Cataloging-in-Publication Data is available.

ISBN: 0-7867-1271-6

Book design by Simon M. Sullivan

Printed in the United States of America
Distributed by Publishers Group West

To Joe and Sam

Acknowledgments

Electric Dreams is a book built upon a mosaic of individual memories; my thanks and appreciation go to everyone who graciously shared with me their stories, materials, and expertise. In particular, I am deeply grateful to Harold Miller and Eric Ryan for their enthusiasm, support, and invaluable assistance, and for submitting to my ceaseless questions cheerfully and with good grace. Many thanks also to: John and June Parker, Randy Shillingburg, Darrell Worley, Henry Campbell, Doug Miller, George Hawkins Sr. and Jr., Norman Joyner, Mary Keeter, Daniel Shields, Keith Edwards, Kelly Daughtry Manning, Jennifer Robbins, Katrina Deloatch-Smith, Pershield Deloatch, Neil Vann, Donny Lassiter, Stephanie Martin Jones, Tim Stauffer, Erick Vann, Anna Collier, Corey Powell, Theresa Williams, Ivory Richardson, Clyde Parker, Darrell Parker, Harold Parker, Walt Purdy, Bob Batson, William Hall, Bob Oldham of the Science Museum of Virginia, Hank Amann, Mark Potter, Lynn Wilson, Carol Hedspeth Lowe, Bill Sawyer, Dave Roop, Kevin Curtis, Roy Southard, Cindy Dickerson, Janet Castellini, Mike Duoba, and Bob Zickefoose.

Thank you to Ann Regn for starting me down this road; to Tim Seldes; to Phaedra Hise, Dean King, Constance Costas, Wendi Kaufman, and Doug Childers for their sage advice and for listening to all my other ideas; to Paula Kettlewell, though she wishes it to be known that she cannot condone "alright"; to Bill Craig, who knows his NASCAR; to the crews of Mas-Tec Power from North Carolina who restored our electricity thirteen days after Hurricane Isabel blew through town; and many, many thanks to Joe and Lee Sites.

Thanks to Mike Tidwell of the Chesapeake Climate Action Network for his professional assistance and for exemplifying the idea that changing the world begins at home; to my wonderful and savvy agent Jennifer Lyons and the always helpful Katie LaStoria at Writers House; to my editor, Will Balliett, for sharing my vision for this story and for bringing extraordinary dedication, a sense of humor, and an unerring eye to editing it; and thanks to a terrific team at Avalon, including Claiborne Hancock, Don Weise, Holly Bemiss, and Lorie Pagnozzi.

Finally, a thank you to all of the great teachers everywhere, the ones we never forget.

"If each one of us took a little bit of responsibility, then together we could change the world."

—Harold Miller

"That car has some get-up-and-go and it don't make no racket."

—Richard Petty

NEITHER A MOVIE STAR
NOR A SURFER BE

Baby-faced, with a bookpack slung over one shoulder, Eric Ryan entered Northampton High School–East on the first day of school, looking like someone dressed out of his father's closet.

Hallways that just yesterday had drowsed in late-summer stillness were filled this morning with the surge and noise and crackling hormonal buzz of hundreds of teenagers: the squeak of sneakers on freshly waxed floors, the rattle and bang of lockers, chatter, laughter, greetings called out. There was that unmistakable back-to-school energy in the air, the eagerness, the feeling of everything starting new again.

Eric headed for his classroom, with curious glances and a few open stares following him all the way. Obviously, you didn't get a lot of new faces from year to year at Northampton–East, or for that matter probably anywhere else here in Northampton County, North Carolina. He smiled and said hello in a general sort of way as he threaded a path down the hallway.

Then a cluster of boys, idling down the hallway toward him with the studied indolence of young men trying to give the impression that they were too cool by far to care, spotted him. They drew to a halt in front of Eric, blocking his way just enough that he would have to step sharply to one side or the other to get around them. Eric could recognize a territorial confrontation when he saw one; he had no intention of conceding the advantage to this would-be alpha pack. He stood his ground and offered the boys an affable nod to make it clear that he fully expected them to give way to him.

They remained.

"What's with the tie, man?" one smirked at last, giving a jerk with his chin in Eric's direction.

"Yeah," snorted the others. Every mob has its yes-men.

"I'm a teacher," said Eric easily. "We wear ties."

The boys froze, faces wiped blank of bully arrogance. Clearly, they'd taken him for a new student rather than someone with the almighty power of the in-school suspension. In the long second or two that followed, Eric could practically see the gears spinning, the boys wondering how bad this was going to cost them, and on the very damn first day of school too.

"Don't you gentlemen have a class you should be getting to?" Eric finally offered magnanimously.

And they were gone. There might have been a "sorry" or maybe a "thanks" thrown over a retreating shoulder, but it was swallowed by the crowd.

Not the first student encounter he would have chosen, thought Eric. But he would mark this one in the success column nonetheless.

Twenty-six years old, an honors graduate of the University of California at Berkeley, with a degree in social science, a thesis on environmental racism, and a full slate of premed courses on his transcript, Eric Ryan was the new science teacher at Northampton–East, a fact not obvious from his appearance.

A few months earlier, in the crowded hallway of an East L.A. high school where he'd been interning, Eric had pressed the receiver of a pay telephone to one ear and stuck a finger in the other and said yes, he would like very much to spend the next two years teaching science at a high school in the flat, sparsely populated, cotton-and-peanut country of northeastern North Carolina.

"You understand this isn't California now? You know what you're doing, son?" asked Henry Campbell, the principal of Northampton–East, at the end of their conversation.

Sure. Changing the course of his life.

Somewhere between noncommittal, twenty-year-old premed student and this morning, Eric had gone through his Searching Period. He dropped out of college, worked construction, made an unsuccessful stab at shipping out for an Alaskan fisherman's life, dropped back in to college, changed his major, graduated, went backpacking, and ended up spending a year teaching part-time in an alternative school for troubled youths. He learned useful things there, like the fact that not all of your students will always find your every word a pearl of wisdom and inspiration, and some of them won't ever do their homework.

But the stint in the alternative school had led him to Teach for America, an organization born of the idea that talented young college graduates who wanted to change the world could start with a couple of years serving in America's struggling rural and inner-city schools where there weren't enough teachers to go around. TFA had led him here.

Opening the door to his classroom, Eric left behind the bustle of the hallway, plopped his books and papers down on the laboratory bench that would be his desk, and studied the roster for his first class—sophomore biology. It was a big group, thirty kids who in a few minutes would go from names on a list to faces, attitudes, the beginnings of individual identities. Who might be his troublemaker, who his too-eager-to-be-teacher's pet, who his quiet genius, who the know-it-all, who the kid who would struggle all year for a hard-won D, who the one who would look like a deer in headlights whenever called upon to answer a question, and who the one who would sit sullenly in the back radiating resentment and committing petty vandalism upon the furniture?

His students began coming in, first a trickle of the prompt, followed by a steady stream. Eric greeted them as they entered; some said hello back, and some looked awkwardly at their feet and scurried to take a seat, while others were too busy gabbing with their friends to take more than the barest notice, or simply stared curiously at him as though he were the first and oddest of the experimental results they expected to encounter in the coming months. Finally the stragglers wandered in.

Eric hiked himself up so to sit on top of his desk, his legs dangling over the front.

"Good morning to all of you," he said over the lingering talk and the shuffling of feet and notebooks. The students before him might have been any random assortment of teenagers. The boys ran to slouch and untucked T-shirts and ambitious wisps of facial hair. The girls were neater, with fitted jeans and styled hair, and like girls everywhere, appeared light-years ahead of their male classmates in poise and self-possession.

They looked up at him expectantly, if a touch warily; he remained to them an Unknown Quantity, the New Guy, whose quirks and standards, mannerisms and attitudes, had yet to be established. He and his grade book would hold a piece of their fates in the months ahead. Would they come to trust him? Like him? Dread him? Resent him? Would he be fair-minded or arbitrary, a pushover or taskmaster? And he did look awfully young to be a teacher.

"I'm Mr. Ryan," said Eric, "and as all of you no doubt know, I am new here at Northampton–East. I moved here this summer from California. I look forward to getting to know all of you."

He left the introduction at that. He didn't bother to tell them that he'd come with TFA. Exactly how he'd gotten here didn't matter, and he didn't want, most of all, to give the impression that he regarded himself as assigned to some kind of hardship duty in the hinterlands. Instead, he moved on to laying out the ground rules and expectations for classroom conduct and coursework. He talked about respect. He called roll and gave an overview of what they could expect to cover in the coming weeks. Finally, he looked around the room. "Now, are there any questions?"

Hands shot up.

"Mr. Ryan, do you know any movie stars?"

"Mr. Ryan, do you surf?"

"Mr. Ryan, what you want to move here for?"

Figuring that otherwise he'd be spending the whole year explaining that no, he'd never gone out with any of the women on *Baywatch*, Eric took a few minutes to sketch an outline of the real California for them, that it wasn't all beaches and Hollywood. Though he had to admit to himself that their idea of California was not appreciably less accurate than his former notions of North Carolina.

Barely a month ago, before his plane touched down one evening at the Raleigh-Durham airport, all Eric had known about where he was going was that it was poor and it was rural and it was in the South. The picture he had made from these details had been colored in almost entirely courtesy of 20th Century-Fox and a 1974 movie, *Conrack*, with Jon Voigt as an idealistic young teacher sent to an impoverished coastal Carolina community of barefoot, illiterate children and dirt-floored houses.

Packing for his move from Berkeley, Eric sold his 1971 orange VW, Henrietta, decided against bringing his Birkenstocks, and gave his stereo to his sister. He hadn't been altogether certain that his home for the coming two years might not be some rough shack with an outhouse in the back where a CD player, hippie bus, and sandals would mark him as a godless, money-flush West Coast liberal come to stir things up.

Eric's students listened politely as he finished his synopsis of the true California. Then they started their questions again. They seemed most curious—bordering on mystified—about what unfathomable attraction could have induced him to move to Northampton County.

"But there's nothing to do here, Mr. Ryan," they said, as though possibly until this moment he had somehow missed this key point. When you are fifteen or sixteen and have lived all your life in a county with far more hogs than people, and you know that there is a world elsewhere in which soybean and peanut futures don't rate the front page of the newspaper, you may find it difficult to understand how exactly thunderstorms over the cotton fields would be worth crossing a continent for. After all, it wasn't like he had kin here.

"I wanted to experience living on the East Coast," said Eric. "I wanted to live out in the country, in the South."

As explanations went, as far as the students were concerned, this one fell sorely short. They waited for further illumination. None came. Instead, Mr. Ryan got down to business with a little game he hoped might warm things up and start them off on a good footing. Give them a sense that sophomore biology would be something they could look forward to, a little quirky, a little out of the ordinary. He blew up a balloon and batted it at the students. "When the balloon comes to you, say your name and something about yourself!" he called out.

It was a very Mr. Ryan kind of thing to do, his students would conclude when they got to know him better. Unconventional—or if you wanted to put it plainly, a little weird—and nothing any of their other teachers would ever have done. But you went along because, well, it was Mr. Ryan, and he was like that.

Down the road, when he had grown into the knowledge won only with an extended tour of duty at the front of the classroom facing hour after hour of teenagers equally likely at any moment to slip into coma or chaos, Eric himself would look back on this exercise with a rueful wince. Not that it hadn't gone fine; although a few sat with arms defiantly crossed, unwilling to risk sacrificing their cool quotient, most of the students, if not robustly enthusiastic, were willing at least to slap at the balloon and admit to their names. Still, it was such a patently too-eager new-teacher kind of game. By his second year Eric knew to take on the first day of classes like the landing at Normandy; you started working the kids almost the moment they sat down, called the roll like you were reading out a long sentence at hard labor, and you didn't let loose with so much as a twinkle in the eye before the leaves turned. Not all the powers of God nor Man can make adolescents rush eagerly to your door week after week for another helping of the circulatory system or dynamic equilibrium, but if you overawe them on day one there's a decent chance most of them will do their assignments through Christmas.

Though like any teacher, Eric would have to admit that there were moments when he wouldn't have been altogether inconsolable if one or two of his young charges had been struck with a lingering case of the flu and subsequently confined to bed and a lengthy absence from his classroom, on the whole Eric would find his students to be a pleasure. They were teenagers, of course; anything from tomorrow's test to choosing a prom dress was a matter of life and death. But they were mostly attentive and almost invariably well-mannered. They answered "Yes, sir" to his questions, and that took some getting used to, but he liked it. They were far less cynically worldly than students he had known elsewhere. They saw the same movies, liked the same music and television and fashions as kids everywhere else, and they weren't immune to the same kinds of problems, like broken families and drugs and falling in with the wrong crowd. Yet somehow so many of them seemed insulated here from the worst of the racket and hue of the wider world, wrapped in the protective layers of family and community and church on Sunday, and an extended network of friends and relations to keep an eye on them. It seemed nearly impossible to be anonymous, to fly under the radar in Northampton County.

Eric would be surprised to learn how many of his students had never even traveled outside of northeastern North Carolina, and to discover, one day in a class discussion, that some of them were under the impression that in the rest of the United States, just as in Northampton, white people were a minority and most of the population was black.

ENERGY RUSH

Whatever there was to be presumed, conjectured, or rumored about the new science teacher at Northampton–East, it had made the rounds of school long before Eric met with his last class on the afternoon of his first day. Reports ran to the favorable, with the general caveat that he was a little odd, maybe, but in an agreeable way. There was heavy traffic in the debate over just how old he was (or wasn't), and considerable speculation as to the real reason that had landed him in Northampton County—the story Eric himself having put out, that he had come voluntarily and even enthusiastically, having been roundly dismissed as beyond credible. There was much anticipation regarding what might yet be revealed about Mr. Ryan that would notably diverge from the East Carolinian norm, with high hopes for something really good and California out of him, though what exactly that would be no one was quite certain, as it appeared that he did not, in fact, surf, or know anyone famous, or drive a Porsche.

The weeks passed, however, and the demands of school life—homework assignments, team practices, club meetings, tests, social maneuverings, pep rallies and game nights, college applications and driver's ed—soon relegated the matter of Mr. Ryan to not much more than the occasional brief hiss of background noise.

The principal at Northampton–East, Henry Campbell, who had developed a fine instinct for a good teacher after all of his years watching the new ones come, and observing who stayed and who left, who thrived and who floundered, had sized up Eric in that one telephone interview, and his initial estimates were proving accurate— Eric was doing just fine. The students had taken to him, his lessons were organized and his classroom well-managed, and Campbell was altogether delighted to have him.

Then one morning in November, Mr. Ryan came to school wearing a dress. A white dress, a flowery, feminine froth of a dress with a wide lacy collar and splashy floral embellishments, that he had borrowed off the Spanish teacher, Miss Carroll. He had accessorized with running shoes and a strand of cheap costume pearls.

True, it was Switch Day, that part of Spirit Week when boys were supposed to dress as girls and vice versa. It was also true, however, that on that particular Switch Day—and indeed quite possibly in the entire history of the Northampton County Schools, Eric Ryan was the only teacher to show up for work possessed of both a Y-chromosome and a hemline.

The verdict was not yet in on Eric. He was friendly enough, certainly, and enthusiastic. He'd jumped right into the life of the school, no faulting him on that point. In the brief time since he'd arrived—and in this part of North Carolina "brief" was anything short of a couple of generations—he'd made a good impression on everyone he met. But still. There was that free-thinking California pedigree, after all, and though he claimed a girlfriend back home, he had produced no actual supporting evidence on this point, and the fact was that he lived with another man in a house whose former bachelor residents had been a couple of florists. A person could wonder, was all.

The kids mostly laughed out loud at the sight of him, astonished peals of laughter bursting out in Eric's wake as he walked the hallways. Some of the girls—the ones already a little bit sweet on him, because he was young and cute and he *wasn't* from northeastern North Carolina, which was as good as exotic as far as they were concerned—they maybe rolled their eyes a little bit and said, "Mr. RAH-yinnn" with indulgently exasperated giggles. And some of the boys, the ones inclined to regard Mr. Ryan with suspicion for almost exactly the same reasons that the girls liked him, maybe they muttered darkly out by the lockers about what it all might mean.

Not given to self-consciousness, and for that matter not yet well-enough versed in how eastern North Carolina wasn't northern California to recognize the degree of consternation he might have been setting off around the coffee pot in the smoke-heavy teacher's lounge, Eric grinned his way through the minor uproar and even managed eventually to get his students to pay more attention to their lessons than his getup. By the end of the day, though, when the bell had rung, he was ready enough to be done with the dress and the pearls, looking forward to shorts and a T-shirt and maybe a cold beer at home, and laughing it over with his new housemate, Tom Sherry. But first there was the regular Wednesday afternoon faculty meeting in the auditorium to get through. Eric lingered in his classroom for a minute, straightening up from the day's work.

As he was stuffing a few papers into his backpack, the usual end-of-day chatter in the hallway came to an abrupt stop. Eric heard stifled shouts from outside, a girl's high-pitched squeal, footsteps rushing past his door. He looked up and listened, parsing the indistinct array of sounds, hoping it didn't all add up to what he knew perfectly well it did all add up to. A fight.

Eric suppressed a sigh. He'd broken up a fight or two in his brief time in education. He had a wiry distance-runner's build, beefed up by working construction, and he wasn't afraid to wade in and bruise a knuckle if need be. Still it wasn't a prospect he looked forward to. You never knew what you might be getting into when you stepped into the middle of a scuffle. But as his classroom was closest to the parking lot, where all the commotion was coming from, it looked like he was stuck with this one. He headed for the hallway, squaring his shoulders even as he hoped that he'd be able to settle it all with a sharp word and the threat of consequences.

Then it occurred to him that he was wearing a dress.

Well, nothing to be done for it now.

To his relief, when he reached the door to the outside, it seemed the fight had dissipated. The crowd was beginning to drift apart, pulling the apparent combatants away in opposite directions to the tune of a few lingering, unintelligible curses. Eric stood waiting to make sure things stayed quiet; he'd return to his classroom in a minute to write up a quick report, and then scoot on to the faculty meeting.

But then there was a flash of motion. One kid coming back at a dead run, looking like murder or worse.

Amid an outburst of resurgent shouting, Eric, on a rush of adrenalin, pushed past a couple of students, took a few running steps, and launched himself at the aggressor in a full-body tackle. The two of them hit the blacktop with a hard thud. Eric's pearls scattered.

The dress came through miraculously unscathed. The police cruiser came for the troublemaker, a student who appeared to have been making free with psychoactive substances. And thereafter, the question of Eric Ryan seemed to be settled satisfactorily for all concerned.

NORTHAMPTON

Not long after arriving in North Carolina, Eric bought himself a secondhand pickup, '87 Toyota, in red. Accustomed to California's clotted freeways, the sprawling subdivisions piled one on top of the other, he could hardly get enough of the sheer open space in this part of North Carolina; there were more people enrolled at Berkeley than inhabited the entire 536 square miles of Northampton County. He could drive along, elbow propped in the open window, and acres could pass between houses, and five or ten minutes tick by, and sometimes even more, before another vehicle might come along headed the other way. And every now and then, someone sitting out on a front porch, someone Eric didn't know and probably never would meet, raised a hand in a leisurely wave when Eric drove by.

The first day Eric had traveled these roads, he'd been riding shotgun in Tom Sherry's Honda, watching mile after mile of fields, cotton and peanut, soybean and corn, rolling away in all directions across a nearly flat countryside interspersed with scrubby marshlands and thick stands of pine and oak like towering green walls. Eric, so recently transplanted from a California burnt brown by late summer, was mesmerized by the runaway, pell-mell riot of growing things here in North Carolina, the pallet of shades from palest chartreuse to deep evergreen, the vines running rampant over fence lines and wrapping around tree trunks and utility poles, everything shoving and twisting in a greedy rush up into the sunlight. Kudzu smothered whole swathes of the roadside and fell in dense, impenetrable curtains of broad leaves from the tallest trees.

Tom, a Colby College graduate going into his third year with TFA in North Carolina, easily negotiated a tangle of indistinguishable two-lane roads, pointing out landmarks and quirky local features: "That's a dance club," he said, waving toward a small, white, cinder-block box of a building that might equally have served as a road crew's storage garage; "That's a family cemetery," he said, directing Eric's attention to a single, enormous shade tree, surrounded by a small iron fence, standing alone in a field.

Single-story bungalows with rusting metal roofs sat propped a few feet off the ground on square brick piers instead of foundations— that would never fly back home in the land of the earthquake. Front porches were populated by anything a body could sit on: a broken-down sofa here, a wooden swing there, lawn chairs, and the occasional bench seat out of a car. There were fading pink and turquoise trailer homes and new-model double-wides with carefully landscaped front gardens. There were low cinder-block houses and red-brick ranchers, and sometimes it appeared a family had simply moved fifty feet forward on a piece of property, built new, and left the old home to raze itself in slow collapse beneath an overgrowth of vines. There were weather-worn barns, some of them sagging into ruin too. Eric caught an occasional glimpse as well of a graceful farmhouse with dormered windows and tall chimneys, set at the end of a long drive.

Neither precious nor manicured, the country they were passing through offered no quaint bed-and-breakfasts or pricey antique shops. It wasn't Hollywood bucolic, it wasn't the kind of setting you could imagine filled up with weekenders searching for fresh air and asking for arugula at the farm stands.

That was fine by Eric. He thought it was a beautiful place, working land, land that had been lived on without being worn out.

Every dozen miles or so, the road would take them through a small town; they hadn't hit one yet that amounted to anything more than a few blocks of houses clustered together with maybe a two-pump gas station, a couple of shops, and a grocery no bigger than a convenience store. No McDonald's or 7-11, no mini-malls, no cul-de-sac neighborhoods.

On the other hand, the towns weren't quite Andy Griffith's Mayberry either. You could get away with calling the unadorned countryside "rustic," but these little burgs were testimony to a former prosperity now lost, with empty main-street storefronts, shuttered banks, and homes dating back to the 1920s and '30s, solid and respectable like the matronly members of a ladies' garden club, but now weathered and worn, with once-white paint peeling from sagging porches and dry-rotted gingerbread trim.

"This is Scotland Neck," said Tom as they slowed for one brief sketch of a town. "This is Rich Square," he said as they passed through another. "This is Woodland."

As they headed along yet another nondescript stretch of two-lane blacktop, Tom suddenly announced, "Well, here you are," and swung into a semicircular drive to pull up in front of a squat, beige building. "Northampton High School–East."

Eric just looked for a moment before getting out of the car, taking it in, absorbing the details of the place, like a hopeful groom meeting the bride for the first time on the eve of an arranged marriage.

Northampton–East was a bunker of a single-story building, brick and cinder block, from the mid-century, fallout-shelter school of design. Two rectangular wings joined by a covered breezeway, it sat like an "H" turned on one of its long sides, in the middle of a big flat patch of open ground. There were towering, gangly pine trees at its back, a crabgrass lawn out front seared brown by the August heat, and an empty asphalt parking lot on the left as they'd entered the grounds, which had been colonized here and there by a few determined weeds.

It was so quiet he could hear birds calling, and the air was filled with a strange whirring—the sound of dog-day cicadas, the sound of late summer.

Eric could go in and have a look around, Tom said, check out his classroom, introduce himself to the principal and whoever else was about, take his time.

"I'll be back to get you," he called, driving off with a wave.

The trip here, dodging along one snaking, no-shoulder road after another, had left Eric vaguely adrift, with no real idea where he was. Now, standing alone in the silence and hot sunshine, he savored the not unpleasant thrill of such complete disorientation, a feeling that every possibility lay open for him.

He stepped inside the high school. The front door banged shut behind him, the noise echoing in a lobby suffused with the scent of floor wax and the hushed, expectant feeling of a school waiting for students.

The administrative office, however, was churning busily on through the ceaseless academic tide of official documentation and duties, the reports, the transcripts, the supply orders and budget reconciliations, the class rosters to be composed. A typewriter clacked away and the phone rang.

"Hello," said Eric to the woman sitting at the typewriter. "I'm Eric Ryan. I'm . . . the new science teacher."

"Well, hello there," she said, smiling.

She seemed perfectly happy to set aside whatever she'd been working on, asking him when did he get here, was he settling in all right, how did he like North Carolina so far, probably it wasn't much like California, was it—as though of all the many matters she must certainly need to attend to today, none was of greater moment than Eric Ryan, who had just showed up out of the blue.

"Now, let me get Mr. Campbell for you," she said after a minute or two of this. "You just hold on a sec."

She slipped away and in a moment returned in the company of an older man, in his late fifties or early sixties perhaps, a man of ramrod-straight bearing who looked like he could stare down a hurricane. Eric got the immediate impression that Henry Campbell was a man who chose his words with deliberation, though at the moment he was beaming, reaching out to envelop Eric's hand in a warm shake and expressing himself delighted to welcome Eric to North Carolina and Northampton–East.

And he was. Finding a new science or math teacher had become a near-annual ritual for the principal. They came, and then they went, because they could go, because everyone wanted science and math teachers, and what could Henry Campbell say to keep them in Northampton when they told him that Raleigh had offered more money or Charlotte was recruiting—the barbecue's better here?

It took a certain kind of person to be willing to come a stranger to Northampton County and stay long enough to find a place here. As he turned Eric over to the vice principal, Mr. Campbell was hoping, as he always did, that Eric Ryan would be one who stayed.

With the vice principal, Eric was guided through the two wings of Northampton–East. The school had been built in 1964, and apparently hadn't come in for much in the way of major renovations since; it had that careworn look of several decades of heavy use. At last they came to the door of Eric's classroom, the light was thrown on, and the vice principal slipped politely away to leave Eric to make himself at home.

It was a little cramped for a laboratory, and the walls were scuffed, the paint job in sore need of refreshing, and the blackboard ghosted with the remnants of marks that could no longer be fully erased. But Eric and his *Conrack*-fueled imagination had been prepared for tar-paper walls and the kids sharing a couple of battered old desks, and instead he found rows of entirely serviceable laboratory benches fitted out with sinks and gas nozzles, and a microscope camera, even lasers. He peeked into his supply room, and then he stopped to take a longer, surprised look and wasn't sure whether he ought to laugh or break into a run; from what he could see, accumulated on the shelves appeared to be enough volatile chemicals to blow a large chunk of the school halfway to Raleigh. That room would need some thorough inventorying, he thought, backing out carefully.

Standing there, breathing in the faint aromas of chalk dust and unstable compounds, it occurred to Eric that the place he'd been trying for months to frame in his imagination had been realized in *this* classroom, this blackboard, those laboratory benches, this particular supply room that had suddenly become his responsibility. The corridors outside his door led to places that would soon be mapped into his memory—the cafeteria, the library, the gymnasium. The empty seats would be filled by students, every one a stranger to him right now, people he could pass in the street with no glimmer of connection. But within a month, six weeks, they would become a familiar procession of names, faces, quirks, habits, and mannerisms. Eventually, he knew, it would be hard to remember *not* knowing them.

DAMN YANKEES

M r. Ryan's students had never had a teacher quite like him, and it wasn't just that business with the dress, either. He had zeal, he had zip, he had enthusiasm; he was so excitable, always jumping around and whooping, hopping up to stand on top of his desk, and slapping a big "AWESOME!" on the page if you turned in a good lab report. He'd tease and joke too, say "yaawwl" back at them with exaggerated slowness, and when they'd ask him how old he was, he wouldn't tell.

At the same time, if you went to him with a question or a problem or a concern, he would focus all his attention on you and make you feel that whatever you had to say was important to him, that he really wanted to hear it and cared what you thought.

Mr. Ryan was a kind of human Cabinet of Wonders to them, constantly springing odd and unexpected things upon them. Every other classroom in the school had a blackboard, but Eric dispensed with his and propped in its place a dry-erase board, the first many of his students had ever seen, and certainly the only one they'd seen fashioned from a piece of coated pressboard otherwise normally used for a shower stall. He liked to go about lessons in unusual ways as well, getting his kids to act out the busy life of a cell, for example, with the mitochondria in hard hats and a kid pushing a shopping cart for the endoplasmic reticulum. Or he might assemble them in the parking lot and drive his truck back and forth in front of them while dropping tennis balls out the window, to illustrate vectors and projectile motion and the concept of unequal forces acting on things.

He required all his students to keep journals, posing questions for them to respond to, which some days had a scientific angle and some days did not; he wanted them to question and ponder and imagine. A boy in one class aspired to be a punk-rock guitarist, so Eric let him bring his guitar and Eric brought his harmonica, and before class started one time they did a quick jam for the other students, who gave each other looks that wondered, "Are teachers supposed to do this?"

You'd see him with the white stick of a Dum-Dum sucker protruding like Popeye's pipe at a jaunty angle from between his jaws. He made regular pilgrimages to the Wal-Mart in Roanoke Rapids to maintain the supply of candy he kept on his desk for his students, too, in delicious disregard of the standard schoolteacher's policy of treating classroom consumption of fireballs, Mary Janes, and butterscotch drops as the gateway drug to a life of gutter-dwelling dissipation.

Eric did everything he could, too, to make the world beyond northeastern North Carolina tangible to them; he brought a jar of ocean water from California so everyone could say they'd put their fingers in the Pacific. When he flew to Vermont for the weekend to visit a friend, he came back to school carrying a foam cooler full of snow.

Sometimes he even shook them up a little bit, like the time he scrawled an enthusiastic "Bitchin'!" on Kelly Daughtry's journal entry.

Kelly stared at it, thinking, "I can't show this to my mother."

After class, she approached Mr. Ryan tentatively. "Um, Mr. Ryan," she said, very gently, as though to a small child or a dubious madman, "I don't think you're supposed to *swear* in school."

Eric suspected he might not always be grasping all the nuances that came with hauling yourself across the country and plunking yourself down uninitiated in a place like Northampton, where you could meet people who'd gone their whole lives hardly ever venturing past the county line and sometimes not even as far as that. Once, early in his time in Northampton, Eric had gotten lost while driving the web of back roads. He knew he was only a mile or two from the high school, and he stopped at a house to ask directions. The people there, who clearly had lived in that house for many years, conferred among themselves for a moment. Then they turned to him apologetically. Sorry. They didn't know.

Unless you were Eric Ryan, chances were that if you lived in Northampton County you'd either been born in the neighborhood or were attached by blood or marriage to someone who had. Coming new and kinless, Eric understood he'd stepped blind into the middle of an intricate and invisible tangle of personal histories and local lore and customs and the long memories of families who knew all each others' relatives as well as they knew their own.

It took Eric awhile to figure out that you went to the back door when you were stopping by people's houses for a visit, and for quite some time he had no idea what people meant when they spoke of the "boot" of the car. He made the mistake of wondering out loud to one of his classes about all the treehouses oddly scattered around the woods and fields; after the students finished hooting with laughter—and that took awhile—they told him those were deer stands for hunters. He learned that homes flying a flag displaying nothing but a stylized "3" or "9" or "22" next to the Stars-and-Stripes were declaring their loyalties to a particular NASCAR driver. He found out that Ralph's was where you went for barbecue and hush puppies, and a BC Powder was what you took for a headache. He acquired a taste for sweet tea and for that handy and presciently gender-neutral word "y'all." He decided that the smaller the church-house, the more unabashedly exuberant a name it was inclined to display—Holy Ghost Power of Deliverance, Inc., or Faith Tabernacle Oasis of Love International Church—and that the Lord popped up with some regularity in casual conversation, appearing not as a distant and inscrutable deity but rather more like a venerable and well-loved member of the family, a fixture in daily life, referenced often, who could be relied upon for good advice and a firm hand of support when it was needed.

Nobody told him that while Henry Campbell went by "Jake" among his intimates, no one could remember anyone in the past twenty-four years at Northampton–East actually presuming intimacy enough to call him by that nickname, or even by his first name, or by anything other than "Mr. Campbell." Eric did not know this every time he said "Good morning, Jake" and "See you tomorrow, Jake." Mr. Campbell, who was well satisfied with Eric Ryan, just smiled and said "Good morning" right back.

Eric was from California, after all, famously a land of oddballs, weird ideas, and loose morals, and for his misfortune of not having had the good luck to be raised right in North Carolina, the prevailing sentiment seemed to be that he was more to be pitied than censured, and his lapses overlooked.

Fortunately, Eric didn't mind laughing at himself. He didn't mind when people teased him for his West Coast ways, when they'd ask about California as if its customs and people had originated in some distant solar system, when they'd shake their heads in mock resignation and sigh, "You are such a Yankee," a term that until then Eric had no idea anyone used anymore outside of a history class.

"Well, there are Yankees and damn Yankees, you know," they'd tell him with a guileless smile. "And the damn Yankees are the ones who come here and stay."

He was pretty sure they were joking.

Northampton–East lay a few miles from the county seat of Jackson, where the courthouse square was listed on the National Register of Historic Landmarks, and a few miles from Woodland, where Eric found a place to live—with his fellow TFA Tom Sherry. The two of them rented a house together, a six-bedroom pile of a 1920s mansion, pretty much the last place where Eric would have pictured himself putting his feet up in North Carolina. Wandering through it the first time, Eric stared around in amazement, feeling as though he'd entered a museum. It was stuffed to the gills with antiques and oil paintings. Someone's Civil War hero, in full Confederate officer's regalia, stared commandingly down from a portrait in the hall. There were white columns out front and a screened porch on the side. In the attic—a classic attic, enormous and shadowy—a huge whole-house fan rumbled deafeningly when you turned it on.

Woodland, too, came as a surprise. Like nearly all the local towns, the whole of it could be counted in blocks, but it revealed itself to be a stronghold of socially progressive Quakers and a hotbed of environmental activism of all unexpected things; the town was in the thick of fighting a pitched battle against a corporate monolith determined to put a hazardous waste incinerator in Woodland's collective back yard. Friend had been pitted against friend in the fight. At a critical public hearing the year before Eric arrived, proper Southern ladies lay down on the public thoroughfares in protest, two dozen highway patrol cars and a police bus with bars over the windows were called in, and arrests were made. One of the town's Quaker residents ran for mayor on an anti-incinerator platform and won by three votes in a bitterly contested election.

When Eric arrived in Woodland, the proponents were still pressing their case by arguing that the incinerator would augur a more prosperous future for the community, and what other industry was going to bother with a place like theirs? The opponents remained staunch, taking umbrage at the presumption that the town was so poor and so desperate that it should ransom its clean air for the sake of a handful of jobs and a corporate name on the county tax rolls.

Still, Northampton was one of the poorest counties in North Carolina, a fact the people who lived there got tired enough of hearing. Its population had been in steady decline since the 1950s, and by 1990 there were fewer residents in the county than in 1900. Median household income lagged by more than 30 percent behind the state as a whole, barely half the adults were high-school graduates, and fewer than 10 percent had completed college. The booming university-technology center of Raleigh-Durham-Chapel Hill, with its high-paying information-economy employers, lay barely two hours to the west, the tourist-rich beaches of the Outer Banks an hour to the east, but somehow, the prosperity of the souped-up New South continued to elude Northampton County, and not only Northampton but this whole northeastern region, struggling along year after year, getting by without ever quite managing to get ahead.

Yet for all the dispiriting statistics, the homes in need of painting, or the cobwebbed windows of empty shops, Northampton County defied you to call it forlorn or forgotten. There were late-model pickups on Northampton's roads, satellite television and VCRs, computers at the high school, microwave meals at the Be-Lo market in Jackson. The economic boosters maintained a cheery confidence, and whatever the census reports said, you rarely heard anyone in the county itself talking as if theirs was a lost cause.

When church was letting out on Sunday; when Eric drove by a family reunion, 150 or 200 people strong, everyone in matching T-shirts, with barbecue smoking on a big grill and long picnic tables dressed up with checkered cloths and covered dishes, and a passel of kids chasing each other under the trees; when he never saw a person homeless and sleeping in a doorway; when the local paper devoted entire columns to who visited whom at the rest home, and who gave a pantry shower or bridesmaid's luncheon to the just-wed Mrs. Smith (and by the way, buy one half-gallon of Yoo-Hoo, get one free at the Food Lion in Ahoskie), he knew there was no poverty of community here.

Eric had lived in four different cities in his life, none of them the ones that either of his parents had grown up in. He'd lived in seven different counties, eight homes, and three apartments. That made him not in the least atypical; almost everyone he knew had relatives scattered like buckshot across the globe and could name a list of zip codes they'd occupied by the end of college.

But in Northampton County, families had roots down to the bedrock. They could show you where their granddaddies and great-granddaddies had been born, and sometimes that meant just pointing to the bedroom over their heads. They could name cousins by the dozens, aunts, in-laws, lifelong friends, first loves, youngest children, all of them living within thirty miles. People hung on, made do, got by here because this place meant "home" to them in a profound and enduring way—it lived in them as much as they lived in it. Even the kids lured to Raleigh or Charlotte by the promise of more jobs, more excitement, often came drifting back, put off by the noise and the crowding, by having to worry about locking their doors, by living where neighbors stayed strangers. They'd return home and say, "Yeah, I lived in Chapel Hill once," in a way that made it clear they were in no hurry to repeat the experience. They'd marry and watch their own children running around happily blowing dandelion puffs and wading in a muddy spring stream with the children of people they'd gone to high school with, and wonder whatever made them think they'd find something better somewhere else.

It wasn't hard to see what had brought them home. As the weeks and months of his first year in North Carolina unfolded, Eric would come to love how people here said "Have a nice day" like they really cared if he did, when back in Berkeley you'd have to deconstruct a line like that for its ironic subversions. He loved the North Carolina accent, the way it took a word and stretched out the vowels like pulled taffy until the consonants were just little props straining to hold up those languishing o's and ah's, the way it added syllables where there weren't any and dropped them where there were, so that "now" came out as "nye-oh" but "Eric Ryan" ended up more like "Erk Rhine."

He loved the thick heat of summer that lingered far into the autumn months, the air hanging sluggish and dense with humidity, and he loved the quiet of the evenings, when mist pooled in every hollow and dip, hovering ghostly over the fields. He loved how deer and wild turkey would slip from the shadow of the woods at twilight, and the way spring thunderstorms came crashing over the cotton fields like the wrath of God. He loved, too, how frogs hopped by the heedless, amorous hundreds onto the roadways after those storms, and the way, just at that moment when darkness washed over the last wisps of an August day, the fireflies would rise up from the fields to jewel the evening with winking pinpoints of yellow-green light.

He loved these things, and the stillness that settled over the empty hallways of the school when the kids were gone at the end of the day, and how no one ever seemed to worry about being in a hurry for anything, how they'd sit down for a chat like they had all the time in the world and would be perfectly happy to spend every minute of it on you. When Eric first arrived, in the few weeks he had to prepare before school started, people had kept stopping by his science classroom to welcome him, and it took them each a couple of hours to get done saying hello.

That first year at East flew by in a blur of getting the hang of it all. There were lessons to prepare and students' names to be learned and tests to be graded and grades to be entered and six-week report cards to be filed and parent-teacher conferences to attend.

Eric was not immune to that unnerving, new-teacher's niggling suspicion that he was staying only one trick ahead of his students. To them, he was the one with the answers, because standing at the front of the classroom with the "Mr." before his name and the grade book on his desk conferred upon him that authority. Eric knew, though, that his last science classes at Berkeley were four years in his past, and it was amazing how much you could forget in that time, all the fine details and sharp edges. Many nights found him with a textbook propped on the edge of the bathtub, revisiting Newton's laws and reacquainting himself with the whats and whys of the Doppler effect.

And then, God help him, eager and enthusiastic as he was to make himself part of the life of the school, Eric was an easy mark for the head basketball coach, who talked Eric into agreeing to be the clock-keeper for the entire basketball season—girls' and boys', varsity and JV, four to five hours straight on game night of pushing a button and people yelling at him and the refs getting after him, with the rules, as far as he was concerned, so needlessly complicated. If he were in charge of hell, this was the job he would hand out to the backsliders. In the spring he turned with relief to coaching track; running was something he understood, a sport of austere parameters of speed and distance.

In his own long runs each morning, Eric watched the subtle shift of days and seasons across the landscape, autumn slow getting off the mark, hardly making any headway until nearly November, when finally it brought out its paint box of scarlet and persimmon and canary yellow. Then winter like a seedy bus terminal—drab, and no place you'd want to spend more time than you had to, the trees bare and the cornfields stubbled with dead stalks, but the weather rarely getting cold enough to produce more than a raw, slushy rain. Spring rushing in on daffodils and sprays of forsythia, elbowing February impatiently aside.

Some weekends he might drive up to Virginia Beach because he missed the ocean, or to Durham because he needed a dose of university-town life: the bookstores stocked with the works of obscure philosophers and poets; the funky little alternative groceries where you didn't have to explain that tempeh was a food. He was looking less for fermented soy than a place where on occasion he could feel grounded in familiar things.

Eric regularly got together with the other TFAs, too, throwing his sleeping bag into his truck and heading for some other pinpoint on the eastern North Carolina map, where there'd be a cluster of idealistic Ivy League types on a weather-beaten back porch, drinking lukewarm beer and trading war stories from a first year on the front lines of rural education. They shared the travails of policing gum and negotiating school politics and living hours from the nearest possibility of takeout Thai, while on those porches Eric learned to smoke, because the flare of the lighter, and the smoke drifting away into the darkness, and the cigarette passed from hand to hand, seemed indispensable to those nights.

Then somehow, the year was over. The hallways emptied again, and in the quiet the maintenance staff set to sweeping up the lingering flotsam of forgotten notebooks and abandoned papers and candy wrappers. Eric turned in final grades and turned off the lights in his classroom. He packed up his things in the big house in Woodland and said good-bye to Tom Sherry, who was moving on after three years in North Carolina, and to Jake Campbell, who was retiring. Then Eric left the cotton fields and the kudzu behind and drove home to California.

HAROLD MILLER
HAS A PLAN

Eric spent the summer in Santa Monica, sharing a house with some California buddies. He saw his girlfriend. He bought a surfboard. He got a beach tan. Despite more than nine months living without the wail of car alarms or the cold embrace of the Pacific, or for that matter, a halfway decent slice of pizza within a two-hour radius or even two stoplights within twenty miles of each other, he didn't have any trouble falling back into synch with left-coast life.

In August, though, when he drove into Northampton County again, with his surfboard in the back of the truck, it felt like coming home too. What had been a rush of the unfamiliar a year before was now a welcome: the thick, lush heat, the meandering back roads, the flat countryside and the fields ripe with late summer, the first warmly sincere "You have a nice day now, hear?" in a languid North Carolina drawl, and then Northampton County, and the nineteenth-century Greek Revival courthouse in Jackson with its white Ionic columns, the high school and the still-quiet hallways and his classroom waiting for him, and finally his students crowding in to their seats on the first day of classes, some of them taller, or with different hairstyles, or with that slightly stiff, self-conscious bearing of a kid dressed in new school clothes.

It felt good to be back, comfortable, like slipping into a favorite sweater on the first cold day of fall. The weeks fell smoothly into place, the reliable rhythms of school life set in motion. He was Mr. Ryan once again, with a tie around his neck and a year's worth of lesson plans in the filing cabinet, and that don't-smile-until October policy so successfully implemented, and so much a departure from the amiable goofball Mr. Ryan of the previous September that students who were enrolled for a second class with him said hesitantly, "Gee, Mr. Ryan, you're different . . . did something happen to you?"

"We've got work to do," was his only reply. "It's time to get to it." Then he'd duck into his supply room at breaks to laugh at himself, at this sham of a serious Mr. Ryan.

Looking back on his first year as time he'd spent working out some of the kinks (balloon batting!) and the rough edges ("Bitchin'!") and learning a few hard-won lessons along the way (that business with basketball season sprang to mind), Eric was settling down to dedicate himself uncompromisingly this year to his classes. Then, on a late September morning, a knock came on his door, interrupting second-period biology. As it was not the first of the small intrusions upon the day's lesson, a note of aggrieved resignation may have found its way into the manner in which Mr. Ryan said, "Yes, come in."

Harold Miller stuck his head in and said, "Excuse me, Mr. Ryan. We're going to build us an electric car and we're going to win that competition. Come see me after class and I'll tell you all about it." Then he shut the door.

For a moment, everyone, students and teacher alike, stared bewildered at the closed door. Then the students looked at Mr. Ryan, and Mr. Ryan looked back at his students. Then they all laughed. Eric had no idea what Miller was talking about.

* * *

Harold Miller was a big guy with a big laugh and a Tar Heel accent as thick as sorghum syrup, born in Mt. Airy, where the Blue Ridge Mountains come ambling down from Virginia. For twenty-four years, he had been teaching auto technology at Northampton–East, but he had been immersed to his elbows in automobiles nearly all his life. When he was young, his family moved to a close-knit Norfolk, Virginia, neighborhood where the NASCAR #10-car driver, Bill Champion, lived next door, and the #8 driver, Joe Weatherly, was just across the street. Harold grew up with a torque wrench in his hand and a grease rag tucked in a pocket, in backyard garages pungent with rubber, oil, gasoline, and grease.

At twelve, Harold started working at a service station. By the time he could drive (legally), he had bought his first car, a 1950 Ford, and was going in for some dirt-track racing, his buddies coming around Saturday evening after the station closed to give their cars those last tweaks and final adjustments they hoped might wring out for them a winning something extra later that night at the track.

In high school Harold was taken on as an apprentice in the shop at Kline Chevrolet. By his mid-twenties, that 1950 Ford was some twenty cars in his past and Harold was moving steadily up the ranks at the dealership, learning everything he could from everyone he worked with along the way. Anything he might have missed, they covered in the classes Kline sent him to at the General Motors Institute in Michigan. By the time he'd risen to service manager, he'd done it all, from oil changes to fleet sales, and you would have been hard-pressed to find a thing worth knowing about an automobile, in sickness and in health, that Harold Miller didn't know.

When he was coaxed away to his teaching job at East, it was with the promise that if he stayed long enough in Northampton County to wear out a pair of shoes, he'd never want to leave. That proved true for a man who loved fishing the slow-rolling rivers and riding his horses through fallow fields and green forests, who enjoyed nothing so much as the unhurried leisure to sit and swap a few stories. And if those stories should run to the tall side or gather a flourish of broad embellishments over time, well, everyone ought to know that if you want the plain facts in fifty words or less you shouldn't ask a Southerner.

With a sunny and unflappable disposition, Harold turned out to be well suited for teaching teenagers. At school he was always surrounded by a cluster of kids, all of them laughing along with him. Most of them liked him so well that they never tried to mess with him, and with the just plain ornery ones, Harold could back up his bonhomie, if need be, with an implacable firmness and the brawn that comes from wrestling with automobile engines and transmissions for most of your life, so they rarely bothered trying him either. He had a knack—a gift, really—for finding with every kid some ineffable harmonic balance of mentoring, discipline, inspiration, and instruction. When they left Northampton–East, they didn't forget him. If you walked a block or two with Harold in Jackson or Weldon or Roanoke Rapids, soon enough one of his former students would be coming across the street, smiling and waving and crying, "Mr. Miller! Mr. Miller!"

What with a couple of generations of those students having passed through his classroom, and Harold Miller being the kind of guy who'd never met a stranger, it sometimes seemed as though he knew everyone in Northampton County and all their cousins as well. He couldn't go five minutes in this part of North Carolina without running across someone he could pass the time of day with and tell two loosely true stories about, and whether you'd seen him every day of your life or only met him once, he'd say, "How you doin'?" like you were his dearest long-lost friend and fold you into an exuberant, back-slapping hug.

In short, if you happened to drift within the Miller orbit, its gravitational pull defied resistance, and often enough Eric Ryan found himself basking in Harold's hearty cheer in the hallway or the cafeteria or when by chance they happened to meet in that great crossroads of humanity, the restroom.

Life as a first-year teacher, though, had been far too frenetic to leave Eric much spare time for chewing the fat with Harold in the leisurely North Carolina fashion, and the location of Eric's and Harold's classrooms in the two separate wings at East paralleled a symbolic and not unusual divide between the vocational and academic programs at the school. Theirs, then, was a friendly but largely passing acquaintance. So what Harold might want with him, Eric couldn't imagine as he headed over to the auto shop later that September afternoon. Certainly, Eric was intrigued: an electric car? a competition? It sounded interesting.

On the other hand, you didn't have to know Harold Miller very well to know that he was famously an idea guy, and that like a lot of idea guys, over the years he'd had a lot of ideas. If he gave you two over breakfast, he'd have three more by lunch and a couple ready to hand you for dinner. He was one of those people forever coming up with unlikely proposals and ambitious schemes: once, for example, he tried to put together a plan to refine ethanol from kudzu.

With Harold, though, inspiration outstripped execution by a considerable margin, so that at any given time he was likely to have a half-dozen or more projects in various stages of indefinite and chronic incompletion. His degree of disorganization was legendary. Ask anyone who knew him, and they'd tell you.

Harold would cheerily admit that organization was not his strong suit. His passion was teaching—never mind protocols and paperwork. But if his methods defied the imposition of any kind of coherence but his own, his results were beyond reproach. Harold never had any problems placing his kids in jobs, and as far as Henry Campbell was concerned, gainfully employed graduates trumped any want of order in lesson plans.

After two decades of Harold's occupancy, however, the Northampton–East auto shop built especially for him had undeniably attained a high plane of entropy. Manuals, papers, tools, grease-stained boxes rattling with dissociated parts, wires, engine components, and materials whose origins were lost in the mists of time and intended applications entirely beyond discernment, had colonized every available surface. Small drifts of oil absorbent, a substance not unlike cat-box filler, gathered in the corners and against the edges of things and under tables and shelves. Those ubiquitous, brown, pulp-paper hand towels that seemed to appear in every bathroom of every school in the known universe, here floated out of the trash cans to remain wherever they came to rest. As the crowning glory, or final blow, depending how you looked at it, the cinder-block walls of the shop were painted an electrifying yellow, an arresting kind of strobing goldenrod that remained imprinted on the eyeball long after you'd left the room.

To be fair, in his march to chaos Harold had been ably assisted by a small army of teenagers—a population never known for an overly scrupulous tidiness—going about the messy business of disassembling cars. Still, as far as Harold was concerned, if you had to step over an object or two to get where you needed to go, well, it wasn't going to hurt you, and if you needed something, he could certainly rummage about and see what he could come up with, because probably he had one, and if he didn't, there must be something else he could make do the trick.

Entering Harold's classroom at the end of that September day, Eric took it all in with a glance (and a mental note not to hire the auto technology teacher to organize Eric's laboratory supply closet) before giving Harold a friendly greeting and a "So, what's up?"

"We're gonna build an electric car!" said Harold, so excited he seemed nearly incandescent.

Maybe he didn't look like anyone's idea of an environmentalist, this autoshop teacher with his Garth Brooks cowboy hat and his clip-on ties. But it was precisely his lifelong association with internal-combustion vehicles that had led Harold to an increasing discontent with them and their manifold shortcomings.

They were insultingly inefficient, for one thing. An internal combustion engine operates by blowing up a volatile mixture of fuel and air and then harnessing the explosion, as well as possible, to a crankshaft; this is about as precision-tuned an approach as throwing strained peas at a baby in hopes that some of the stuff will make it into his mouth. Fill up the gas tank, and at best only about 20 percent of what's put in will actually go toward moving you down the road: of the rest, most is simply lost, blasted off the engine block and out the rear at broiler temperatures.

"You took the heat came out your tailpipe, you could heat your house," Harold would say to his students to illustrate the point. You might just as well drive along throwing money out the window, and that didn't set right with Harold, who came from the kind of people who didn't countenance foolish waste, who saved bacon drippings for the cornbread, used empty cans to hold nails, made relish out of the green tomatoes left in the garden at the end of the season.

Even before the evolution of electronic-controlled this and computerized that, vehicle systems had been made ridiculously complicated, noisy, smelly, greasy, clanking, whirring, tangles of hoses and belts and fans and tubes and pipes and gaskets and filters and seals and pistons and valves, most of which existed for the sole purpose of keeping the engine from choking to a halt or cooking itself into cataclysmic failure, and yet all of which parts and pieces themselves might at any moment seize up, burn out, overheat, spring a leak, slip out of synch, crack, clog, shake loose, and otherwise surrender to wear, tear, rust, and decay. In the hope (though not the guarantee) of avoiding the worst and most expensive of these contingencies, owners were advised to lay out for oil changes and tune-ups and regularly scheduled service visits. When Harold had worked at the auto dealership, the mechanics had referred to those 20- and 40- and 50,000-mile checks as "gravy work." There was a lot of gravy filling up the coffers of dealerships and local garages and the parts suppliers and manufacturers, and a cynical person might even suspect that the automakers had a powerful incentive to layer as much under the hood as possible.

At what price? Back in Harold's years at Kline, there had been many busy days when all the bays on both floors of the two-story service center were full and engines were rumbling hour after hour, turning the space hazy with exhaust. The mechanics—guys who weren't given to fussing over discomforts, guys who would shake off a contact burn or a finger sliced by the slip of a tool—would rub at their temples and curse piercing headaches, and everyone in the service department knew that the mechanics who regularly worked the second floor, where the air was worst, called in sick more often. The first-floor guys joked that they were just a bunch of pantywaists up there, and nobody seemed all that concerned, but Harold wondered, even then.

In the mid-1960s, when new models began arriving in the showroom with the first, basic pollution-control mechanisms, Harold started connecting those headaches and health problems in the shop with that exhaust the mechanics were breathing in by the lungful. The more he learned about what was actually coming out of a tailpipe—the carcinogens, the hazardous gases, the lead—the harder it was for Harold to believe that this was the best that human ingenuity could do.

He was teaching in Northampton by the time the OPEC oil embargo of 1973 ushered in gas lines, and odd-and-even rationing, and everyone suddenly worrying about how we were too dependent on foreign oil and saying how something should be done.

Since then, a couple of decades had passed, the United States had just gone to war in the Gulf, and still people were talking about how we were too dependent on foreign oil, only now the U.S. was sucking it up faster than ever, driving more vehicles more miles, smogging up the air, and dumping tons of greenhouse gases into the atmosphere. Now there were ozone alert days every summer in Charlotte and Raleigh. It didn't seem to Harold like any progress had been made at all.

When he stood up in front of a fresh new crop of students every fall, he couldn't help but think about how he and the other teachers, and the parents and the preachers and all the rest of the adults, were always talking about how you needed to be responsible and do the right thing. But what example were they setting, wasting so much of the world's resources and fouling the air and the water and the earth they'd be leaving one day to these kids and to their children and grandchildren to come?

"It don't make sense," he would say. "The Lord gave us a brain to use to figure out what's right and wrong."

Harold couldn't put a finger on just when he'd started favoring the idea of electric vehicles. But in his early days teaching, in the 1970s, he'd involved some of his students in a project to rehab a few golf carts. One group worked on an electric cart and another on one that was gasoline powered; a spirit of friendly competition arose, a challenge to a race on the school track was issued. The boys on the gasoline team souped up their engine and figured it for a sure bet, but the electric team built in a bypass to run power directly from their batteries to the motor, and when the driver flipped the switch to activate the bypass, to everyone's surprise, including Harold's, that boxy little cart shot down the track and left the gasoline team fuming in its wake. As the electric zipped almost noiselessly along the far side of the track, Harold watched with the distracted air of a man unexpectedly waylaid by his future.

Soon enough, building an electric vehicle became one of the more frequently mentioned of the schemes Harold was forever proposing. He even tried, once, to scavenge together something with parts from a junked and rusting forklift, abandoning the plan only when it turned out that most of the wiring was rotted through and too much rain and weather had rendered the rest of the components unsalvageable.

If only, Harold liked to imagine, he could somehow find a few spare months and (less likely) some extra funds. Labor, he could round up easily; you could always find kids interested in figuring out how to make something go fast.

Give him that chance, and he'd prove that electric vehicles could be so much better, so much more elegantly simple a solution to the transportation question, more efficient by far than gasoline vehicles and better for the air and the earth. No exhaust fumes filthing up the atmosphere. No oil or antifreeze to spill into the waterways. No need for a muffler—there was nothing to muffle. No need for tune-ups—there was nothing to tune. No radiator, no spark plugs, no hoses. No tailpipe, no fuel tank, no pistons.

In place of all that complexity, an admirably minimalist system: a pack of batteries wired to a motor with a single moving part. The batteries powered the motor and the motor turned the transmission and the transmission turned the wheels and Bob's your uncle.

When you stopped, the motor stopped. When you went, the motor went. A freeway packed to the horizon with EVs stuck in a traffic jam would be as silent as a parking lot. And when you got home—plug it in and fill it up for a buck in your own driveway.

"If I gave you an electric car to drive for a week, you wouldn't want to give it back," Harold would assure his friend and tennis partner, John Parker, whenever their conversation turned to the subject, which was often, because it was one of Harold's favorite topics, and because for years John and Harold played each other nearly every week, and sometimes twice in a week, and because when they were together they usually ended up spending less time addressing the ball and more dreaming out loud about how they'd solve the world's ills.

John was Northampton born and bred, from a Quaker family full of educators and progressive thinkers. He was in college when he first met Harold, working summers as a lifeguard at the local pool where Harold was president; he taught Harold's son Doug how to swim. He followed in the family footsteps and went into teaching himself—math and physics—at Northampton–East. He'd had plenty of opportunity, therefore, to observe Harold in action, both in the classroom and outside of it.

John knew there were people who dismissed Harold as the good ol' boy autoshop teacher with the endless crazy notions. If you didn't count Harold, there probably wasn't a person in Northampton County who would give a minute's credence to electric cars. But John had come to believe that Harold was one of the smartest people he knew, someone with the vision to see before anyone else the potential in ideas and people alike.

Harold was the first to insist that the school system needed to get into computers. Back when the earliest PCs, the ones with only a few K of memory, were straggling to the market, Harold had talked John into taking a class with him at Radio Shack, the two of them hunched over the little Tandys, Harold hunting and pecking one key at a time at the instructor's directions. Harold could transform the dry abstractions of textbooks into lively, hands-on lessons; John had liked to invite Harold to stop by his physics class for an inimitable Miller demonstration in circuitry and the speed of electricity and the path of least resistance.

"Don't nobody let go," Harold would warn the assembled circle of students linked together hand-in-hand to the secondary ignition system—the spark plug part—Harold had pulled out of a car and would hand-crank to generate a current. And as he was setting things up he'd say, like he was musing to himself, "Some days this works and some days it don't, and I hope this is one of the days when it do work," and some of John's students who had heard a few things about Mr. Miller would start shooting each other nervous looks, wondering if their last vision of this earthly life would be two minutes from now in physics class.

As soon as Harold started cranking, someone always did end up letting go, getting a little tingling snap of a shock, no worse than a spark of static electricity, for failing to heed instructions. Cue hearty laughter all around, then they'd all want to do it again. It was a classic Miller lesson—entertaining, interactive, succinctly instructive, and unforgettable. John only half-worried that one day Harold was going to electrocute somebody.

Now John was in administration as director of instruction for the county schools, and there was a new science teacher at East, an excitable, idealistic California kid known for jumping up on his desk and for one time coming to school in a dress, but also for really devoting himself to his students. Who happened, in that way that people intersected in Northampton County, to be living now in John Parker's house.

The Parkers had gotten to know Eric when Tom Sherry started bringing his housemate to the Friends Meeting in Woodland, where the Parkers attended. When Eric and Tom were moving out of their house in the spring, June mentioned casually to Eric, "We've got an upstairs, you're welcome to stay there until you find a place."

Eric took the offer, threw his things in his truck, and relocated to the two-story frame house built in 1863 by an earlier generation of Parkers. But if the plan was to make a temporary way station of the Parker home, soon enough it became impossible either for Eric or John or June to imagine he might actually move again. When Eric returned from California at the end of the summer, he settled into an upstairs bedroom with a capacious, comfortable sleigh bed and a view over the surrounding fields, and though he wasn't quite so young as a son to John and June, nevertheless he soon became less boarder than adopted member of the family, and it suited June just fine to spoil him a bit, even.

Eric and John started running together in the mornings, dubbing themselves the George Running Club, in honor of their town of residence, the microburg of George, named after John's great-grandfather, George Parker, and boasting a population of maybe fifty if you included John, June, Eric, and anybody who happened to be visiting from out of town. The George Running Club convened at six on the broad front porch of the house, where swallows nested in the eaves, and set off into the dawn.

As they ran, Eric and John liked to muse on the world and its troubles, large and small, in rambling, philosophical conversations surprisingly reminiscent, John realized, of the kinds of discussions he enjoyed with Harold. Eric and Harold? Nothing like each other, you might think, from a once-over of their resumes alone. If he hadn't known them both personally, John might never have seen it. But on a particular late September morning, just before John, feeling rather like a genie with a wish to grant, picked up the phone in his office to call Harold in the shop at Northampton–East, it was Eric's name that came to mind.

"Hello!" said Harold, snatching up the receiver with one hand while sorting through a pile of something with the other.

"Harold, it's John. Listen, I got to ask you something. You've been talking electric cars all this time, you think you could actually build one?"

Harold stopped sorting, but he didn't miss a beat. "Does a cat have climbing equipment?" he asked.

"Well, then," said John, "I'm going to get you your chance."

FAITH

arold thought he might have died and gone to heaven, except that heaven bore a remarkable resemblance to his shop at Northampton–East and Harold thought that God would probably expect him to keep things at least a bit neater. Had John Parker really just asked Harold to put together a team to build an electric car?

It was a competition, explained John, for high school student teams from the mid-Atlantic region, to convert standard automobiles into electric-powered vehicles. He didn't have a lot of details, he'd only just heard about it himself, but he understood that it was enough of a big deal that the Department of Energy was involved.

"There's no money in the budget for this—the team will probably have to raise most of the funds," said John.

Fine. They'd figure that out.

"I'm going to invite some of the other high schools in the area to join in, too, if they want."

Certainly. Many hands make light work. And if John wanted Harold to take on a hardened crew of recidivists from the prison down in Maury as well or, for that matter, promise to turn three backflips at the homecoming dance to get this project off the ground, Harold wouldn't object.

"And I want this to be a co-curriculum project," said John. "I want you to work with the science teacher, Eric Ryan."

Who was standing in Harold's classroom now, later on that same day, pressing for elaboration

"You and me," said Harold, "are going to put together the team and build an electric car."

And here was the part the kids were going to love. Here was the part Harold really heard in his conversation with John: Come April, they would load up their car and take it north to Richmond, Virgina. They would have a chance to test it there against all the other teams' cars in a final event. A final event hosted right smack on the track at Richmond International Raceway—a famed three-quarter-mile oval where drivers like Dale Earnhardt and Richard Petty had helped make NASCAR history.

"Just think about it," said Harold, with a faraway smile on his face. "Our kids, with a car they built themselves, driving it on the track at Richmond."

To Eric, the details between "put together the team" and "take the car to Richmond" seemed awfully fuzzy. Still, he could see right away what a great project this could be. It would take hands-on education far beyond jars of ocean water and coolers full of snow. And he had been in North Carolina more than long enough to know that for plenty of people around here, NASCAR bordered on a religion, the way so many New Yorkers take credit for the Yankees and Los Angelenos live and breathe the Lakers. In or out of season, NASCAR made the sports news nearly every day, and in the parking lot at East it seemed as though half the trucks and cars had a bumper or window sticker with a favorite driver's number or other show of fealty to the National Association for Stock Car Auto Racing. Maybe it was because NASCAR's roots, or so the story went at least, were in the whisky-running moonshiners racing around up in the mountains during Prohibition. Or maybe it was because the first official NASCAR race took place in Charlotte. So many NASCAR drivers lived in North Carolina or ended up moving there that the ones who didn't sounded like they had anyway; in the unlikely event that a NASCAR team ever recruited a driver out of Kazakhstan or Patagonia, a month on the circuit and he'd be talking like he'd never been more than fifty miles from Raleigh in his life.

What a thrill it would be for a group of their students to build a car and then have a chance to run it on a NASCAR track. And really, even if you didn't care for NASCAR, who wouldn't be excited by the prospect of getting out and driving on a real racetrack? It would have to be some serious fun.

As to what it would take to get there? Eric hadn't a clue.

The inaugural mid-Atlantic high school electric vehicle challenge had been born in the mind of one Walt Purdy, early in the preceding spring, in the grandstands of Phoenix International Raceway in Arizona.

Purdy was watching the APS 500, an event, sponsored by the electric utility company Arizona Public Service, that was considered the leading national electric vehicle competition—although, without in any manner discrediting the work of Arizona Public Service in putting the thing together, that "leading national" status wasn't exactly a hotly contested title. Electric vehicles being a pursuit of the passionate few, if Walt Purdy could have collected a dime for every one of the EV competitions existing in the U.S., he'd have been hard-pressed to scrape together enough for a cup of coffee.

Nevertheless, for the participants—including hobbyists and college teams and professional engineers—the 500 certainly appeared to be a rollicking good time. With the EVs themselves making nearly no noise at all, even up in the stands Purdy could hear the whooping and cheers of the teams down on the track.

Purdy was director of educational services for the Edison Electric Institute, the PR and lobbying muscle for the nation's investor-owned electric utilities. EEI's mission was to voice the concerns, represent the opinions, and press the goals of its members. Purdy's job at EEI, though, was to develop energy information to provide to schools and educators. In that he had come on board at EEI during the very week in 1979 of the Three Mile Island nuclear incident—a moment when the electric utilities might safely be said to have been suffering a credibility problem—it never surprised him when his overtures to schools and teachers were sometimes given a chilly reception, or that his motives were openly treated as suspect. Educators do not want to be made patsies to industry spin-doctoring. In the work he'd done for EEI, therefore, Purdy, himself a former teacher and principal, made it his aim to keep his materials educationally sound and scrupulously free of ideologies and agendas, and did not concern himself with pitching the utilities' interests or parroting their positions. Give people knowledge and let them make up their own minds, had always been his policy.

It had been Purdy's observation over the years that electricity, being everywhere in modern life, had apparently rendered itself invisible; most people never seemed to think twice about it until the power went out, and surprisingly little on the subject of energy appeared in most textbooks and standard classroom materials. Where did it come from? How was it made? How did it work?

Who knew? It just magically emerged from the socket when you plugged in a cord.

To this informational void Purdy had addressed himself while at EEI, but now, looking a short distance down the road to retirement, he was searching for a bigger idea, for a truly captivating and engaging something he could create that could stand as a legacy of his life's work.

Sitting at the raceway in Phoenix, he realized he'd found his inspiration. What if, thought Purdy, he could create an event like this just for high school students, a competition to support math, science, and technology education by combining all three within a single exciting project, setting teams of students to the task of converting a conventional vehicle into an EV.

In the next few months, Purdy pulled together his electric vehicle challenge with miraculous speed. There would be multiple competition categories, not just speed or distance, but also design, even an oral presentation, so that winning would demand a range of accomplishments and wouldn't simply be a matter of who arrived with the fastest car. A final event at a professional racetrack would give the teams an unforgettable setting for testing their conversions against each other. If it was a success, this inaugural event could serve as a template for others around the country. That was Purdy's big vision.

Since he was making it up as he went, Purdy decided to locate this first competition where he could keep a close eye on things from his D.C. office. So he invited electric utilities in the mid-Atlantic region to sponsor teams and reap the benefits of the good publicity and community relations that could come with supporting an educational competition. He asked the Department of Energy's Center for Transportation Research at Argonne National Laboratory in Chicago to bring the needed technical expertise to assembling and overseeing the rules, vehicle specifications, and safety inspections. He set his sights on Richmond International Raceway as the location for the final event, and with the help of Virginia Power, headquartered in Richmond, secured it.

With utilities signed on and the raceway reserved for the end of April, it was time to bring on the schools.

Randy Shillingburg was attending a meeting at Virginia Power headquarters one day early in the fall when he first heard mention of a high school electric car competition, or a race, or something along those lines. There would be teams from around the region, he heard. The Department of Energy was involved. Virginia Power had volunteered to serve as host.

Randy was a community relations representative for North Carolina Power, working out of an office in Roanoke Rapids. Despite the name it went by, North Carolina Power was not actually North Carolinian, except in territory. It was in fact a division—and the only non-Virginia one—of Virginia Power. It covered an area that ran from around Roanoke Rapids, a few miles south of the Virginia line along the I-95 corridor, and stretched east to the coast and down the Outer Banks.

Virginia Power had decided at some point, for the usual inscrutable reasons to which businesses with a very large number of employees with "vice" in front of their titles are given, that each of its "service territories" should have its own corporate identity. Conveniently, good political relations were served as a result by the tactful absence of the word "Virginia" from the amoeba-like foot the utility had extended far into its neighbor to the south.

Nevertheless, it was perhaps inevitable that people who worked in the North Carolina division sometimes got the feeling that their standing within the company was in the nature of the redheaded stepchild. It didn't help that the corporate headquarters were located in the fast-growing Richmond region, while North Carolina Power's territory encompassed no major cities or even particularly large towns, and with the exception of the summering destinations of the Outer Banks (which a lot of Virginians seemed to regard as a piece of honorary Virginia turf that only happened to be hanging off the coast of North Carolina) consisted mostly of nominally populated farm and forest land. Whether accurately or not, some of the power people down in North Carolina suspected that a lot of the power people up in Richmond thought *everyone* down in northeastern North Carolina was a straw-chewing hick.

If you were inclined to take that suspicious view, you might have wondered whether someone at Virginia Power, in the interest of looking good on the home turf, was trying to stack the deck for the electric vehicle competition. Because the schools that Shillingburg heard the company was inviting to compete all happened to be in Virginia, and all happened to be prestigious educational and technical centers, magnet schools known for their excellence, for their state-of-the-art facilities, and for the strong partnerships they maintained with leading local industries. One of them, Thomas Jefferson High School for Science and Technology, in Alexandria, was considered among the best science and tech schools in the whole country, a place with top-drawer resources and corporate sponsorship and mentoring programs, where nearly all the seniors could count on multiple college offers.

Shillingburg, however, did not intend to let this plan pass unprotested. How about North Carolina schools? he asked. Shouldn't there be some from the company's North Carolina territory?

To this, the power company at first gave what amounted to an indulgent corporate chuckle. The question hardly needed to be asked, did it? The state of affairs in northeastern North Carolina was no secret. They were poor down there, and there was almost no industry to speak of, much less anything you'd call high-tech. Textiles, tree products, and peanuts—that about covered it, didn't it?

That an invitation had not been extended to that region's schools was not a deliberate slight but rather a frank appraisal of economic realities. Where would a team from North Carolina Power's turf find the funds it would need, or the facilities, not to mention the expertise? It wouldn't exactly be a fair competition for such a team, now would it?

The rules for this competition were being put together by the most advanced transportation research division of the U.S. government—this wasn't going to be some kind of rubber-band and chewing-gum affair, something a couple of farmer boys could put together in the barn on a Saturday night. Was it really very likely, then, that a single school from that hard-pressed northeastern region would step up to the plate, commit time its short staff didn't have and resources its anemic and overstretched budget couldn't muster, for a competition in which clearly any team it put together would be so grossly, even cruelly out of its league?

These were the obvious answers to Randy's question, but not the ones he intended to hear. People forever wanted to write off his part of North Carolina as Beverly Hillbillies–backward, as though they were all still bathing out of tin buckets and plowing with mules. Randy knew differently. Randy could cite, in particular, the case of Tech High, a technology summer camp for rising high school sophomores that he had dreamed up a few years earlier in a brainstorming session with his boss. The first Tech High, launched at

Chowan College in Murfreesboro, North Carolina, had proved such a bang-up success that eventually three more were established—all of them at colleges in Virginia. Who, then, Shillingburg could say, was the progressive-thinking innovator, and who the follower? Whose kids could be better suited for a science-tech project like this electric car competition?

Immediately after coming home from that meeting in Richmond, Randy went to his territorial vice president and said we need to be included in this competition, and the territorial vice president went to his superiors and said we need to be included in this competition, and they were both in manner as determined and undissuadable on this point as a couple of snapping turtles with a firm fix on a passing duck, and so at length Randy was granted the go-ahead—an indulgent oh-very-well-if-it-will-make-you-happy kind of go-ahead—to prospect for any interested schools in the North Carolina Power territory. Not that a clamoring crowd of volunteers was anticipated.

"Let it be on your own head," went unspoken.

Randy knew who he would call first. John Parker had worked closely with Randy setting up Tech High and also creating a staff development program for area teachers called the Roanoke Valley Math, Science, and Technology Alliance. Say the words "integrated curriculum" around John, and you could see the gleam in his eyes. Tell him his students could have an opportunity to prove their hands-on ingenuity by going up against the best of the region's science-and-technology schools, and John would ask, "Where do I sign?" before Randy had finished saying "electric vehicle competition."

And so it was.

DOUBT

As a Quaker, John Parker was deeply committed to the principles of nonviolence. If, however, there was any time when he was sorely tempted to abandon that commitment, or at least to get really, really ticked off, it was whenever he heard someone suggesting that the solution to what ailed American education was more testing.

"Standards" was the rallying cry of the testing movement, but as far as John was concerned the only standard that standardized testing established was the dangerously deluded notion that all the different and complicated challenges of successfully educating any and every kid who walked in the door of any and every public school could be managed on the cheap with a one-fits-all solution.

Tests were easy to order up, easy to quantify and track from year to year, easy to point to as a way of saying, "Look, people are being held accountable. Something's being done." But what, really, was being done when you pretended that testing could be the quick cure for vexing and pervasive inequities between students and communities and school systems?

In a public school, you couldn't pick and choose your students. You had to take them as they came, whether they were well- or ill-prepared, whether cared for or neglected at home, whether they were surrounded by books and every material thing they ever might need or lived in a house where the electric bill didn't always get paid. It was ridiculous to suggest that the child whose parents, no matter how devoted, were minimum-wage hourly employees with high school diplomas and no health insurance, started school on equal footing with some suburban kid whose parents were college-graduate business executives with gym memberships and a three-car garage. The suburban family father's car breaks down, he takes one of the other ones to work and complains about the repair bill over dinner. The other family's car breaks down, it's the only one they have, and as there's no money to spare right now to fix it, the mother misses a couple of days of work because she has no way to get there, and she loses her job. And yet both students are presumed equally able to concern themselves undistractedly with the Roanoke Colony or long division, and in two or three or six months to spit that information back out on a test, as though children's brains were blank hard drives into which data could simply be inputted and withdrawn at will.

Testing ignored the challenges of finding enough good, qualified teachers for rural school districts like Northampton County, where salaries were lower, where it was a thirty-minute drive to the nearest mall, where nearly 80 percent of the students qualified for the federal free-lunch program, and children uncooperatively refused to leave at the classroom door all the personal issues and consequences wrought by endemic economic hardship. Testing did not take into account that studies showed that even middle-class students performed worse in economically disadvantaged school systems.

Testing set the standard that whatever their lives might be like outside school, you could accurately measure every student's knowledge, abilities, and accomplishments with a couple of hours spent filling in circles with a No. 2 pencil. It set the standard that learning was a dry procession of facts and formulas, dates and names and diagrams for rote memorization, that every question already had an answer and only one right answer, A, B, C or D, and that the only thing that mattered was getting the question right, or wrong. That there were no gray areas, no need for critical thinking, hypotheses, and trial-and-error, no "you're on the right track, now see if you can go back and figure it out."

How should students drilled on the standards of yes or no, right or wrong, black or white, confront the complicated, open-ended essay questions of life itself that waited for them on the other side of the school doors? How would testing inspire those students to reach beyond themselves?

In North Carolina, the Wright brothers, a couple of bicycle mechanics from Ohio, were so highly revered that "First in Flight" was printed on the state license plates. If ever there was a case of trying and failing and trying again, of asking questions that had no answers yet, of success in the face of long odds, who better exemplified it than Wilbur and Orville with their unlikely bid to fly?

Those were the kinds of standards John believed in. Not to stuff students full of information uniformly cut and dried and stamped out like a pack of crackers, but rather to pose them challenges intriguing enough to spark that bottomless hunger to learn and to master. To fire them to reach beyond their own expectations. For a lot of kids growing up in Northampton County, it was going to take a great deal more than knowing the capitals of all fifty states to give them a leg up in the world. It was going to take more than boxes, charts, and bullet points, education served up like broccoli or bran flakes because it was good for you. Northampton's students—all students—needed better than that. Every kid deserved his own Kitty Hawk.

The electric car competition was the kind of project that John believed could change a student's life. It could give a kid reason to care about ingenuity and perseverance and a true mastery of difficult subjects—the physics of friction and motion, the chemistry of energy, the principles of aerodynamics and acceleration, and the fundamentals of amps, watts, and electromagnetism. It would break across traditional school boundaries, combining resources and talent, science classes and vocational-technical, the kids who were good with their hands and the ones accustomed to working just with their heads, as a team, to learn from and appreciate each others' knowledge and abilities. It would make the students look beyond the world of northeastern North Carolina, to understand the science of air pollution or the politics of transportation. It would be fun.

John was one of the opponents fighting the hazardous-waste incinerator plan in Woodland, and it made him angry when the proponents argued that dirty industry was the region's best hope for economic growth because the kids out of Northampton schools simply couldn't manage the kind of high-tech skills that were elsewhere in demand.

Here was a chance to prove otherwise. If they could build an electric car, and if they could get it to run, and if they could get it to Richmond, go up against schools from across the region, these students might have a shot at demonstrating talents too often overlooked and under-recognized by bar charts and computer printouts. They would have an experience and an accomplishment they could point to, something real and tangible they could take pride in, one that wouldn't pronounce them a success or failure based on a percentile calculated in some faraway testing service headquarters. And how might that resonate in all their lives?

But looking around his classroom a few days later, Mr. Miller sensed a degree of skepticism among the members of his audience, the collective enrollment of Auto Tech I. In his students' faces, Harold read a nearly unanimous consensus of "Huh?"

Jennifer Robbins, for one, was not at all sure she liked what she was hearing.

Honey blonde and vivacious, Jennifer had the good looks and warm personality that would win her the homecoming queen's crown in her senior year. But you wouldn't want to make the mistake of writing her off as some pretty bubblehead. She was smart and driven, and she didn't believe in doing things halfway; if you weren't going to give 100 percent-plus effort, the way Jennifer saw it you might just as well stay home. When it came to Jennifer's expectations for Jennifer, 150 percent was more like it. Her schedule was loaded up with hard-core college prep classes in this, her all-important junior year, the year for laying down the grades the admissions committees would be scrutinizing most closely in the coming fall.

Jennifer wasn't the kind of girl, therefore, you'd expect to find enrolled in Auto Tech I. But the high school had just switched that year to a new schedule that left Jennifer with one free period to be filled, and with nothing else academic available to cram in, she'd committed that period to Auto Tech I. Jennifer had never been afraid to shove up her shirtsleeves and mix it up with some hard work and grime; she was here in Mr. Miller's class hoping to equip herself to take the firm upper hand in daily negotiations with the

Rustang, her fulsomely oxidized '86 Ford Mustang. She was here to learn how to change her oil and adjust the timing, speak with authority on overhead cams, diagnose trouble in the exhaust manifold.

But now Mr. Miller had just told the class they would be spending the year building an electric vehicle. An electric vehicle was not in Jennifer's plan. Jennifer wanted to say (though she wouldn't, of course, because she'd been raised right not to speak disrespectfully to her elders), "Hey, wait a minute."

Jennifer wanted to ask, "How is this going to relate to *my* car?"

"Y'all pass this around," said Mr. Miller, holding up a picture that looked as though it might have come from a magazine ad or a brochure. "This here's an electric vehicle GM is developing. They're calling it the Impact."

The picture moved from hand to hand around the classroom, each student holding it and scrutinizing it uncertainly.

It looked like a car, but not like one anyone had ever seen on a road in Northampton County. It was sleek and streamlined and futuristic. Batman might drive it for those times when the Batmobile was too conspicuous. You couldn't really imagine running over to Ralph's for some takeout barbecue and hush puppies in a car like that.

"Does Mr. Miller expect us to build *that?*" Jennifer wondered.

Donny Lassiter, his long, lanky frame draped into a seat near Jennifer's, took the picture and, looking at it, thought that everything he'd always heard about Mr. Miller and his wild ideas must be true. From a farming family, Donny was taking Auto Tech I because he thought it would help to have a general grasp of the inner workings of the engine-driven agricultural equipment he had to work with. Now it seemed that their auto mechanics teacher expected them to make a car from the ground up—and by the coming spring no less. It was a notion not appreciably more unlikely than some others he'd heard that Miller had been known to propose in his time.

Erick Vann, always agreeable and willing to go along with an interesting proposal, nevertheless wondered, "Now how are a bunch of country boys like us going to pull off something like that?"

Whereas in Auto Tech II, when Neil (no immediate relation to Erick) Vann heard Mr. Miller say "electric car," he thought of a golf cart. Something that would tootle around a parking lot at old-lady speed. When Mr. Miller said that the automotive classes would be *building* an electric car for a competition, Neil thought he was probably kidding them. The way Neil heard it, Miller had been talking electric cars for so long that around Northampton County the subject had gotten to be a minor joke.

As a rule, Neil never hesitated to express an opinion. As a rule, Neil always had one to express, which was why people sometimes said of him, "You know Neil . . ." and didn't have to say anything more to make it clear what they meant. At the moment, however, Neil didn't know what to think. The picture of the teardrop-shaped Impact was making its way around the room, and though obviously it wasn't a golf cart, just as obviously it wasn't something a bunch of high school kids were going to be building either. But Mr. Miller sounded really serious about the idea, like it was more than just the usual Miller talk.

"Mr. Miller," someone finally said doubtfully, voicing the thought on everyone's minds, "we gonna build a car like this one in the picture?"

Actually, explained Mr. Miller, they were going to *convert* a car, a regular car—gut it and rebuild it as an EV. It would have an electric motor, and it would run on batteries instead of gasoline.

On *batteries?* scoffed the students. A real car? Batteries were for *toys.*

Now the whole plan sounded more preposterous than ever. And here Mr. Miller was telling them how when they were done (not *if* he said, but *when*) putting together their car, they were going to take it to Richmond and win.

Win wasn't a word you heard thrown around all that often in Northampton County. In the kids' experience, the only thing the county ever got recognized for winning was the race to the statistical bottom. Who would be the poorest county in North Carolina this year? Who would have the lowest ranking on this scale, the worst scores on that one?

There were those in Northampton County, therefore, who would have advised Mr. Miller to adopt, at least openly, at least with his students, a more modulated and less ambitious tone. After so many decades of disappointments, of being one of the state's perennial also-rans, the best policy to pursue, they would have suggested, was to keep heads and expectations low. What you don't promise, you can't be faulted for failing to deliver.

Harold Miller wouldn't have listened. Expect everything from yourselves, was his policy. Build an electric car? Of course they could do it. Of course they could win.

"Ain't no point in showing up if you ain't gonna do something," was all he would say.

Never mind that he had no idea, at the moment, what other teams they might be going up against. That he couldn't guess how much money they might need or where they would possibly hope to find it. That Harold wasn't even precisely sure what retrofitting a car as an EV would entail. That he would be coordinating this project—that he would be making it up as he went—with that California kid of a science teacher and a still-unidentified group of students from Northampton–East, as well as teachers and students as yet unknown from three other high schools spread across two counties, who had responded to John Parker's invitation to join the team. Really, how hard could all that be?

It would simply add to his determination, then, when he learned how they had been shoehorned only at the last minute into a competition that otherwise hadn't planned on inviting them, how the whole of northeastern North Carolina had initially been written off as a collective noncontender even before the first electron was fired.

YOU CAN'T KEEP
A GOOD CAR DOWN

For a guy from Berkeley, Eric Ryan wasn't all that mellow. Notwithstanding that he knew not all that much about cars and next to nothing about electric vehicles, Eric had decided before he'd even walked out of Harold's classroom after that first brief meeting that if he had any means within his power to make it happen, they were going to have a team and a car to take to Richmond in April. Eric dove in to finding out everything he could as quickly as possible on the subject of electric vehicles.

There was a nice irony to the situation; Eric had crossed a country thinking that North Carolina would offer him the antithesis of all things California, and in the end, electric vehicles—one of the most contentious issues stirring up the California political scene—had chased him down to Northampton County.

Not long before Eric moved to North Carolina, and over the vociferous and continuing objections of the auto industry, California had declared its intentions of plucking the EV from the dustbin of history and putting it in large numbers in the garages and driveways and vehicle fleets of the state's driving public. It was a bold gesture, and for the few and the dedicated EV enthusiasts it was a thrilling turn of events, a surprise comeback for a piece of transportation technology long presumed, if not quite dead, then the nearest thing to it, like a has-been sitcom star, aging and bloated, seen only on late-night infomercials.

The golden age of the EV might be said to have reached its apex in April of 1899. That was the month that a Belgian, Camille Jenatzy, operating La Jamais Contente, an electric-powered vehicle closely resembling a torpedo on wheels, set a world land-speed record, clocking in at just over sixty-five miles per hour, or in metric terms breaking the one-hundred-kilometer-per-hour barrier for the first time. Five months later, an electric cab in New York City would nab the dubious historical honor of being the first vehicle to off an American pedestrian, one H. H. Bliss, struck dead at Seventy-Forth Street and Central Park West and thus ushering in a new century in which the two-footed would take permanent backseat to the four-wheeled.

Although future generations of schoolchildren would read the history of the American automobile as the inexorable rise of Henry Ford and the Model-T, in fact the electric car was introduced to the consuming public at roughly the same time as the gasoline vehicle, in the waning years of the 1800s. For a brief historical moment the two appeared headed for a dead heat, with the outcome by no means a certain thing. Gasoline cars were widely derided as noisy and smelly, and before the development of the electric (note the irony here) starter motor they were unwieldy to start as well. Notwithstanding H. H. Bliss, clean and quiet-running electrics were promoted as sophisticated and elegant, and in particular, just the thing for the ladies. Even Henry Ford's wife drove an electric car.

That state of affairs didn't last long.

The subsequent precipitous decline of the electric vehicle was attributable in no small part to the same problem EVs would still face at the end of the twentieth century in competing with gas cars; with gasoline you could go a long way on a few gallons and fill up again in minutes, whereas an electric vehicle was powered by a large and unwieldy pack of batteries that needed hours to recharge, took up a lot of space, and wouldn't get you as far. Adding to the EV's troubles, in the early 1900s gas was cheap and electricity wasn't, and because the electrical infrastructure was spotty at best, with large segments of the U.S. still without a grid to connect to, the plug-in car had decided disadvantages when compared to an auto that ran on gas. With a big country waiting to be explored, gasoline gained the edge.

The notorious matter of the Selden patent helped seal the EV's fate. George Selden, an attorney from Rochester, New York, applied in 1879 for a patent on an invention he'd never actually made—an internal combustion vehicle. He managed, whether deliberately or by accident, to keep the patent from being issued until 1895, at which point, unlike in 1879, automobiles were becoming a viable means of transportation.

A few years later, an electric vehicle company—unimaginatively known as the Electric Vehicle Company—bought the patent from Selden. What the company's executives wanted with the Selden patent has never been clearly determined. This was a time, though, when almost anyone with a garage, a couple of screwdrivers, and a little know-how could set up in the car-making business, and if you built fifty or a hundred, that qualified you as a major auto manufacturer. The Electric Vehicle Company's main business was making electric cabs and the batteries to run them, but its owners seem to have been suffering from a bad case of mergers-and-acquisitions fever and outsize ambitions, which may or may not have included the possibility of hedging their bets by moving into building gas vehicles as well.

Whatever their long-term plans, they immediately went ahead and tried to capitalize upon their purchase by brashly demanding, under threat of legal action, that all makers of internal combustion autos pay a licensing fee to them as holders of the Selden patent. Remarkably, quite a few of the gas automakers acceded to this demand, even banding together with the Electric Vehicle Company to form the Association of Licensed Automobile Manufacturers (ALAM). On vintage vehicles from this era you can commonly find a small brass plaque that reads "Manufactured under Selden patent."

One staunch holdout (or maybe just a sore loser—the ALAM was said to have turned him down for membership) was Henry Ford. He went ahead and made his cars without the ALAM's okay. A lawsuit ensued, and while it dragged on through the courts, the Electric Vehicle Company collapsed, dogged by allegations of financial chicanery and rumors that its batteries were no good. The company's owners were painted in the press as fat-cat monopolists, the "lead cab trust." The courts ended up ruling against the patent holders. The reputation of electric cars was sullied by association, putting the EV well on its way to quaint historical artifact, in which twilight it would linger for decades, while its upstart near-relative made a progressively more troublesome nuisance of itself.

At first it was hard to see a downside to gassing up and going. The open road called, and soon enough, Americans answered by the tens of thousands, then the hundreds of thousands, then the millions. The Sunday drive, the road trip, the family vacation, Route 66, celebrity endorsement ("I like action!" said Ginger Rogers in a 1939 ad plugging the DeSoto), the suburban dream. By 1943, Los Angeles had its first recorded incidence of smog.

It was a word that soon enough would become synonymous with the city. But at the time, with no one clear on what smog was or where it came from, it was labeled, in a nice piece of unintended irony, a gas attack.

Internal combustion vehicles were not, of course, the only cause of air pollution, but unlike a factory or a power plant, vehicles always concentrated where people did. As their numbers in the U.S. grew from a mere 8,000 in 1900 to more than 180 million by the early 1990s, their contribution to turning the air toxic grew accordingly. From fumes vaporized out of the gas tank to exhaust smoking out the tailpipe, trucks, cars, and buses spit out all manner of deadly delights: among other things, carbon monoxide (the reason why you don't want to lock yourself in the garage with a running car); nitrogen oxides, which can be thanked in part for lung-burning smog and acid rain, too; volatile organic compounds (also major contributors to smog) and other assorted offenders, including formaldehyde and the known carcinogen benzene; sulfur dioxide (acid rain again); and collectively, billions upon billions of pounds of carbon dioxide, one of the "greenhouse gases" taking the heat these days for global warming. For years, until leaded gasoline was substantially phased out, vehicle emissions were also a major source of atmospheric lead pollution. Top it all off with a nice haze of lung-damaging particulate matter (the sooty gray stuff from diesels and dirty-burning cars), and in some areas, stepping outside for a breath of fresh air went from pleasant exercise to oxymoron.

California was the first place in the country to venture an official effort at trying to do something about its air problem, with the creation, in the late 1940s, of "pollution control districts," though it would be several more years before Dr. Arie Haagen-Smit would scientifically identify smog and its precipitators—nitrogen oxides, hydrocarbons, and sunlight.

The federal government needed another couple of decades to decide conclusively that air quality was a national issue and that perhaps something definitive ought to be done to address the matter before whole areas of the country disappeared into a smutty brown cloud and people started dropping dead on street corners. In 1970—not coincidentally, the same year as the first Earth Day, and following a summer in which for days on end a large part of the East Coast was blighted by a massive, foul haze—the Clean Air Act was passed, signed into law on the last day of the year by President Richard Nixon. It was an aggressively ambitious and wide-ranging piece of legislation that, among its significant features, set upon the auto industry particularly stringent demands and deadlines: in particular, to reduce the aforementioned hydrocarbon, carbon monoxide, and nitrogen oxide emissions by 90 percent within five years.

The Clean Air Act's crafters freely acknowledged that the automobile technology necessary to achieve the Act's goals did not yet exist. The idea was to light a fire under the auto industry and force it to put its resources and engineering ingenuity to work cleaning up its products, a task for which it previously had demonstrated no noticeable enthusiasm.

By this time, however, the freedom to go wherever you wanted, whenever you wanted, in a personal transportation capsule as big and fast and powerful as you could buy had come to seem like one of those inalienable American rights. Thus, the Clean Air Act did indeed get the auto industry people fired up, but not quite in the manner the lawmakers had intended. They took it as a shot across the bow. *If this now, what next?* seemed to be their sentiment. With all the upheaval of that day, the antiwar protests and the kids turning on and dropping out and declaring their contempt for "the establishment," what nefarious long-term agendas might be lurking beneath this blithe talk of clean air? Rumblings had even been heard in some quarters about doing away with the internal combustion engine altogether.

The automakers' lobbyists and lawyers were thrown into the breach, and the battle was joined. Impossible! they cried. It couldn't be done! they insisted. They'd be driven out of business, the economy would collapse, life as we knew it would come to an end.

And yet, in spite of foot-dragging delays, and challenges, and dire predictions at every turn that would have made Cassandra look a paragon of sunny optimism by comparison, somehow—miraculously!—new automobiles got progressively cleaner and Western civilization remained standing. And for a while at least, the nation's air, taken as a whole, improved as well.

Meanwhile, though, the number of people and vehicles and the distances they traveled all kept going up, and not in direct proportion, either; in California alone, between 1970 and 1990 the population increased by half, but the count of registered vehicles nearly doubled and the miles traveled went up by 120 percent—to a stratospheric 242 billion miles. Just in California. Even with all the gridlock.

With those kinds of numbers to contend with, cleaner wasn't going to be clean enough when it came to vehicle emissions. In some places, air quality that had been fine before actually started to decline. And now there was growing unease as well over the question of global warming, and the finger of blame pointed once again at the good old American gas guzzler. Drastic measures were called for.

In 1990 the Air Resources Board of California's Environmental Protection Agency threw down the gauntlet, enacting what was known as the "ZEV mandate," which required that by 1998 two percent, and by the year 2003, ten percent, of all new automobiles sold in the state would have to be "zero emission vehicles," or ZEVs.

A ZEV, as its name implies, is an automobile that doesn't emit; it goes without gassing the planet. On that front, the choices were limited to a field of one; at the time that the ZEV mandate was passed, and indeed for the foreseeable future, for all practical purposes the only producible ZEV was a battery-powered electric.

Technologically speaking, an electric car was a fully feasible proposition. Although the EV passenger automobile had slunk into obscurity in the early 1900s, its basic components—motor and batteries—had continued in use in various other applications, where they were fine-tuned over time. Gas automobiles depended on the battery-powered starter motor to turn over the engine and get it going. Industrial forklifts, whizzing around factories and warehouses, ran on a motor-and-battery setup, as did that iconic emblem of leisure, the golf cart. The gas crisis and rising environmental awareness of the 1970s even breathed a little life back into the electric car itself, fostering the odd backyard hobbyist and a few small businesses in the work of converting standard automobiles to EVs.

But practically speaking, electrics suffered from an image problem. They seemed irrevocably tied in the public mind with golf carts, scant distances, and penny-ante power. In 1990, when the ZEV mandate was passed, there were fewer than two thousand registered EVs in the entire country.

If, however, the mandate should be successfully carried out, thousands of such vehicles could be driving California's roads by the end of the decade. And as drove California, so sooner or later would drive the rest of the country. Those both in favor of and opposed to the mandate knew that. Soon New York, Massachusetts, and other Northeast states with their own air and acid-rain problems announced that they planned to adopt the ZEV regulations for themselves.

EV, environmental, and public health advocates all cheered the ZEV mandate and the states pledging to follow in California's footsteps. To no one's surprise, however, the auto industry immediately resumed its standard howling chorus of agonized protests, the cries of "impossible" and "economically unfeasible." The deadline was too short. The technology was incompatible with consumer demand—people didn't want a car they had to plug in, didn't want a car that took hours to recharge, didn't want a car that could travel only fifty or at best one hundred miles at a go.

The ZEV hullabaloo raged on across the decade, a war waged by ad campaign, press release, legal action, and backroom lobbying, peppered by volleys and countervolleys of reports, statistics, and surveys, along with further confusing acronymic proposals regarding LEVs (low-emission vehicles) and ULEVs (ultra-low-emission), TLEVs (transitional), SULEVs (super-ultra-low) and PZEVs (partial ZEVs). Each side assailed the other's science, questioned its research, and impugned its motives. For the average observer, it was impossible to sort out all the details, much less know which side to believe.

The auto people insisted that technology simply couldn't be ready anytime soon for market-level production, that battery range was too limited, that the cost would be too high for consumers and still the industry would lose money anyway on vehicles they said would cost tens of thousands of dollars more to build than regular automobiles. Jobs would be lost. The economy would suffer. It was a familiar refrain reprised from the 1970s. Yet how could they have responded otherwise? Theirs was a vast industry, from suppliers and manufacturers to the Jiffy Lubes and Pep Boys and corner gas stations, all dependent upon the construction, care, and feeding of the internal combustion vehicle. Electric vehicles needed hardly any of that—no fill-ups, no tune-ups, no gazillion inscrutable parts to replace, no gravy work. From their point of view, EVs didn't signal opportunity, they portended disaster.

On the other side, the ZEV proponents, not without reason for suspicion, suggested that the auto people, with a documented history of efforts to foil every new attempt at regulating their industry, were mounting a conspiracy to sink the mandate. They were trying, accused the ZEV advocates, to suppress demand and sabotage the EV's chances of catching on with the public through a veritable smear campaign of badmouthing and negative PR, overestimating the price and underestimating the capabilities of electric vehicles. GM was particularly difficult to figure, praising its prototype Impact as the car of the future and then turning around and suing the California Air Resources Board to overturn the mandate.

Harold Miller had picked up that picture of the Impact—the one that he'd shown his class—at a presentation he'd attended the year before, given by GM, to plug the new EV. But when he'd shown real interest, he'd met a miasma of obfuscation.

When would the Impact be available? asked Miller.

They couldn't say.

How much would it cost?

They couldn't say.

Could he buy one? He'd pay cash.

They couldn't say.

Could he put his name on a list at least?

He gave his name and never thereafter heard a word from GM.

Fine. Harold didn't need GM anymore. Harold had his own EV production plan in the works—if you could call two teachers with a nodding acquaintance, and no team, no money, no car, no parts, not even a textbook between them a plan.

THE BOYS IN BOSTON

Not everyone in Northampton County shared John Parker's esteem of Harold Miller's methods. Not everyone could look at Harold ("You ever seen his classroom?") and Eric ("Wasn't he the one came to school in a dress one time?") and hear "electric vehicle" ("What kind of a damn-fool idea is that?") and manage the leap of faith to believe that the two of them could take this project from zero to sixty, much less get it across the finish line in time. But John Parker's boss, the school superintendent, believed in John, and believed what John believed in, which was that northeastern North Carolina's kids could prove themselves against anyone.

Bureaucratically induced torpor is the order of the day in most school systems. Every contingency moves sluggishly through its designated policies, procedures, and paperwork. Nothing short of a bomb threat, boiler explosion, or outbreak of the plague should be expected to hasten things along, and requests for funds, in a district short on same, can be assumed generally to be subject to a particularly dilatory pace. So it was a measure of the superintendent's support that when John Parker went to him and said *I need money to send two teachers to a conference in Boston next week,* he got it. A commuter-flight-and-two-to-a-budget-hotel-room sum was pried loose from a carefully husbanded staff development fund.

The conference, sponsored by the Northeast Sustainable Energy Association, was all about alternative transportation; Eric had stumbled across some information about it while in the early throes of his crash-course research on electric vehicles. By one of those serendipitous bits of timing with which we are sometimes blessed, the conference was scheduled to take place in just over a week.

"Maybe I should try to get up there," Eric mused out loud to John Parker. John made the maybe a definitely.

"Meet me at my house in Murfreesboro Friday after school," Harold instructed Eric.

Although they had left reasonable time for the ninety-minute drive to the Norfolk airport in Virginia, where they would catch a flight to Baltimore and then change planes for Boston, Eric arrived at Harold's home early and antsy to hit the road. "Rush," however, was not a word that ever had been part of Harold's vocabulary; even where "come on and set a spell" amounted to the unofficial regional motto, Miller brought an exceptional degree of dedication to the policy of taking life at a measured pace. The man didn't have so much as a strand of hurrying DNA in his body. It took Eric about thirty seconds to throw his backpack into Harold's truck, and then Eric was ready to roll, but Harold was still puttering around for all the world as though they had nowhere to go and nothing on the agenda.

You can take the guy out of the West Coast go-go, but you can't take the West Coast go-go out of the guy. Not even in northeastern North Carolina. Waiting and waiting to get under way, Eric couldn't understand what was taking so long. In the near future, he would learn that Harold's sanguine indifference to the ticking clock was so widely infamous that it had earned itself a label: *Miller Time.*

Once they got going, things didn't necessarily improve from Eric's point of view. Most of the route to Norfolk lay along a two-lane road that rambled through flat tidewater countryside of farm fields and patchy woodlands. Neither the road nor Harold had any notion of proceeding with haste, and while the time remaining until their plane's departure steadily diminished, Harold chugged his truck along with comfortable respect for the speed limit, all the while discoursing amiably on this and that subject, pointing out the occasional item of interest as they passed it by. Eric wanted to jump out of the truck and start pushing.

At last they merged onto a four-lane highway. Now they could make up some time, Eric thought with relief. But no, Harold hardly nudged the accelerator past the angle he'd held it at for the last hour, while a steady stream of cars zoomed up behind them, whizzed past, and accelerated into the distance.

They arrived at the airport at virtually the minute their plane was scheduled for takeoff; the two having settled on a plan that Eric would race ahead and try to hold the plane while Harold parked and then brought their stuff, Eric flung open his door and fairly flew into the terminal. He bolted through the small concourse searching for their airline's ticket counter. Fortunately, there weren't many to choose from, and no lines at any of them. Eric gasped out his plea.

"Oh, don't worry, sir, the plane's been delayed ten minutes," said the ticket agent. "You have time."

A few minutes later, Harold appeared at a pace somewhere between a brisk saunter and a purposeful stroll. He didn't seem in any degree concerned, nor did he appear surprised to hear that the plane had so conveniently been held up. Things worked out, that's what Harold believed. And Eric would find that around Harold it was true; somehow, even when (usually) things didn't come about quite as planned, they came out all right.

The two made their way through security to their boarding gate and sat down. Nothing seemed to be happening yet. Eric decided he'd make a restroom run.

Immediately after Eric walked away, the plane was called. Harold told the airline agent his friend would be along in a minute, and then he followed the agent's directions and ambled through a doorway to find himself standing outdoors on the tarmac. A dozen yards away their plane waited. It was a twin-engine job, a turbo-prop puddle jumper.

"Uh-oh," said Harold.

In the life of a teacher and farmer in Northampton County, one not given to wanderlust but rather to an abiding contentment with the quiet pleasures of rural living, riding his horses, fishing, and hunting turkey on occasion, there wasn't much call for regular air travel, and it had been awhile—a good long while—since Harold had boarded a commercial flight. He couldn't say that he was alto-gether sanguine about making his return to the blue yonder in quite so modest an example of contemporary aviation technology.

Well, that's what made life an adventure. He ducked on board and found a seat, settling himself as best he could in the cramped space, sticking his legs out into the aisle since there was no room for them anywhere else.

After a few moments, the flight attendant—it was a touch sur-prising there even was a flight attendant on so small a craft—leaned over him and said, "Excuse me, are you Mr. Miller?"

Yes, he was.

There was a Mr. Ryan, the flight attendant said, who was held up inside the gate, saying Mr. Miller had his ticket.

Oh Lord, thought Harold, feeling in his pockets, and sure enough, there it was, Eric's ticket. Poor Eric, the kid had been in such a fired-up hurry already, he was probably in a hundred-horse-power swivet right about now, thinking Harold was going to fly off to Boston without him.

Harold untangled himself from his seat, got off the plane, and crossed back over the tarmac and into the terminal, where Eric waited at the boarding gate, laughing. What next?

"Where you been, boy?" Harold laughed, handing him the ticket and giving him a reassuring clap on the back.

Once more across the tarmac, and at last they were on board, wedging themselves into their seats while the engines revved loudly. The preliminaries were completed, seatbelts latched, and finally the plane rolled down the runway, launched into the sky, and began plowing noisily northward.

Eric let out a long breath of relief. He tried to imagine how, in the coming months, they were going to coordinate this project and manage to coach a group of students from four different schools through rebuilding an entire car, with the minor consideration, among other issues, that at the moment they didn't even have a car to rebuild. And it wasn't as though the kids could jump right in and put the vehicle—when they got a vehicle—together. Even the most car-savvy of the students, the ones who had grown up with engine grease under their fingernails, would have to learn a whole different set of concepts and skills and applications. And the college-prep kids, who'd been tracked into the realms of the cerebral, were going to have to learn how to translate abstraction into two-aught wiring and vehicle weights and all sorts of other tangible applications.

Eric, of course, had been one of those academic kids, groomed in abstract intellectual inquiry. He loved the liberal arts at Berkeley, the pursuit of learning for learning's sake, but he'd loved also the beautiful, mysterious order of the pure sciences. He'd always thought, too, that he'd been well and thoroughly grounded in those sciences, having waded his way through demanding courses densely packed with theory, put in his hours in laboratories and lectures and in the library, filled page upon page with equations and analyses. He could—if you gave him a minute—cite you chapter and verse on electromagnetism and Ohm's law and rotational force and friction.

But as he sat on the plane thinking about what he'd learned so far about electric cars—not that much yet, he'd had hardly a week to take on the topic—it occurred to him that despite all the facts and formulas he'd crammed into every recess of his brain, and even despite being enough of a hands-on guy that he'd replaced the starter motor in a car of his own, if one of his students should ask him how an electric motor actually worked, what its parts were and what they did, he couldn't say. He really didn't know.

It was a piece of applied learning entirely too practical ever to have cropped up in the classes he'd taken, in which, without anyone ever stating as much, it was somehow broadly understood that studying how everyday things actually worked, and taking them apart and putting them together to see what made them tick, was the business of a different order of schooling altogether. As though it would diminish the intellectual value of your learning to point out in plain terms that an electron's charge, a subject abstrusely analyzed in your textbook, was what ran your refrigerator.

Thus, Eric had to admit that he was probably better prepared to explain a particle accelerator than to describe how the electric razor he shaved his face with every day operated.

He said as much to Harold, turning to him almost in wonder to observe, "I'm teaching physics. I use electric motors all the time. But can you believe, I don't think I really know how an electric motor works?"

Harold didn't look shocked or disappointed or even rib him in that usual Harold way. Eric would learn that about Harold, watching him work with his students; he never demeaned, he just said, "Let's go figure this out then."

On the plane, in just that way, Harold took out a pencil and a piece of paper and started explaining about motors, about permanent magnets and armatures and brushes and the left-hand rule of thumb. He used the pencil as a prop and to sketch, and he talked about RPMs and torque, and all the time he spoke with the quiet, focused passion of a true expert, someone so unfailingly intrigued by his subject that he would never tire of sharing it, never grow weary of explaining it on the fifth or tenth or five-thousandth iteration, the way an artist could spend a lifetime exploring the composition of light. Not at all like a teacher gone jaded from a quarter-century in the classroom.

Eric was starting to see that Harold Miller, on casual acquaintance, was a deceptive piece of work. All that good ol' Carolina boy heartiness, that unassuming "we're just folks, y'all" manner, tended to commandeer your attention, so you might not recognize right off just how smart he was. Eric was beginning to appreciate why John Parker had tapped Harold for this project. It wasn't only because Harold was an agreeable guy who happened to know a thing or two about electric vehicles.

They arrived at Logan Airport after dark. Neither Eric nor Harold had ever been to Boston before. They had a car reserved, a map, and general directions to their hotel.

"I'll drive," said Eric firmly.

Harold wasn't sure how he felt about that proposition, and he was even less sure when they hit the expressway, Eric swooping and weaving through the traffic. California driving, Harold guessed. "Clean and jerk" is what he would call it—the clean pass and the quick jerk back into the traveling lane. As if the Boston drivers weren't bad enough by themselves. Harold wedged his arm against the door to steady himself and hoped he'd live to tell the tale.

Their hotel was north of the city, and somehow—by a small miracle, thought Harold—they found their way there, through a nighttime blur of lights and highway interchanges and confusing signs, without incident or injury.

They had left Northampton still sultry in the grip of a reluctantly departing summer. In the morning, they awoke to a perfect New England autumn day of crisp air and blue skies. Last night's highways were not so bewildering in the light, though Eric still insisted on driving.

Eric had brought his video camera to Boston; if his students couldn't come along, he'd bring the trip home to them. He'd taped the electric-eye flush mechanism on the toilet in the Norfolk airport bathroom, and for contrast he'd dutifully recorded the less technologically advanced urinals at Logan. As they drove to the conference, he handed the camera to Harold to tape the trees bright with fall colors, the rock formations by the roadside, the overhead highway signs.

Finally they arrived at the convention center. Entering, they stood for a moment, looking about in wonder.

A crowd of several hundred milled among the usual display

booths and other conference trappings. The cars, however, were an unusual touch; full-sized vehicles were scattered around the big hall, each one surrounded by a small knot of people. The hemp-and-tofu crowd, early embracers of the idea of alternative-fuel transportation, had turned out, not surprisingly, in substantial numbers. Perhaps less expected was the business-suit contingent that thronged the floor. The ZEV mandate, it seemed, must have sparked not only a burst of fresh hope among the diehards who'd championed EVs through all the lean years, but also a flare of interest among people more typically concerned about quarterly earnings than air quality. Could it be that finally there might be money to be made in the green transportation business?

Harold Miller felt like a horse in fresh clover. Everywhere he looked there were cars, motors, parts, batteries, cables, tools, things he couldn't begin to name, thingamabobs and whatnots and whoosywhatsis galore, an arena-sized tinkerer's toy shop. And Eric—not that there wasn't any time when it didn't seem like he was excited about *something*—but right now he had that particular, glowing, kid-on-Christmas-morning look.

They plunged in. They wanted to see everything and talk to everyone.

"I'm Harold Miller and this here's Eric Ryan," Harold would say as they moved around from table to booth. North Carolina accents being in notably short supply in the room, Harold hardly needed to add that he and Eric hadn't driven in that morning from Concord or Worcester. Nevertheless, "We're from Northampton County, North Carolina," he'd say. "Well, Eric here is from California, but we're trying our best to make a Carolina boy outta him."

Eric paused by a Trojan battery demonstration, studying with interest a cutaway of a lead-acid battery. There was a series of flat lead plates evenly spaced in parallel inside a plastic casing. The battery was a few inches longer, deeper, and taller than a standard automotive starter battery and weighed more, apparently, than an overfed kindergartener. For all that, Eric saw from the accompanying materials, it only produced a trifling six volts. How many of those would it take to make a car go?

Meanwhile, Harold was contemplating a display of electric motors. Harold had worked with electric motors in various forms all his life, but never with one designed for moving a car. It was surprisingly small, really—like a big coffee can, nine inches in diameter and fifteen inches long.

When Eric rejoined him, Harold had spent thirty seconds talking with, and therefore undoubtedly already making a lifelong friend of, Bob Batson, the man with the motors.

Bob thought it was nice to see some people here from outside the region. He also thought it was nice of Harold to bring one of his students along. It took him a few minutes to understand that Eric was a teacher too.

Bob ran a business called Electric Vehicles of America, selling complete EV conversion kits as well as all the individual parts and components. Bob was one of those stalwart enthusiasts with high hopes for the future of the electric vehicle, although he never could understand why anyone persisted in believing that the big automakers, with their billions invested in the internal combustion automobile, would be the ones merrily to lead the way to an EV future. Kicking and screaming and dragging their feet would be more like it. A big car company would sink a few million dollars, several years, and a couple of dozen engineers into turning out a single prototype. With that kind of time and money, Bob could convert an entire fleet of vehicles, and you'd be driving them around town while the big company's engineers were still twiddling with their CAD blueprints.

Eric and Harold could see that if they wanted to learn about making a car over into an EV, Bob Batson was clearly their man. He'd brought a converted Chevy S-10 pickup with him to the conference, and he showed Harold and Eric around it, explaining what everything was and how it went together. Eric whipped out his video camera to document the tour.

Eric and Harold told Batson about the EV competition. Of course they wanted to win, they said, but mostly they were setting their sights on the goal of helping their kids to complete a vehicle, to have something running in time to take it to the competition.

"What you want to do, then, is have your car ready a month before," advised Batson. He told them about a school up in Vermont, St. Johnsbury Academy, how the students there had converted a VW Rabbit two years before to run in the Tour de Sol, an anything-green transportation showcase started in 1989 as a New England road rally for solar vehicles. The kids at St. Johnsbury finished their car a month ahead, said Bob, and thus earned themselves time enough to test it, tear it apart, and put it back together, and they ended up winning in the "open" category. Bob Batson thought that month for troubleshooting probably made the difference.

Harold and Eric took Bob's advice to heart. "One month early" would be their mantra.

By the end of the day, Eric and Harold had harvested armfuls of brochures, flyers, business cards, convention-tchotchke giveaways, photocopies, notes, names, and ideas. Over dinner that night, and late into the evening, they sorted through it all, trading information and materials back and forth. From the dizzying abundance, they began putting together a picture of what they were going to be up against in the months to come.

To convert a car—when, if, they got one—to an EV, they would need to disembowel it of every piece and part of the internal combustion system, from the radiator to the tailpipe. The doors would be taken off, too, and most of the interior removed as well—the seats and carpeting and the like—so that the team could work from the inside. In short, they would strip the car nearly to a shell.

Eventually, some of those parts would be put back—the doors, for example—but first, into the shell would go the components of their electric vehicle: a motor, an item called a controller that would regulate the flow of power to the motor, enough wiring (it seemed) to stretch the length of Northampton County, assorted breakers, switches, contactors, meters, and . . . some other stuff they'd figure out later. Also a charger, for plugging in the car to juice it up, and batteries.

In theory it ought to be simple enough: stuff out, stuff in. In practice, though, Eric and Harold understood that taking a car built to run on a gas-powered engine and making it over into one that would run on a battery-powered motor would be not unlike trying to rebuild a cat as a dog.

A "purpose-built" EV like the GM Impact, the car Harold had shown to his students, was designed with its end in mind. Whereas your standard modern automobile was created to carry about your standard modern automobile systems—your engine here, your exhaust there, your gas tank right in this place. It was not made to be recycled into an EV.

Thus, their empty frame would pose them an elaborate puzzle of What Goes Where. With a conversion, there was no definitive template to follow. Whatever vehicle they started with—the make, the model, the year, two-door, four-door, hatchback, pickup—would determine the particular set of advantages and disadvantages and constraints. These they would have to deal with in solving the crux of the puzzle: figuring out how to place the batteries.

If an army travels on its stomach, EVs go on their batteries. Do what they might to make their conversion as lightweight, as efficient, as aerodynamic as possible, ultimately how much power the vehicle would have, how far it could go, and how fast, would depend, Harold and Eric understood, on the batteries. And for better or worse, the proven standard for EV conversions was the deep-cycle, six-volt, lead-acid battery. To put it plainly, a golf cart battery.

The words "golf cart" do not arouse visions of adrenaline-pumping speed and awe-stoking power. What they lend the mind to imagining is middle-aged guys straining the capacity of their Sans-abelt pants as they roll up for the nineteenth hole.

Nevertheless, it appeared that when it came to electric transportation, there was much to be said in favor of the humble lead-and-sulfuric-acid golf cart battery. When it was connected to a circuit—and essentially, an electric vehicle is a big circuit on wheels—a chemical reaction between the lead plates and the sulfuric acid created a flow of electricity and could continue to do so at a fairly steady rate (which translated to sustained speed) over an extended period of time (which translated to distance). Charging the battery reversed the chemical process and readied the battery for reuse.

A deep-cycle lead-acid battery could go through this charge/discharge/recharge process hundreds of times before beginning to lose effectiveness. It was also reliable, relatively cheap, rugged, and nearly completely recyclable as well. These were the advantages of the lead-acid battery.

The downside was that it was made from lead.

A single six-volt battery weighed more than sixty pounds and took up half a cubic foot of space. To make a car go, however, required a good deal more than six volts—at least *ninety*-six, according to Bob Batson, to get an EV up to highway speeds. Ninety-six volts would mean sixteen batteries wired one to the next, negative terminal to positive, in what was known as a series config-uration—in effect, making one giant battery out of them. Sixteen batteries would command almost eight cubic feet of space. Sixteen batteries would weigh in the neighborhood of one thousand pounds. Not for nothing had EVs earned the derisive nickname "lead sled."

You didn't have to know as much about automobiles as Harold Miller did to understand that safely securing that half-ton of lead and acid without throwing their vehicle wildly out of balance was going to take more than just tossing those sixteen batteries in the trunk and driving away. And you had to wonder how a car hauling around all that weight wasn't just going to poke along like . . . well, like a golf cart. Ought to make for some interesting challenges for an engineering team that would consist of a bunch of teenagers armed with handheld calculators.

FIVE MONTHS

The conference was over. Their bags were stuffed with the materials they'd collected. For these few days, Eric and Harold had immersed themselves among people for whom the language, and technology of EVs were everyday things, sat rapt in seminars, and wandered happily around the convention floor, looking and learning and engaging in long, wonderfully technical conversations. They were nearly giddy with the wealth of the experience and with their utterly serendipitous fortune in stumbling across this gathering at so propitious a moment, before they'd taken more than the barest of first steps toward launching their EV project. Now, armed with information both formal and anecdotal, they felt they might have a chance at avoiding at least the worst of the missteps.

"Now," said Harold, "let's do us some sightseeing."

They filled an afternoon criss-crossing the Charles River in a whirl of bridges, traffic rotaries, one-way streets always headed in the direction opposite the one they wanted, and clearly homicidal Boston drivers. Drive like that in Northampton County, Harold thought, you'd be rushed to the hospital under the presumption of stroke or seizure.

It was a regatta weekend in Boston, slender rowing shells skimming the surface of the river like water bugs. At Harvard, Harold bet one of the guards at the gate to Harvard Yard that he couldn't correctly guess where Eric and Harold were from. The guard pegged Eric right off for a Californian.

"Alabama?" he guessed for Harold.

At MIT, tech mecca, Harold stood looking on in the manner of a fondly indulgent parent as Eric ran around in circles yelling, with his hands up in the air, like a player taking a victory lap.

On the flight to Boston, the two of them had been casually acquainted fellow faculty members from opposite sides of the tacitly acknowledged academic/vocational divide. By the time they returned to Logan Airport to board the plane for home, they had discovered themselves to be more alike than their differences in age and history might have suggested. They had made a friendship, the Northampton kind that would be measured in years and spread itself broadly and deeply through their lives.

Back in Norfolk, getting into the truck with Harold behind the wheel again was a good way to shake the Boston pace and settle once more into Northampton time, as though minutes were actually melting into something looser and more open to interpretation. Still, when Eric arrived back at the house in George, where the Parkers were waiting to hear news of the trip, he put John in mind of a fire just doused with gasoline. The people! The technologies! The hundred-odd bits and pieces of insider dope he'd gleaned in conversations, the names he'd collected, all in scribbled notes. He told John and June about the vehicles, and Bob Batson, and the revelation of spending time with people who dreamed of remaking the way we got around in the world.

In the days and weeks to come, the George Running Club would find itself given over to exclusive preoccupation with the EV effort. Along with everything else Eric brought back from Boston, he came home possessed with a sense of urgency. They had a car to build.

Eric appointed himself the organizational director of the project—obviously, Harold was the car guy, the one with the technical knowledge they were going to need, and just as obviously, he was not your man to make a plan. In the time the two had spent together, Harold had presented Eric with enough ideas to launch a fleet of electric vehicles and to change the future of humankind while they were at it. Inspiring, but as Eric saw it, what they really needed to focus on was a couple dozen kids and one car by April. Actually, what they were shooting for was a car by March. If they were going to stick to Bob Batson's advice to be ready to road test a month before competition, then effectively they'd lost four weeks before they'd even started. That left six months. Take away Thanksgiving, Christmas, exam week, and spring break, and it looked more like five.

Five months to find a car, take it apart, put it back together, and make it drive. Five months to raise funds and solicit donations and collect sponsors. Five months for the kids to absorb the science of amps and watts and volts, electricity and batteries, acceleration and resistance, motors and charge, wiring and welding, and whatever else they'd need to know to get a car to run as fast and as far as they could make it go on nothing but electrons.

It would help, then, if the team leaders knew, officially speaking, what they were supposed to be doing—what the competition would actually entail, and what limitations, requirements, or specifications would be placed on the EV conversions. Obviously, there would be more they would need to take into consideration than just building a car that moved. But what would those things be? So far, details on these points remained in short supply.

Fortunately, and none too soon, an introductory meeting was scheduled to take place at Virginia Power headquarters in Richmond, interested schools to attend. John Parker, Harold, and Eric would go, grabbing a few students to come along with them. They hoped to learn there whatever they needed—anything they could use—to move ahead with the project.

In the meantime, though, they weren't going to waste a day if they could help it.

The northeastern North Carolina high school electric vehicle team (clearly, finding a snappier name for themselves would be necessary soon) established Monday afternoons and Harold Miller's shop as the time and location for its weekly meetings. Five other area high schools had been invited to join Northampton–East on the project—all members of the Roanoke Valley Math, Science, and Technology Alliance, the staff development program dreamed up by John Parker and North Carolina Power's Randy Shillingburg. Only three of those schools had signed on: Northampton–West from Northampton County, and Northwest Halifax and Weldon from neighboring Halifax County.

At Northwest Halifax, the auto mechanics teacher was the first to be approached, but he didn't want to do it. Mary Keeter, on the other hand, said that driving a couple of students some forty miles over to Northampton–East and back again every Monday afternoon for the rest of the school year would suit her just fine. Mary Keeter liked to stay busy.

MizzKeeter, as her name came out under the influence of a North

Carolina drawl, taught Principles of Technology at Northwest Halifax. It was an "applied physics" class—practical applications of science for students who weren't taking college-prep physics.

Mrs. Keeter was formerly a seventh-grade teacher, but anyone who ever has spent any time instructing children knows that the road to madness is paved with middle-schoolers. So she went back to school to get recertified, and right off it became apparent that she hadn't picked a field heavily populated with other women. When she went to a conference, the school district urged her to save money by sharing her hotel room with another conferee, until she pointed out that this would leave her no option but to double up with a man not her husband.

When she volunteered to get involved, then, in the EV project, she'd long since grown accustomed to being the lady teacher amid a crowd of men with clip-on ties and calloused hands. And anyway, Mary Keeter was something of a car buff, an accidental interest that had evolved because she still owned her first car, a 1947 Ford she and her husband paid four hundred dollars for in 1963 when she started teaching and needed a way to get to work. It wasn't an antique when they bought it; it was all they could afford. But now it was nearing its fiftieth birthday, and to keep a car like that going, inevitably over time you picked up a tidy heap of knowledge about what happened under the hood.

Mary Keeter told her principal she would identify some students to invite into the project. By the time she finished sorting through the likely candidates—the ones who would have enough interest and dedication and discipline to stick with it through the whole year—and by the time those students sorted themselves according to who didn't want to miss baseball season and whose parents didn't want them traveling all the way to East once a week, Mrs. Keeter was down to only a few kids. On the October Monday of the first meeting, she loaded them up in her car and headed to Northampton County.

Daniel Shields was in his twenty-seventh year teaching science at Weldon High School—chemistry, biology, and physics, at the moment. Some might consider that enough of a day's work and then some, but Mr. Shields was one of those people to whom sleep always seemed like an extraneous activity needlessly taking up useful hours out of his twenty-four, something to get around to only if there wasn't anything more interesting to do. On top of teaching, he owned an insurance agency, and if you called him at the office at ten o'clock on a Saturday night he might tell you cheerily, "Well, I was just settling down to get to work."

Mr. Shields was already taking part in the Math, Science, and Technology Alliance, so when the EV project came along he looked on it as an extension of his commitment to the Alliance. Just part of the job, really. Sure, he'd round up some students to join the team.

But "I'm too busy," said one. "I have other things to do," said another. "I don't have the time," said someone else.

Mr. Shields explained the idea of the electric vehicle—that it would be a regular car, like any you'd see driving down the road, only they would be making it over to run on electricity instead of gas. This proposal was greeted with considerable skepticism among the students. Eventually, though, he talked Theresa Williams into it, despite her initial insistence, "I am not interested in no cars," and by the time of the first team meeting, a second student as well.

* * *

Before he came to teaching, Norman Joyner, the electronics teacher at Northampton–West High School, was in the Army Airborne in electronics—radar and computers. Mr. Joyner had spent so much of his life amid capacitors and amps and ohms that if you ran him through a CT scan, you might find that his brain had arranged itself into a circuit diagram. He knew electronics the way Harold Miller knew cars. He could strip wire with his thumbnail.

Upon issuing an open invitation, Mr. Joyner was blessed with an overabundance of volunteers for the EV project. He selected just a few—students he thought would be suited for the work and the commitment. If, however, you had asked some of their former teachers at Garysburg Elementary School, they would have expressed considerable surprise that two of Mr. Joyner's choices were Harold and Darrell Parker.

Mr. Joyner was a quietly commanding teacher, someone who gave the impression he had been chiseled out of granite and could subdue a restive mob with no more than a piercing glance. He watched out for his students; he was someone you could rely upon absolutely. He saw something in Harold and Darrell that no one else did, that maybe the two boys didn't even see themselves.

Harold and Darrell were identical twins. They came from a family of tinkerers and mechanics, and they loved gadgets, anything with switches to flip and buttons to push, anything they could take apart and put back together. When they were kids, they made their bedroom closet into an imaginary spaceship, and when they were still in grade school, they built a tree house and wired it with Christmas lights powered by a car battery. They'd grill hot dogs up there. The neighborhood kids thought it was the coolest thing.

The grownups weren't so sure about young Harold and Darrell.

They would say, "Them Parker boys," with a sigh and a shake of the head that said no good could be expected from that quarter.

Most people couldn't tell Harold and Darrell apart, and perhaps that was why everyone usually referred to them as a collective unit, "HaroldandDarrell," or sometimes simply "the twins." The twins sometimes thought of themselves the same way; being with each other wasn't really like being with another person, or even like being with a brother, it was more like a seamless continuity of self in two bodies. They played off each other, quick-witted like partners in a comedy sketch, and sometimes they didn't even have to say things out loud to be traveling along the same thoughts.

Unfortunately, when they were younger, often those thoughts weren't altogether well-advised. Harold and Darrell had been the kind of boys who were too smart, too creative, and too busy for their own good in the absence of rigorous adult oversight. In their early years, whatever notion occurred to them, they were inclined to go right ahead and act upon without further reflection. One day they came to school in their pajamas. Other days, they played their teachers, switching classes and identities, a kind of two-boy shell game. They would provoke their classmates and torment the girls and get up to an endlessly inventive array of mischief and mayhem, and when confronted, Darrell would say, "That wasn't me, it was Harold," and Harold would say, "It wasn't me, it was Darrell," and the trouble was that you couldn't absolutely be sure that the Harold who was pointing the finger at Darrell wasn't actually Darrell himself, after all.

The boys' teachers pronounced them hellions. By the time the twins made it to high school, they'd both been held back two grades. By that time, though, Darrell and Harold had been taken in firm hand by family, particularly by their Uncle Clyde. And while they had certainly done their bit of wandering in the wilderness, the twins discovered that the Lord waits patiently to gather the strayed into his fold. It took Christ and Uncle Clyde to bring the Parker boys to heel, but once their imaginations and energy were given proper guidance, it was almost as though they'd stepped aboard that rocket in their closet and pointed it toward their own futures. They made up the grades lost, and Darrell would end up enrolling part-time in college while he was still finishing high school.

When Mr. Joyner told them about the EV project, Darrell got the impression he was talking about a model car, like one of those remote control toys. That sounded fun enough. If it had a wire or a switch or a fuse, the Parker boys couldn't resist it.

Harold, who was taking electrical trades with Mr. Joyner and considering becoming an electrical engineer, said yes without thinking twice, and for once, impetuousness served him well. Uncle Clyde said he would make sure that Harold and Darrell got themselves over to East every Monday afternoon; he'd bring them himself if need be.

When the students from Northampton–East turned up in Mr. Miller's classroom that Monday afternoon, some of them were surprised to see the kids from the other schools—a small number, true, but strangers, all of them. So much about this whole project remained vague and up in the air that no two students had quite the same idea of what they were getting into, and not everyone had understood it was slated to be a multischool effort. Shooting furtive glances at the newcomers, the East students were feeling proprietary. Their school. Their project. Who were these other kids? What were they doing here?

The East students knew to be on their best company behavior, however. These visitors were *guests,* after all, and to behave rudely to them would reflect poorly on Mr. Ryan and Mr. Miller and on Northampton–East too. The South has strong feelings on the matter of guests.

Meanwhile, the guests themselves perched uneasily in unfamiliar desks in an unfamiliar classroom, casting their own sidelong looks around. They were outnumbered collectively by the students from East, but they weren't a collective themselves; the Halifax contingent didn't know anyone from West or Weldon, and vice versa all around. So they sat and waited.

Then here was this Mr. Miller telling them they were going to take on a future technology that only a handful of people in the country—including the top engineers at GM—were working on. They were going to be part of something none of their schools had ever done before. They were going to be a team. They were going to bring home that trophy from Richmond.

Katrina Deloatch thought how strange it was seeing these unfamiliar faces in Mr. Miller's classroom as he was starting things off with an introduction that was equal parts welcome speech and pep rally. Katrina had attended school and ridden the bus with many of her classmates at East—like Donny Lassiter, for one—since they were gap-toothed primary-schoolers with their lunch boxes and pencil cases clutched firmly in hand.

Taking physics with Mr. Ryan and auto tech with Mr. Miller, Katrina was a sitting duck when it came to the EV project. Even if she hadn't wanted to sign on, how could she have avoided it? If it wasn't Mr. Ryan talking about smog in California or global warming, and how they could bring about real change in the world and in their own futures, it was Mr. Miller talking about what a shame it was that the world was still so dependent on oil and how this competition could help show the world that a different way was possible. And also, of course, how good they were all going to feel when they won up in Richmond.

Katrina liked Mr. Ryan, but like quite a few of her classmates she thought he was kind of weird too: California weird, she presumed. All that business with jumping up on top of his desk—he had a lot of energy. A lot. Every now and then you wanted to say, "It's just physics. It's not *that* exciting."

For Katrina, although she'd be the first in her family to go, college had never been an "if," only a "where." But like Jennifer Robbins, Katrina, with a handy extra space in her otherwise college-prep schedule, decided she could squeeze in Auto Tech I. As a senior, she wasn't coasting by any means, but as far as what the colleges would be looking at in her transcript, the die had been cast, so she might as well allow herself this last chance to take Mr. Miller's class.

Katrina's father worked as a prison corrections officer, but his real love—besides Katrina, on whom he doted—was all things mechanical, particularly automobiles, and Katrina had picked up that interest from him. She'd joke that she was more like her father's son than her brother was, spending hours with her father in the backyard while he worked over some balky engine or fine-tuned a transmission.

Her father was kind of like Mr. Miller when it came to cars, and in fact the two of them—Mr. Miller and her father—went a ways back themselves. Vocational education didn't always draw from the highest concentration of model citizens among the student body, and Mr. Miller usually ended up with at least a couple of boys in his classes whose futures appeared determinedly headed for ten-to-twenty without the option, so Mr. Miller liked to invite Mr. Deloatch to come and talk to his classes and share a few hard facts about prison life, maybe put a kid in handcuffs for a few minutes to give him a sense of what that felt like.

Unlike many of the people Katrina knew in Northampton and in her little hometown of Potecasi, where almost everyone was related to her by blood or marriage, Katrina knew something of the world beyond the pine forests and peanut fields of northeastern North Carolina.

Her mother's family was from New Jersey, so Katrina and her parents and brother visited there, and they also traveled to destinations closer by, like Richmond and Raleigh, where they liked going to the museums and cultural sites. Those experiences didn't make her one of those teenagers counting the days until she could leave this hick town behind and never come back, however; she appreciated the comforts of life in a small community where you knew everyone and didn't have to lock your doors or look over your shoulder at night. Though sometimes, being a teenager, she wouldn't have minded if every single person in her town didn't know her on sight, and her car, so that there was never a chance that her mother wouldn't know where she'd been, what she'd been up to, and who she was with.

Mr. Ryan was talking now, outlining a general schedule the teachers hoped the team could follow in the months to come, discussing how the goal was to have the car ready to drive a month before the competition and how they were going to have to push themselves and stay focused to have any chance of making that deadline.

Kelly Daughtry was taking chemistry with Mr. Ryan. In class, he had been telling the students about emissions regulations passed recently in California; within a few years, Mr. Ryan said, two percent of the vehicles sold in his home state were going to be electrics. Kelly, who was practical-minded, found that hard to imagine. What if you ran out of power miles from an outlet?

Kelly was one of Jennifer Robbins's best friends, and she was in her junior year at East as well. Kelly's mother was a teacher, and Kelly understood that her parents saw high school as an arrow aimed directly at the bull's eye that was college. No matter how many spaces might open up in her schedule, therefore, Kelly would never be so foolish as to propose to her parents that she sign up for auto mechanics or any other class that did not include the word "honors" in its name.

But Mr. Ryan had piqued her curiosity—or maybe just her skepticism—and besides, Jennifer, and Kelly's boyfriend too, who was also in one of Mr. Miller's auto tech classes, kept going on about this electric vehicle competition.

Kelly was no NASCAR fan—watching a bunch of loud cars go around and around in a circle seemed to her like a dumb way to spend your time. But building an electric car still sounded interesting and maybe even fun, so Kelly decided she'd find out about the after-school team that was being put together. There were, after all, a few minutes in her day not yet claimed by class work or studying or sports or other extracurriculars. Her mother said it would be all right so long as her grades didn't suffer.

Mr. Miller was discussing safety now, and the importance of following proper procedures and precautions.

"This is electricity we're gonna be working with," said Mr. Miller. "We want to try not to get anybody killed here."

RULES MAKE
THE CHALLENGE

Bright autumn leaves were beginning to scatter to the ground like confetti, and the weather was showing signs of working itself into its winter sulk, with the occasional dreary day of featureless gray skies and a raw, drizzling damp. On one such morning, Harold, Eric, John, and a few students headed up I-95 to Richmond for the first informational meeting, ready to find out, finally, exactly what they'd signed on for.

The meeting was being held at Virginia Power headquarters, a large, boxy, contemporary brick-and-glass building within a suburban office park of nearly indistinguishable large, boxy, brick-and-glass buildings, each lapped at the edges by its own black sea of asphalt parking lot. It was in the thousands of square miles of parking lots just like these across the country that the most visionary of the EV advocates imagined scores upon scores of commuter electric vehicles resting in the shade of solar panel arrays, charging pollution-free from the sun while their owners toiled in the office buildings.

There was no such future on display at the moment at Virginia Power. Nevertheless, among the power companies signed on as sponsors for the EV competition, perhaps none was so strongly interested in the electric vehicle's potential as Virginia Power.

All the electric utilities would stand to gain, certainly, if a growing number of consumers started driving plug-in cars. More people using more electricity sounded good, and better yet, most of them would be using it when there was more electricity available for use. Peak demand for electricity generally was made during the daylight working hours when homes and stores and offices and schools and businesses were lit up and churning away. At night, when large portions of the population turned off the lights and went to bed, millions of meters settled into a lazy, low-demand spin. From the point of view of power company number crunchers, it truly was darkest before the dawn, when the electric utilities had the capacity to put out electricity but few customers were in need of it. EVs, though, would typically be charged at night. Assuming that the solar-paneled-parking-lot future the visionaries imagined was still a very long way off, if not an impossible dream altogether, electric vehicles dangled the promise of increased demand in the dark hours and thus more buoyant balance sheets. Millions of EVs could be plugged in through the night without demanding any more power than the utilities already could supply.

Then, too, it was a rare power company that couldn't stand some significant burnishing of its environmental record with a clean-air technology. Virginia Power, for one, had a serious coal habit, and if you put together the toll from extracting and then burning the stuff, it wasn't a very pretty picture. In fact, EV detractors liked to point out that electric vehicles couldn't really be called "clean" at all if they were being charged from polluting sources like coal-burning plants.

True enough, but hardly a resounding argument on behalf of defaulting to the internal combustion status quo. Logic would conclude that it would be far easier to clean up and control emissions from a few hundred stationary power plants than from hundreds of millions of automobiles buzzing around the country. Electric vehicles themselves put out no emissions while operating—unlike gas cars. Electrics used no energy, gave off no heat or pollutants while sitting stopped in traffic—unlike gas cars. What's more, electrics did not render a nation hostage to the whims of autocrats and dictators who happened, by the luck of the geological draw, to be sitting atop an ocean of oil—unlike gas cars. Anything that could make electricity—including wind and solar power and perhaps, one day, hydrogen, the vaunted, if forever just over the horizon, fuel of the future—could charge an electric. As long as the sun continued to rise, the Earth would have a viable source of electric power, but gas cars ran only on gas. And gas was made from oil. And while the rate of consumption was continuing to accelerate, worldwide oil supply was expected to peak and begin declining in a matter of decades. Not good news for a nation where demand already equaled more than a quarter of the entire world's annual production, with two-thirds of that fill-up being funneled into transportation.

Sadly, though, this wasn't the most gripping of stories, written in pie charts and dire predictions and of the sort that people didn't really want shoved down their throats, when every day the news delivered more of the same, another and another and another tale of looming global catastrophe of enormous geopolitical complexity, and meanwhile there were the kids to fetch from school and dinner to get on the table and bills to pay, and couldn't someone who was qualified figure out a workable solution to this mess and get back to them?

Early in the previous year, before any whisper of the EV competition was in the air, Virginia Power, wondering if they couldn't do just that—help make a solution happen—had dedicated a small division, fewer than a dozen people, under the heading of "Conservation," to investigate EV technologies. The ZEV mandate and the GM Impact made it seem possible that the electric vehicle's time had come, and with the support of a few key individuals with clout in the company, including the president, the members of the Virginia Power future technologies team joined the leading edge of research and development. They traveled constantly, meeting with battery companies and auto manufacturers, looking into charging protocols and energy storage and examining the prospect of what was known as distributed energy generation, when power production might be revolutionized, localized to a more efficient system of smaller, neighborhood-level generators to serve the needs of these plug-in cars.

Much of what they were exploring was likely years, and even decades, from practical application, and thus there were some, quite a few in fact, at the company who were less enthusiastic, who thought the conservation team's pursuits were the proverbial money pit.

Yet Virginia Power itself, the very company, was the legacy of a groundbreaking joining of electricity and transportation—the world's first commercially viable, city-scaled electric street railway. Designed by Frank J. Sprague, a former employee of Thomas Edison, the railway was put into service in Richmond, in 1888, by the Richmond Union Passenger Railway, a privately financed enterprise with its own power-generating station. It proved conclusively that this newfangled stuff called electricity could be successfully harnessed to move large numbers of people around a city with speed and efficiency, and other systems in cities elsewhere soon began appearing. Though EVs would come and shortly thereafter go, electrified mass transit continued to spread around the world and still moves millions of people every day. Meanwhile, over the course of a few decades and several corporate evolutions, the Richmond Union Passenger Railway turned into the Virginia Electric Power Company.

In a sense, then, the company had turned full circle to reinvest itself in electric transportation, and at the moment when word came from Walt Purdy at Edison Electric Institute of his plans for the high school EV competition, it occurred to the people involved in these matters at Virginia Power that the story of electric vehicles—why we needed them, how they could benefit us, and also how much fun they could be—might go over much better if it came packaged in the triumphs, tribulations, and dedication of teams of high-schoolers. It would be a feel-good story that would move beyond polarized politics and get people excited about electrics, while helping shake the common misperceptions that the vehicles were esoteric, experimental, and impractical. What would say This Could Be You more succinctly than the sight of someone's sixteen-year-old zooming around in an EV he'd helped build himself?

A number of the utilities Walt Purdy approached voiced some initial skepticism. What benefit would it bring them to sponsor a bunch of kids fiddling around with a secondhand car? Where would be the payoff in teenagers clanking around a racetrack in a sorry parade of old beaters?

Virginia Power, however, signed on immediately and offered to act as host. It was their people who sat down with their hometown neighbors, the Sawyer family, owners of Richmond International Raceway, and helped secure the track for the competition. The Sawyers hadn't been unreceptive to Purdy's initial overtures. They could see it would be a great thing to do in the community, good for the kids and good exposure for the racetrack too.

Still, they hesitated. They expressed concern about the long list of technical and logistical details that went with putting on an event like this, details that would call for a lot of bodies on the ground to see them through, when, after all, the track had a big race in March to plan for, eighty thousand people expected. "We're kind of busy," they said.

Virginia Power said, "We'll see to those details."

The Sawyers said, "Welcome to Richmond International Raceway."

Virginia Power didn't stint; it committed a couple of staff members full-time to the EV competition. The company of course held high hopes for sparking interest in EV technologies. Just as importantly, though, Virginia Power understood that since this event would be taking place on its home turf, then regardless of whom the official sponsors might be, in Richmond, at least, Virginia Power was going to be the name people recognized, the name they would associate with the inaugural high school electric vehicle challenge. Virginia Power, therefore, planned to take a firm hand in making sure that things went swimmingly.

Unfortunately, the line between a firm hand and high-handedness can be a matter of perspective when multiple parties with sometimes diverging agendas are working very hard on the same project. From EEI's perspective, Virginia Power was the host, and thank you very much indeed for volunteering, but with all due respect, please remember this wasn't a Virginia Power event. It was a multi-utility, educational event for which EEI, Argonne National Laboratory, and the Department of Energy were the sponsors, and EEI, Argonne, and DOE ought to be the final arbiters on decisions made.

In the months to come, as the April date drew nearer and the pressure mounted, feelings would run high and some heated exchanges would develop between EEI, Argonne, and Virginia Power. All of them wanted the event to be safe, to be a success, to be right, but they didn't always agree on what that meant or how to go about achieving those ends.

On this drizzly October morning, however, of the first meeting for the schools, the Virginia Power conference room buzzed with happy anticipation and the rumbling bass note from a preponderance of male voices.

Harold Miller was "How you doin'?" and shaking hands and slapping backs all over the place. He was in his element, joshing and back-and-forthing with a 500-watt grin, introducing Eric and the students around in a blur of powerful handshakes, friendly braggadocio, and hearty laughter.

"Y'all might as well go on home right now, because you know there ain't no chance you're gonna beat us."

"Ahhh, you just know you got no chance to win if we're there."

"Boy, I was winning races when you was still in diapers."

And so on. Eric could see that some of these teachers obviously shared a history. They'd met before at conferences and continuing-education programs or events and competitions with VICA—the Vocational-Industrial Clubs of America.

The meeting was called to order. Everyone took seats.

"We've got competition," said Harold under his breath, as he and John and Eric sat down with their students.

Harold was worried about Southern Wayne, another North Carolina high school, being sponsored by Carolina Power & Light. Harold knew they built race cars in the Southern Wayne shop during the summers and nationally acclaimed drag-racing cars too. And Person County High School, another CP&L team, Harold knew they had plenty of NASCAR talent in their part of North Carolina.

Nearly all the schools were unfamiliar to Eric, but as the meeting got under way and the different teams were introduced, Eric noticed how many of those schools had "vocational" or "science" or "technical" in their names. He could take a guess at what that meant in terms of the facilities and the resources they were probably working with. More, he'd bet, than a cramped, cluttered shop and a single, dust-encrusted PC and hoping they could beg anything with four wheels and a steering column.

Nevertheless, to be one among these schools from across the mid-Atlantic region, North Carolina to Pennsylvania, filled the group from Northampton with excitement and a sense of possibility. This competition clearly was going to be much bigger than anything they ever had participated in before. Thanks to their advocate at North Carolina Power, Randy Shillingburg, the perennially discounted schools of northeastern North Carolina were getting a chance to play in the big leagues. At least that was the plan. Even Harold, the sunniest of optimists, looked around the room, feeling, on the one hand, that it was all so close, this wonderful opportunity, just at the edge of their grasp, but wondering, on the other hand, how they ever were going to manage it. From Boston they'd come away understanding that the absolute barest-bones conversion ran about six thousand dollars, not including whatever the vehicle itself might cost. Add in the expenses to transport the team and the vehicle to Richmond and to house and feed the kids and the teachers for the days of the competition, and assume that there might be costs they couldn't yet anticipate, and easily they could be talking at least ten thousand dollars. Which was ten thousand dollars more than they had at the moment.

* * *

At the front of the Virginia Power conference room, the usual welcoming remarks were being made, the blah-blah-blah about this unprecedented partnership for education and etcetera, etcetera. All very good and respectable points, but you got the feeling that the competitor had already been roused in the educators assembled here, that they were chafing with impatience politely held in check, like a pack of hound dogs straining at the leashes for the moment they'd be let loose for the hunt. They wanted rules, they wanted guidelines—they wanted to get started.

Finally, the overtures and preliminaries were completed, and the sure signal was given that it was time to get down to business—photocopied materials were handed around. Everyone immediately began leafing through the pages, scanning ahead.

An EV conversion expert, Mike Brown, author of the guide *Convert It!*, had been flown in from California, along with technical people from Argonne. In the audience, notes were scribbled, and an attitude of rapt attention prevailed as the parameters of the inaugural high school electric vehicle challenge were outlined.

The operative word there might have been "inaugural"; another way to put it would have been: "We're still hashing out the details."

This much was established: the competition would be divided into six categories. Five of these—efficiency, design, oral presentation, range, and acceleration and handling—would be sponsored by the Department of Energy, which would be providing the funding and resources for the events themselves as well as prize money for the top finishers. Teams would be recognized for a win in any one of the individual categories, and teams whose total score in all five placed them in first through sixth place would receive a cash prize.

There would be awards as well for things like sportsmanship and safety and for "press on regardless," recognition for that team— there was always one of them—with bottomless bad luck but boundless good spirits anyway.

To win the overall competition, however, a team would have to place solidly in all or most of the categories. It wouldn't be enough to make a fast car or a car that could go a long way. It would have to balance those qualities and be well designed, handle smoothly, and accelerate briskly too. The oral presentation would demand poise and presentation skills and the ability to articulate what the team had done and why. Purdy had included that element in order to encourage teams to bring in students—girls, even—who might not traditionally have taken interest in an auto mechanics project but who had that all-important talent for standing up in front of a crowd without being struck dumb with terror.

On the final day of the challenge, there would be a speed event that the Department of Energy would have nothing to do with—a race, also with cash prizes, that would be judged separately from the other five categories and be sponsored by the participating utilities. Because while the DOE had many interests in supporting the inaugural high school electric vehicle challenge, one of them was not being the putatively responsible party when Junior came out a few limbs for the worse from a high-speed pileup on turn two.

Why the utilities, for their part, had agreed to take it on was anyone's guess. Electricity, cars, teenagers, a racetrack—it all looked like one big lawsuit in search of a plaintiff. It was a wonder the proposal ever made it past the firewall of corporate attorneys.

Which brought the organizers to their next point. Safety.

The people from Argonne would be responsible for determining rules for the competition and specifications for the vehicles. Their mission, in simple terms, appeared to be to forecast all conceivable manner of doom, disaster, and worst case scenarios and then figure out how to avoid any such contingencies with a rigorous body of protocols and precautions. Oh, and also to make everything fair.

"The first thing we're going to do," said the Argonne representative at the meeting, "is inspect." Every vehicle, he explained, would be gone over by a persnickety—not the word he used, but the meaning he made clear—technical team to verify that it complied with all design and safety requirements. If there were any problems, any shortcomings or oversights, anything not performing correctly that might affect the vehicle's safety, and it couldn't be fixed on the spot, then that vehicle wasn't going anywhere. In particular, if a team's EV went even a pound over its gross vehicle weight rating—let there be no confusion on this point—it was going to spend the rest of the competition resolutely sidelined.

Mandated for every vehicle, a gross vehicle weight rating (GVW in shop-talk shorthand) indicates the maximum load, including its own weight, that a vehicle can safely carry. The GVW is conveniently noted on a sticker on the driver's side doorjamb of a vehicle in case you are thinking of converting it to an EV, or more typically so that if you are contemplating, say, loading the entire offensive line of a football team into a Honda Civic to take them to lunch at the All-U-Can-Eat buffet, there is a basis on which to consider, strictly in terms of poundage at least, whether this is a good idea. Exceed the GVW and you risk the possibility that the strain will overload the brakes—not a good thing—or accelerate fatigue on essential structural elements, increasing the possibility that some key part of the vehicle might come asunder at an inopportune moment, like on a curve at seventy miles an hour. This, the Argonne representative made adamantly clear, was not going to happen under Argonne's watch at the inaugural high school electric vehicle challenge.

When the time came for questions, the room bristled with raised hands, and as the Q&A session proceeded, it afforded Harold and Eric with an unexpected boost of confidence. Even if they had nothing else going for themselves in the way of state-of-the-art anything, at least it was clear that they didn't seem to *know* any less than anyone else in the room. Possibly, thanks to that Boston trip, they might know more. Wouldn't that be a kicker?

What everyone seemed most concerned about was time. Would there be enough? Could there possibly be enough, with less than even a full school year to figure out the conversion and get it completed with a team of *teenagers*?

It will have to be enough, said the organizers, because it's what we have.

FINDING MR. HAWKINS

Someone suggested "Past Gas." But by the next Monday gathering of the four-school EV group, consensus for a name for the team had gone in favor of ECORV: Electric Cars of the Roanoke Valley. If less colorful than the alternative, ECORV at least posed no risk of unfortunate homonymic misconstructions. The success of the project would depend on the good graces of many people, such as members of the school board and potential donors, and, alas, you couldn't count on all of them having a hearty appreciation for indelicate puns.

That settled, the students clamored to know what had been learned at the meeting in Richmond. Armed with the handouts distributed there, Eric and Harold were ready to tell them. Except that the handouts ran to thirty double-sided, single-spaced pages, densely packed with what seemed at the moment like an overwhelming list of rules, specifications, and requirements—weight bias, vehicle lean, throttle return, bleed-down devices, conductor routing, incidental contact, rollover protection. All of it was laid out in a volley of linguistical firmness: *must; no; cannot; may not; not permitted.* Clearly, the technical people at Argonne were not a waffling bunch.

"There's a lot of safety features we'll have to put in," Harold told the students, not adding *as if we didn't have enough to figure out already.* They would have to build a steel roll cage for the interior, add a five-point racing harness for the driver, safety netting for the driver's side window, mount in a fire extinguisher, tape the headlights.

Roll cage? thought the kids, perking up. Harness? Fire-resistant driver's suit? Maybe there was going to be more to this battery car than they had been thinking.

Harold was getting ahead of himself. They didn't have a car yet, but he was firing out what-ifs and how-abouts and what-says right and left, a human Gatling gun of ideas. He had the rules and regulations in hand, and already he was trying to figure the angles, work the gray areas. It didn't take much to rouse the former Saturday night dirt-track racer in Harold Miller.

"We could save a lot of weight," he said, for example, to Eric, "if we could build that battery box out of plastic."

In that game of "whither the batteries" that went with converting to an EV, typically some of the pack ended up where the most space was available—inside the passenger compartment. You could not, however, simply toss them into the backseat like so many bags of groceries. In all circumstances in an EV, the batteries had to be firmly secured, but when they would be sharing interior space with the human occupants, they had to be fully enclosed within a box as well—one permanently installed in the vehicle, and usually made out of metal. In the event of a disastrous crash (now *there* was a scenario everyone really wanted to contemplate), the box was supposed to contain any sulfuric acid that spilled from the batteries. The box also allowed for controlled venting of the small, but nevertheless potentially explosive, amount of hydrogen gas given off when the batteries were being charged.

What if, Harold was thinking, you could make that box from something lighter than metal, and something, too, that would be nonconductive, so you wouldn't have to worry about the possibility of an electrical short between the batteries and the box?

There was a company in Roanoke Rapids called Airmold that made injection-molded plastics. Maybe, said Harold, they could talk Airmold into molding them a plastic battery box. And Harold was thinking, too, that a belly pan would be nice to have, something smooth to run under the bottom of the car to cut down on wind drag and give the vehicle an aerodynamic edge. Maybe Airmold might help them with that too. No use not asking.

"I'm not shy," said Harold.

Late in the afternoon on the last Friday in October, Harold, Eric, and John headed to a meeting Harold had arranged with an engineer at Airmold. When the three arrived, the engineer, George Hawkins, offered to show them around the plant.

If Harold Miller had ever gotten to a point without further ado, it wasn't because he'd meant to. As the foursome wandered the plant, he marveled at length over the features and componentry and technical gadgets and asked Mr. Hawkins reams of questions, so that Harold, John, and Eric had all learned almost everything three laymen might master in a single evening on the science and technology of injection-molded plastics before Harold made the first mention of the EV project.

Watching Harold in action—first in Boston and then at the meeting in Richmond and now here with George Hawkins—Eric was beginning to appreciate that there was something to Harold's gift of gab. Harold was an epicure of the human race. He liked people of every type and flavor, and he had a sincere and apparently bottomless curiosity about anyone he met. If it seemed that Harold took the long way to go about things—Eric would have made reasonable small talk and then cut to the chase himself, thinking otherwise he would be needlessly occupying Mr. Hawkins's good time—maybe, at least with Harold, the indirect route took you farther.

Eric had to admit that Mr. Hawkins certainly didn't look as though he felt his time was being wasted. He was listening with interest and absorption as Harold described the EV competition, the categories the car would be tested in, and how they were trying to figure out ways to cut weight to counterbalance the addition of all those lead batteries.

When Harold finally finished describing his ideas about the battery box, George said that unfortunately he didn't think Airmold could help with it—among other things, the cost would be prohibitive.

"But tell me more about this project," he said. He was intrigued by it. Maybe he could give them a hand with it, he suggested.

Almost before they knew it, George had them gathered in an office and was throwing down numbers and figures, stuff about efficiency and speed and acceleration and friction, page after page scrawled out in the engineer's arcane language of symbols. The idea, he told them, would be to focus on making the car as efficient as possible so that it required the least amount of force possible to travel down the road, and here was how they could calculate efficiency for whatever car they ended up with.

"Look at what has worked in the past," he also suggested. "Have there been other competitions? What kind of car won?"

To an outside observer it might have seemed a strange scene, these four men animatedly chattering long into the night over an inscrutable hieroglyphic of slashes and letters and formulae.

Eric and Harold had gone in search of plastic and come away with George Hawkins instead. They hadn't begun to assemble a car yet, but in ways they couldn't imagine they were putting together the framework that would make building it possible.

Meanwhile, they needed a car. They needed it soon. They needed it cheap. Free would be even better.

When you're looking for a free car, you understand that your options may be limited. Nevertheless, the vehicle had to be not so light that it couldn't carry the added weight of the batteries, nor so heavy that with those batteries it would end up wallowing along like a heifer stricken with the bloat.

Mr. Miller swept aside a stack of manuals, binders, and miscellaneous papers, sat Jennifer Robbins down in front of the phenomenally dusty computer in his classroom, and instructed her to go looking through a database program called *Mitchell on Demand*, which would yield a list of vehicles that fit whatever parameters were specified—make, or model year, or, in this case, gross vehicle weight.

"Pull anything less than twenty-five hundred pounds and more than eighteen hundred. See what you find," said Mr. Miller— instructions, it turned out, that could not be faulted for being too exacting.

Her initial reluctance forgotten, Jennifer had started catching Mr. Miller's and Mr. Ryan's excitement. Sometimes in Northampton County it seemed like you only ever heard about what couldn't be done—what there wasn't enough money for, what list the county had landed at the bottom of yet again. But Mr. Miller and Mr. Ryan talked as though they suffered not a single doubt that a bunch of kids like Jennifer and the other students, who weren't even thinking of themselves as a team yet, could build a car and win the competition.

Every time Jennifer had a few minute to spare, she sat down at Mr. Miller's computer, stabbing at the grubby keyboard, squinting at the smudgy screen until she felt like her eyes had gone permanently crossed, crawling through page after page the program produced for her. Who would have known so many cars weighed more than eighteen hundred pounds and less than twenty-five hundred? From that vast category she had to cull only those vehicles widely enough produced that even in an underpopulated place like Northampton someone might have an extra one of them around. Also she had to narrow her selection to anything that would be old enough that someone would be willing to let it go for cheap, but not so old that it would be verging on an ancient ruin, making spare parts, if they were needed, hard to come by. With all that, it still turned out to be a lot of cars. Gamely, though, she started calling dealerships in the area, the small ones that were hardly anything more than a garage with a side business, and the bigger ones as well, explaining the team's story, sketching broadly what they were looking for in the way of a vehicle.

There was a reason Harold had picked Jennifer. Jennifer, he knew, would get the job done. She was equal parts sweet voice and implacable determination. She was hard to say no to.

While Jennifer was trying to hunt down a car, Eric was taking George Hawkins's advice and researching what was known to work best, what was definitely a dead end, what kinds of cars, batteries, components were most favored in building conversions. When you had five months, no experience, and a team of teenagers, it wasn't time to start reinventing the wheel.

With the list of names, contacts, and sources he'd collected in Boston, Eric called Arizona, Massachusetts, New Hampshire, Washington, California, everywhere and all over, digging up any useful tidbit he could glean that would help the team make the right decisions and avoid the wrong ones.

He'd paid for a separate telephone line to be installed in his bedroom upstairs at the Parkers' house. For hours in the afternoons after school Eric would lie on his sleigh bed, watching the evening drop across the fields outside and making calls. Honestly, John and June thought they'd never met anyone who could spend as much time on the telephone as Eric Ryan. Suppers in the Parker household started sounding like a technical conference, as Eric reported what he'd learned for the day.

He was driving himself batty over batteries at the moment. The competition rules said they had to use lead-acid and they couldn't have more than ninety-six volts in their battery pack, so the standard sixteen six-volt golf cart batteries would do them. But there were so many different battery manufacturers, and of course it would be too easy if there was just one kind of six-volt lead-acid battery. Instead, there were flooded and sealed and absorbed glass-mat. There were ones rated for this number of amp-hours and that number of amp-hours—how long, under ideal conditions (and when were conditions ever ideal?), the batteries could go if current were drawn at a steady rate. Since the higher the rating, the heavier the battery, you had to calculate whether the theoretical additional time was worth the additional weight. And then just to complicate things further, the rules said ninety-six volts max, but they didn't mandate six-volt batteries. Eight twelve-volt batteries would add up to ninety-six just as well.

Six volts were the standard for conversions, Eric understood, because they were designed for range, for giving sustained speed over a sustained distance, and that's what you wanted for a car you were planning to drive around for your regular use.

Twelve-volt batteries were usually made with more and thinner lead plates than six-volts. With more lead surface area to react with the sulfuric acid, they could put out significantly more current than the six-volts for roughly the same weight. The advantage there was obvious—taking out eight batteries would also take off maybe five hundred pounds, and more power with less weight ought to mean the team's theoretical car would go faster and handle better—maybe giving the team an edge in the acceleration event and the race.

There were more considerations, however. With their thinner plates, most twelve-volts couldn't withstand nearly as many charge/discharge cycles as the six-volts could handle. And to further complicate the issue, although sixteen six-volts would weigh roughly twice as much as eight twelve-volts, it was one of those perversely vexing battery things that the twelve-volts discharged more rapidly than the six-volts, so the heavier battery pack might give the team better results in the range event and possibly also the race.

A quick lesson in electricity: watts, or power, equal amps (the amount of current flowing through your circuit) multiplied times volts (the pressure forcing that current to flow through your circuit). Think of a soda straw full of milk. If your six-year-old blows gently on that straw (lower voltage), the milk will dribble out onto the table. If he blows hard (higher voltage), that same amount of milk will splatter his baby brother across the table. So if power (watts) equals amps (the milk in the straw) times volts (the pressure forcing that milk through the straw), then if your kid blows hard enough (volts), even a small amount of milk in the straw (amps) will be sufficient to annoy his brother (power!).

The harder he blows, though, the sooner the milk will be gone.

Just so, for the competition this was the bottom line: they could go far, or they could go fast, but they weren't going to go far, fast.

One or the other, power or range, twelve-volt or six-volt. Whichever they chose, they were going to have to live with the decision. Batteries could take months from order to delivery, so even if they made their goal of getting the car on the road by late March, there would be neither time, nor the money anyway, for changing if what they picked turned out a disappointment.

Cross your fingers? Flip a coin? Instead, Eric pulled in Harold's son Doug, a whiz with a PC, who taught computers at Northampton–West, to extend the search for an answer into that strange new frontier, the Internet. Doug—who'd nearly been stupefied with shock upon hearing the news that finally, really, honest-to-God and truly his father was going to be building one of those electric cars he'd been singing about since Doug couldn't even remember when he hadn't—Doug wasn't going to miss this project. Doug deserved, after all these years listening to his father go on, and on, and on about EVs, to be part of this project.

He came back to Eric with reams of printouts. In the end, all of it took them right back to where Eric had started. What has worked best before? George Hawkins asked. What's everyone else using? What offered the best possible balance of power and range?

FALSE START

*G*_olf cart_ batteries?

The kids were not impressed.

Mr. Ryan was scribbling all these equations on the board and explaining why they added up to sixteen six-volt golf cart batteries. But amps, volts, watts, whatever—he was not winning over his audience with his arguments. From the look on many of the students' faces, he might as well have suggested they run the car on gerbils harnessed to exercise wheels. "Golf cart" was not the rallying cry for a group steeped in NASCAR.

No matter. Until they got a car, the issue was purely academic.

Then word came from Alan Vester Nissan. A car! The dealership had one, an old Datsun, a 240-Z. It was pretty much a beater, but if the team wanted it, they could have it.

Did they want it? A free car? A Z-car? Of course they did, said Mr. Ryan.

A few day later the car was dropped off at East, a 1970s-vintage Datsun. Eric's excitement dimmed a few watts when he got his first look at it. There was some limited evidence to suggest that at one time the car had been painted red, but rust had since flagrantly colonized the vehicle from hood latch to tailpipe. Speaking of ancient ruins.

Oh, but it was a Z-car, sleek and low-slung and sporty even in its diminished condition. It looked like a car built for speed, like a car that could go somewhere and do something, even if admittedly it might shed a few pieces of itself along the way. And most importantly, Eric knew the kids could get excited about working on a car, driving a car like that.

The car arrived on a Friday afternoon after school, when almost no one was around. Horace Burnette, one of the school's two janitors, was standing with Eric giving the Z an appraising once-over. Horace had been one of the very first people to welcome Eric to East, stopping by his classroom to give Eric his first introduction to the three-hour Southern "hello." They had discovered (the kind of detail a Southern hello gives you the leisure to get around to) that they shared the same January day of birth, so whenever they saw each other in the hallway, one was certain to hail the other with a "happy birthday!"

Now Eric glanced over at Horace. What do you say . . . ? Eric suggested, with a meaningful nod at the Z and a jingle of the keys in his hand.

So they took it for a test-drive. Spitting and smoking, rattling and clanking, it charged around the parking lot and out to the street with surprising vim. Eric was just thinking of really putting the pedal down when reason asserted itself and he and Horace recognized that the car was almost certain to expire just when they'd gotten themselves a long, hot walk from school. The car coughing and sputtering, Eric steered it back to the lot, where they parked it again.

What did it matter what kind of shape the engine was in? The engine was coming out anyway.

When the students saw it on Monday, they said, "Cool!" Eric looked at it and thought, "Cool!" Irrational exuberance ran high for the rust bucket.

Harold Miller took one look at it and thought otherwise. Harold had seen a lot of cars in his life, and he knew that if you get a car that has been banged up and knocked about, you can hammer out the dents and fill in the divots, straighten the frame even, if you have to. Rust is another matter. Rust means replacing parts, and they could hardly expect to find a couple of pristine fenders or a door panel for a 1970s Z-car lying around in someone's backyard.

Besides, the car was hardly big enough for two people and a pack of Saltines; where, Harold asked, were they going to stuff all the batteries?

Keep looking, Harold advised.

Eric knew Harold was right. The EV was like a different language; what made sense in a gasoline car didn't necessarily apply when you went electric. And the rust clearly had long since passed through the cosmetic and entered the systemic stage. Still, reason faltered in the face of romance. Eric wanted the kids to choose a car they could love.

For the time being, at any rate, they would keep it around, because a team that has nothing does not get rid of whatever something it happens to get. Who knew in what manner that Datsun might yet serve? It might even be that it would end up the only option they had.

So she sat in the parking lot, and though sullied she might have been, she was not so far gone a beauty that she did not prove, soon enough, too tempting a siren for Harold's student Neil Vann.

By his own admission, Neil was prey enough to mischievous curiosity that had he been a cat, he would have needed all his nine lives. Somehow it just happened, after school had let out for the afternoon and no one seemed to be around, that Neil found himself in close proximity to the Datsun, and somehow it just happened that Neil figured out he could start up the car with the key from his own truck. Sensing an opportunity to be seized or forever lost, he took the Z out for a smoke-belching joyride, spitting gravel around the parking lot.

Alas, where he made his fatal error was in letting a friend give it a whirl too, because inopportunely, Mr. Ryan happened upon this illicit exercise. Mr. Ryan was not pleased. Mr. Ryan thought the amazing coincidence that Neil's key worked in the Z was neither amazing nor a coincidence nor, as Neil seemed to have taken it, a sign from the gods not to be ignored. A pointed discussion ensued, closely followed by a verdict of a week's in-school suspension.

When it came to Neil, though, possibly his most aggravating quality was his ability to be so charming and funny that just at the moment when everyone in the room was ready to deal him blows, and it had been determined that bread and water and a month in irons was about what he had coming, he would manage somehow to turn everyone's ire to amusement. In negotiations with Mr. Miller he talked his sentence down to a couple of days. The truth was, for all that his methods and manner were unreformably Neil, the kid was good with his hands and smart around mechanical things, and the project needed him.

George Hawkins agreed the Z should be the car, if not quite of *last* resort, then at least not first. Look for what has worked before, he reminded them, sending Eric back to his research to compare with Jennifer's list. Realistically, they had to acknowledge that they were hardly in a position to name their demands—they would have to take what they could get, and maybe that would end up being the Z. But if they were going to keep searching, they might as well be able to give an idea of what they were hoping for.

George Hawkins had called not long after his first meeting with Eric and Harold and John, offering to stop by Harold's shop at East to see if he could help. He'd be happy to advise on technical matters, and he also happened to be a dab hand at welding, which the kids were going to need to learn to build the battery box and the roll cage when the time came.

Harold was delighted to welcome George on board. Harold liked guest speakers and visiting experts. They broadened the kids' horizons, and they were always a change of pace, which kids loved.

Eric would come to think of George Hawkins as the true engineer's engineer, a man always with a pencil at the ready in his shirt pocket and a calculation when you needed it. With the studied and deliberate manner of a person drawn to precision and a reliable order, George was not someone to countenance shortcuts, the fudge factor, or cutting once without measuring twice. He was, in short, Harold's polar opposite.

Upon his first sight of Harold's auto shop, then, it might be going too far to say that George Hawkins was actually struck dumb, but it was a near thing. Harold's shop was to George like a vision of the apocalypse.

It's a delicate business to walk into another man's working space and set about suggesting how it ought to be changed, but as George saw it, if this project was going to come off, both for efficiency and safety something needed to be done. He broached the matter diplomatically with Harold, observing that he might offer a few . . . suggestions for shaping up the shop for working on an EV.

Harold made a magnanimous, sweeping gesture that took in the crowded tabletops and shelves, the dust and debris, the oil stains and disorder, and that might equally have meant "Be my guest" or "Best of luck to you."

A lesser man might have quailed at the prospect before him; George started with the staples.

There were a couple of workbenches on wheels in Harold's shop, on which you could set down a part you were tinkering with or set up components for a lesson. Since nearly everything you might fiddle with from a car seemed to ooze something, whether it was oil, grease, or gas, Harold would get big rolls of paper from Georgia-Pacific, which had a plant in Conway, and he'd tear off long continuous sheets and throw them down on the benches and slam in a dozen staples or so to hold them in place, and when the sheets got too greasy or torn or otherwise besmirched, he'd just rip them off and lay down some fresh ones with a few more staples.

As a result, Harold's workbenches bristled with years' worth of bent and broken and twisted wood staples, probably thousands of them, protruding from the benches like some strange exercise in abstract industrial art. It was to these that George decided to address himself first, with the mission to remove each and every staple in order to restore the working spaces to an uncluttered state of *tabula rasa*-dom.

Harold might have imagined that straightening things up would mean shoving aside the extraneous clutter and perhaps giving the place a once-over with a broom. Stepping back into the shop from his classroom, where he'd been distracted by some other matter, Harold took in George, methodically prying staples loose, and stopped short.

"What the heck is he doing?" murmured Harold to Eric in astonishment.

Eric had long ago decided that Harold Miller must have a negative blood pressure, but would this be the moment that would prove even Harold had his limits? Were they about to witness one of those epic and legendary confrontations, like the immovable object meeting the unstoppable force?

Harold just laughed. He laughed as if the whole business of George Hawkins and the staples were a clever and genuinely amusing joke played on him. Then a student asked a question and Harold turned his attention to answering and that was the end of the matter.

It took days of devoted effort on George's part to remove all the staples, but he persevered, proceeding steadily and patiently, and when the last of them had been plucked out, he showed the students how to lay the paper on the bench and fold it into sharp corners neatly tacked down at the edges. He made suggestions, too, for setting up separate working areas for different tasks in the conversion process—welding here, wiring there, batteries in this place, everything ordered and safe, with the proper tools nearby. And slowly, almost as if by osmosis, his influence insinuated itself into the life of Harold Miller's auto shop: items were used and put back where they'd been taken from; historical oily spills were at last given their due, and if the tide of entropy was not entirely turned, its progression was for the moment stemmed.

Another man might have taken offense, bristling in territorial indignation, but Harold chose instead to see a paradigm shift. They were putting gas and its grunge and grease behind them. "We're going to be working with clean technology, we need a clean shop," said Harold.

"Mr. Hawkins here, he's our quality control," Mr. Miller started saying. "They weren't gonna learn that from me."

A CAR WITHIN THE MEANING OF THE WORD

The first week of November was already crossed off the calendar. A month gone in the five, and still no car better than the Z had appeared.

"All right, give me that phone," said Jennifer Robbins. "I'm getting us a car."

Jennifer happened to know some of the people at Pope Motors in Rich Square, and Mr. Miller thought he must have taught one Pope or another nearly every year since he came to Northampton.

What they didn't know—and why should they have?—was that Pope (though not the same Pope) had once been one of the biggest names in electric vehicles, back when electrics enjoyed their brief rise to glory on the threshold of the twentieth century.

Is it an omen if you don't know about it? Jennifer called the guys at Pope, armed with her list now further narrowed according to the George Hawkins what's-worked-before standard and by model year, weight, and the likelihood that there would be more than one or two extras kicking around Northampton County. They said, "Oh sure, we can help, we'd love to help, give us a little time and we'll see what we can come up with."

What they came up with, shortly thereafter, they said the team was welcome to, free. It should fit within Jennifer's parameters, too. Oh, and, um, by the way, it had been totaled. Twice, actually. "Do you want it?"

The car arrived at East on a flatbed. It appeared to have undergone in its life more body work than an aging Hollywood starlet. Not as much of a wreck as might have been expected for a twice-totaled vehicle; nevertheless, it had seen better days, and it hadn't seen them recently.

Katrina Deloatch took a long hard look at it.

"We're going to drive an *Escort?*" she said.

The twice-totaled, 1985, two-door Ford Escort hatchback sat in Mr. Miller's auto shop, as sexy as an overstretched panty girdle. It was a faded white, with the squat and solid unloveliness of its species, the mid-80s compact. It appeared to have come out the worse in altercations with various solid objects large and small, leaving it pockmarked like the surface of the moon. Its interior, a fresh-scab shade of red, was cracked where it wasn't split, flaking where it wasn't peeling, and pulling up where it wasn't sagging down. Among the members of the team gathered in the shop and giving it a skeptical appraisal, it excited all the enthusiasm aroused by mayonnaise on day-old white bread.

"That car is ragged," pronounced Donny Lassiter.

"Total hooptie," agreed another student, conferring upon the Escort the favored local term for "sorry jalopy."

If it had been difficult before for the students to share Mr. Miller's confident predictions of a resounding victory in Richmond, now, looking at the Escort, it was pretty much impossible. It was hard to imagine beating a bicycle around the parking lot.

Neil Vann knew the girl who'd owned it before, and what he knew of the car's history of hard knocks didn't bode well for its future.

"What kind of junk have we gotten into now?" wondered Neil, the car going a long way toward confirming his estimation of their chances of pulling off this whole project. There wasn't a chance he'd be tempted to sneak off for a joyride in this clunker.

Erick Vann heartily seconded that verdict.

After the precedent set by the Z, they'd been imagining something, you know, a little hotter, something with some muscle. Or at least something that didn't provoke an immediate urge to laugh and leave.

Eric Ryan worried that the kids could never get enthused and excited over an Escort, that it would cast a pall of blandness over everything to come, like inviting a girl on a first date to see your stamp collection.

Mr. Miller, however, thought the car was just the ticket. Go with what has worked before? A boxy compact like the Escort, while admittedly short on glamour, took top marks among EV enthusiasts for convertibility; it was the kind of vehicle recommended by Mike Brown in the book *Convert It.* Plenty of space for the batteries without being too heavy to start out with. Plus, Ford had churned out a zillion Escorts, so even in Northampton it ought to be easy to come by spare parts if they were needed. And the car was a hatchback, which would make it easier to get inside it to work. And it was in decent enough shape. And it was free. And it was already November.

For better or worse, everyone hoping it wouldn't be the latter, the Escort carried the day.

All they had to do now was strip the car, redesign it, put it back together, get it to run, get it to Richmond, and win. Not to mention they still needed about ten thousand dollars. Give or take.

John Parker had asked Harold and Eric to put a figure on what they thought the project would take to complete, from nuts and bolts to meals and lodging, and that was the number they named: ten thousand dollars.

Or so. To converting their vehicle and traveling to Richmond they would have to add, in order to comply with competition rules, the expense of the specialized steel tubing for the roll cage, the five-point driver's restraint, the fire-resistant suit and safety helmet for the driver. Other things, other unanticipated costs, might yet pop up.

John encouraged them to try to keep it more to the ten thousand and less to the "or so," and he said that the team was going to need to do everything it could to raise as much of that amount as possible. Then he said, "But do what you need to do and we'll figure it out," and it was that last part that Harold and Eric chose to hear most clearly.

Harold had already put two of his students, Anna Collier and Stephanie Martin, on the job of fund-raising. The girls worked the phone with a dedication that made Mr. Miller proud. Call after call, business after business, from Georgia-Pacific down to the sole-proprietor operations, they laid out their pitch politely but persistently.

"Hi, my name is Anna Collier and I'm a junior at Northampton–East . . . a team . . . electric vehicle . . . Richmond . . . would you be interested in sponsoring . . . any amount . . . ?"

They plugged away, undiscouraged. Yes. No. Fifty dollars. One hundred. Call back next week, call back when the manager's in. The girls made personal visits to pick up twenty-dollar bills and two-hundred-dollar checks with equal gratitude and wrote thank-you notes to every donor, all their efforts adding up in ones and tens and hundreds.

So when Randy Shillingburg stopped by to let them know that Virginia Power would be providing each of the teams it was sponsoring—including the one from North Carolina—with fifteen hundred dollars in seed money, there was whooping in Harold's shop, and it wasn't coming only from Eric Ryan. If fifteen hundred dollars would barely cover the cost of the motor alone, with thousands of dollars in parts and materials needed beyond that, still it put the team fifteen hundred dollars closer to the possibility of making it to Richmond. And it had a value far beyond its measure in dollars too. For the kids, it was as though this big, powerful company had leaned down and said, "We believe in you." Whether that was true, or whether Virginia Power was merely tossing out corporate pocket change to help give a boost to making sure the whole event came off, didn't really matter. What mattered was that what a month ago had seemed like a farfetched proposition—we're going to build an electric vehicle—wasn't feeling quite so farfetched anymore.

Of course, not everyone saw it that way. Word was getting around the counties now, Halifax and Northampton, about this electric car they were trying to build over at East to race up in Richmond. There were people already, like George Hawkins, Doug Miller, and Katrina's father, Pershield Deloatch, who said, "How can I help? What can I do?" There were parents and businesses digging into their wallets and hunting around their garages for whatever they could give. There were supporters like Pope Motors and Alan Vester Nissan. But there were other people, and John Parker would hear from them in the months to come, who muttered how they couldn't believe anyone would go and give Harold Miller money for one of those damn-fool ideas of his when everyone knew that not a one ever came to anything. They said, "He's gonna take them kids up to Richmond and make us a laughingstock with that old junker of a car; did you hear it had to be carried over to East on a flatbed? And they scoffed, "How's Miller gonna get an extension cord long enough to go all the way around that track?" and laughed heartily at their own wit. And they said, "There ain't no way that car is gonna run, nohow," and this last pronouncement they made with what sounded suspiciously like satisfaction.

To be sure, the ranks of the mutterers were small and in more than one case were comprised of what might be termed lifelong members of the club, people who had missed their calling as choristers in a Greek tragedy. Nevertheless, they were the ones who made it clear that they saw in this electric vehicle project not an opportunity for the kids to prove what they could do, but rather another shot at ending up on the bottom of someone's list.

MANY HANDS

They're calling it the EV Grand Prix," announced Mr. Ryan, reading from the latest newsletter to arrive from competition headquarters, Walt Purdy's office at EEI.

If ever there had been a case of hyperbole, it would have to be the words "grand prix" used anywhere in conjunction with this Escort. But this Escort was what they had to work with, and it was more than time to begin.

If you were a student electric vehicle team working in the shop at Northampton High School–East and you wanted to establish the starting weight of your 1985 twice-totaled Ford Escort hatchback before taking the car apart, you could take it just down the road about a half-mile from the school to the peanut scales.

Which they did, Harold and some of the students. And while they were on the straight stretch of road in front of the high school, they put the Escort through its paces briefly, for a "before" shot of its capabilities. At the moment, the car showed an inclination to buck and shimmy like a go-go dancer at anything approaching highway speed, and as for get-up-and-go, the car had little to speak of; stomp on the accelerator, and it dragged begrudgingly forward in the manner of a teenager rousted early out of bed on a Saturday morning to clean the garage.

And the weight? The peanut scales said about 2,200 pounds. The Escort's gross vehicle weight rating, the nonnegotiable number it could not exceed by competition rules (and, for that matter, safety), was 3,135 pounds. The batteries the team had settled on ordering weighed 66 pounds each, for a total of 1,056 pounds. Add in the motor, steel tubing for the roll cage, battery box, other parts and pieces—another several hundred pounds.

Their first challenge: this car needed to lose a few.

The Escort was back in Harold's shop once again, students gathered around it, most of them still having a hard time picturing how this car was going to become something other than what it was, and particularly how it might become something they wouldn't feel the need to apologize for driving up in.

Harold always believed the best place to begin was to start. He liked to jump into a project without a lot of preamble, preferring the direct approach over the abstract. He believed students learned better by doing; they could sit around all day talking about plans and ideas and concepts, but nothing says "getting down to business" like handing a kid a wrench.

"We got to take this car apart," he announced. "And while we're at it, let's look at how it pollutes, and what we won't need anymore when it's electric."

The gas tank went first. It was a nicely symbolic gesture, going straight to the font of the foul life's blood of the internal combustion engine. There was, however, a wholly pragmatic reason behind the approach.

Most of us, it is a safe bet to say, rarely pause to consider, upon pulling out of the Gas 'n' Go with a full tank, that we're heading down the highway in what amounts to a rolling bomb; pound for pound, gasoline has fifteen times the energy of the equivalent amount of TNT. In practice, this is an interesting but otherwise (one hopes) largely academic comparison—even in an accident, cars don't readily explode, since it's vaporized, rather than liquid, gasoline that goes up with a bang. On the other hand, gasoline is highly volatile—it vaporizes easily. This is why it works in an internal combustion engine. This is also why you don't want to smoke while pumping a fill-up.

If cavalierly handled, the tank on the Escort, still with fuel in it, could provide a too-instructive demonstration of gasoline's explosive potential. As blowing up Mr. Miller's shop and the students therein was likely to bode poorly for the future of the electric vehicle project, Mr. Miller made sure that both the tank and anyone touching it were properly grounded before the removal began. Just in case.

Harold possessed a hand pump for the purpose; they grounded it to the body of the car and then siphoned out the gasoline into an approved container.

"Now," said Mr. Miller, "what you have in that container is a couple of gallons of toxic waste."

They could not let it evaporate—that would pollute the air. They could not pour it on the grass—that would pollute the ground, and kill the grass too. They could not pour it down a drain—that would pollute the water. Gasoline is pretty much an all-purpose poison.

How many hundreds of times in their lives had these kids visited a gas station without ever thinking once about the gasoline itself, except maybe to note its smell? Now, with their half-filled jug sitting there, the enormity of their burden weighed upon them; they couldn't do anything with that gasoline without polluting something. It was like being a murderer trying to dispose of a body.

Finally, they poured it into the school lawn mower, where it would live to pollute another day.

Back at the car, they blew air into the tank to vent the remaining fumes, flooded the tank with water to force any residual vapors up and out, and at last were ready to remove the tank itself.

That went fast. A couple of straps, a few minutes, and Mr. Miller held up the tank like a surgeon displaying an excised tumor.

"We're going to hang this up here in the shop to remind ourselves where we started," he said, and set it aside.

Then out came the rest of the car's innards, and some of its outards: the engine, the fan, the muffler, the catalytic converter, the belts, the hoses, the fuel lines and pump, the pistons and spark plugs and head gaskets, the antifreeze tank, the air filter, the oil pan, component after part after nut after bolt, each one filthier and greasier than the last.

With each item they took out, Mr. Miller and the students would talk about what it did. And then he'd say, "We won't need that in our EV."

The students stood amazed at the heap of what went in to getting a gas car to go. And you could make a vehicle that needed none of that?

In helping to take the Escort apart, Jennifer Robbins felt like she'd learned more about the internal combustion vehicle than a year of lectures would have taught her. And if you wanted to say that those vehicles seemed ridiculously overly complicated, she wasn't going to disagree with you now.

Their twice-totaled hatchback ran on a basic four-stroke, internal combustion engine—the underpinning of almost all automobiles on the road today, and for that matter almost all automobiles ever.

A German, one Nikolaus August Otto, is generally credited with being the first to build a successful version of the four-stroke engine, in 1876. The four-stroke cycle (aka the Otto cycle) consists of an intake downstroke, a compression upstroke, an explosive downstroke, and finally an exhaust upstroke. Whether you have four or six or eight cylinders in your vehicle, this is what is going on inside each one of them.

On the first downstroke, the piston inside the cylinder moves down and a mixture of air and gasoline is drawn into the cylinder. On the second, compression stroke, the piston is pushed back up, packing the already combustible air-fuel mixture to highly explosive density. The spark plug fires, the mixture goes "boom," and the piston shoots back down the cylinder for the second downstroke. Finally, the piston rises once more on the fourth stroke, pushing the exhaust left over from the combustion back out of the cylinder, and then the whole cycle begins again. Harold Miller had an exercise he would conduct with his students to illustrate this cycle, with kids running in one door, and up and down the aisles between the desks, and out the other door, with someone smacking a book on a desk for the bang in the middle.

In an automobile, the piston is connected to the vehicle's crankshaft, translating the downward force of the compression stroke into the rotational motion of the crankshaft, which turns the transmission shaft, which turns the gears, which turn the axles, which turn the wheels. Multiple cylinders, firing successively, keep the crank turning smoothly and steadily.

For years, Harold Miller had been introducing his students to the four-stroke cycle, but now, as they disassembled the engine and examined the pistons and the cylinder heads and the distributor cap, he took them one step further. He asked them to think about everything that was wrong with the system.

A very small amount of gasoline, compressed with the right amount of air, packs an amazingly powerful wallop when ignited. That would seem, of course, to be the good thing about gas, but it's a dubious virtue that has spoiled us filthy.

"It's so wasteful, you can't believe," said Mr. Miller. "You turn on a car; in a couple of minutes that engine is so hot you can't touch it without burning yourself."

And what is that heat? It is the by-product, he pointed out, of that steady parade of mini-explosions going on inside the cylinders, where the temperature may be measured in the thousands of degrees. A great deal of the energy contained in the gasoline is given off in this heat. And yet, the engine has no use for it. Quite the opposite. If an elaborate cooling system weren't built in—pump, fan, radiator, whatnot—the engine would overheat so quickly that it would essentially weld itself to itself, seize up completely, and be ruined.

For the final insult, for all that heat and bluster, the combustion process doesn't even manage to burn all the fuel, converting it instead to a cloud of airborne pollutants. For every gallon of gas, the engine sucks through its system roughly the amount of air that would fill an average-sized room, then sends it hot out the tailpipe bearing its added burden of killer chemicals. Think of a traffic jam, all that air going in one end and out the other of vehicle after vehicle and then down your own pipes and into your lungs.

But because gas gives so much oomph to the ounce, because on a five-minute fill-up and hardly a second's thought we've been free to go larking off on our errands and road trips and wheresoever we want to go, we have made our devil's bargain, uncomplainingly accepting, even embracing in our lust for the biggest, most powerful gas-guzzler on the block, the profligately spendthrift inefficiency of the internal combustion engine.

We are the wife who cannot leave a bad marriage to a rich man because she loves the money too much.

Mr. Miller made the students stop and think about these things, but sometimes they simply nodded, not altogether paying attention, because really, they were having a blast tearing the car apart. What teenager's Inner Anarchist would not rise to such an opportunity? With the gas and engine and exhaust systems gone, they turned to the body and pulled out the seats too, and the carpets and the ceiling panels, removed the doors, removed the hood, removed the hatchback.

In a week, they had the Escort stripped to the bones.

Now the car would go back to the peanut scales for weighing again. Only this time, with no engine to do the work of getting it down the road, human power would be required.

Miller recruited a couple of his bigger boys, and they got behind the car and started pushing—huffing it out through the parking lot and along Route 2 in front of the school and back to the scales. They had reduced the car to about seventeen hundred pounds.

At the moment, they were free to add fourteen hundred pounds before they would exceed the Escort's gross vehicle weight rating. That sounded like plenty of pounds, until you considered that more than one thousand of them were already claimed by the batteries, and then the doors and the seats, the hatchback, everything that would make it look like a real car again, had to go back on too. The way the team understood the rules, the design event would be won by the vehicle that looked most like the car it had started as. The EV Grand Prix wanted to show that you didn't have to give up comfort or style to go electric, and to dispel the EVs undeserved reputation as a tricked-out golf cart.

What that meant for ECORV was that when it came down to the wire, every pound—and even every ounce—might count. Would the team end up with the vehicular equivalent of a kid trying to make weight for the wrestling match by spitting out the side of his mouth before stepping on the scales?

Back down the road went the Escort with the boys pushing behind. Miller would bet the kids up at Norfolk Tech weren't running their shell down the street to weigh it; maybe that meant a disadvantage for the North Carolina Power team, and maybe it didn't. Soon enough, they'd see.

If the Escort hadn't looked like much before, now it looked like . . . less. When Darrell Parker had last seen it a week ago, at the Monday meeting, it was still all in one piece, and he'd wondered then how they ever were going to make anything of it. Now the doors, dingy and dinged, were off and leaning against the wall, and the seats were out as well, looking odd and orphaned where they'd been shoved out of the way, and most of the interior finishing details were gone too, the carpeting and panels piled in their own heaps. You'd see cars that looked like this, propped up on cinder blocks in backyards here and there around Northampton County, and over the years the weeds would grow up around them and the frame rust out and fallen leaves accumulate inside. Would the team's ambitions end up like that, an overgrown pile of junk that Mr. Miller's classes would scavenge parts from for a few years before finally the school paid somebody fifty bucks to haul the rest off to a scrap yard?

Everyone took seats in Harold's classroom to start the weekly meeting. This was the routine they'd established: first thing, Mr. Ryan and Mr. Miller would remind everyone what they had done the previous Monday, talk about anything that might have been accomplished in the intervening week, and then discuss what was planned for today and who would be doing what. At the end of Monday's work, they'd reassemble briefly for the day's progress report.

Mr. Joyner, Mr. Shields, and Mrs. Keeter let Harold and Eric take the lead, set the pace, and determine priorities, and then, when it was time to get to work, they'd sort themselves out to oversee this or that task and the kids assigned to it. It all went surprisingly smoothly, considering that they were five teachers from four different schools, all sharing a classroom and a project. Every teacher has a particular style and way of doing things, and except for Eric, the other ECORV teachers were veterans of many years of doing it their own way. Add to this group George Hawkins, and then George Hawkins, Sr., who came to help teach the kids welding. Add some parents and other relations, drop-ins by Greg Todd, the new principal at Northampton–East, who was a mechanically oriented, hands-on guy himself. Add the pressures of taking on a completely uncharted technical challenge in the face of a fast-approaching deadline. It was hard to imagine how the situation couldn't lead to tension and conflict and territorial skirmishes and clashes of philosophies, and eventually someone shouting, "Well, fine, I wash my hands of the lot of you!" and snatching up his socket wrench and going home.

Somehow, that never happened.

Which isn't to say that dissent never arose. Drawn into debate over where to put this or how to connect that, the teachers and Mr. Hawkins might crowd over the engine compartment with their own measuring tapes and calculators in hand and their ties flipped back over their shoulders.

"I think this might work," one would venture, sketching a possibility.

"Are you kidding? It's never going to work that way," another would say. "Maybe on paper, but not in this car," he would add, launching into an explanation of why, which, depending on who was giving it, might involve several formulas and a discussion of friction and mass, or an anecdote about a Saturday night racetrack and an unforgettable trick learned. After much animated discussion, with resort to scribbling things on the blackboard and perhaps to the consultation of a manual or two, with Mr. Shields scratching the side of his head as he always did when deep in concentration, there would be a slow dawning of nods all around, and someone would finally say, "I think that sounds right—let's go ahead and try that."

The conversations were spirited but never heated, and the kids, listening as they worked at their own tasks, would look at each other and crack grins. When you were a student, you didn't think about whether your teachers were having fun. They were just . . . teachers. Grownups with grade books. The people with all the answers already. You didn't give much thought to whether they derived any satisfaction out of giving pop quizzes (though you suspected they did) or whether there was something they might rather do with a class than teach out of the same textbook year after year. But it was obvious, listening to them all happily arguing with each other, that the grownups were having a good time.

* * *

This afternoon, with the car sitting freshly stripped next door in the shop, Mr. Miller was handing around a couple of canister-shaped objects, about the size of a coffee can but much heavier.

"This here is an electric starter motor," said Mr. Miller, holding one up.

To some of the students, this stated the obvious; to others, it was a first introduction.

Mr. Miller told them to think about the power it takes to turn over a cold engine, to get all that system fired up and moving. "It takes an electric motor to do that," he told them, a little itty-bitty motor like the one they were handing around.

That gave them something to think about—a big engine started up by this motor so small that you could practically hide it under Mr. Miller's Garth Brooks hat.

"And the motor we put in our car," Mr. Miller told them, "only thing different about it is that it's going to be bigger. But it works the same way."

He had one motor disassembled so the students could see what was going on inside, and he explained how it would drive their EV.

Stripped to its essence, as Mr. Miller explained it to the kids, an EV is a big electrical circuit on wheels, powered by a battery pack, with a motor in the middle. Cable the positive pole of battery number one to the negative pole of battery number two, and the negative pole of battery two to the positive pole of battery three, and so on, until each of the batteries is wired to the next in a continuous series, each adding its volts to the whole, each adding its pressure to push the current along the circuit. Ultimately, with a few safety and control features along the way, the circuit is routed through the motor and back to the first battery.

A battery wants nothing so much as to discharge itself, its electrons, like thoroughbreds pent up and pawing at the starting gate, yearning to rush pell-mell to the opposite pole and surrender themselves. The circuit is the course they run to get there; when you press the accelerator in an EV, off the electrons merrily go, diverted through the motor along the way. This is where the magic comes in.

It's one of those fascinating and wondrous happenstances of the universe that electricity flowing through a wire makes a magnet of that wire. If you wind an insulated copper wire around a nail and hook it to two ends of a D-cell battery, you will have constructed yourself a simple electromagnet; you can pick up paper clips and thumb tacks with it. The more coils of wire you add, the stronger the magnet you can make. Now recall the well-known principle that like poles of a magnet repel each other and opposites attract, and you will understand what drives an electric motor.

Inside a motor is a free-rotating, horizontal cylinder of coiled wires called the armature. Surrounding but not touching the armature are a series of magnets. When power flows through the motor it magnetizes the armature, setting it spinning in an attracting/repulsing dance with the surrounding magnets, and in the very act of spinning the armature keeps reversing its own polarity, so that, like someone in an unhappy love triangle, it is perpetually chasing what it desires and fleeing what repels it. Round and round it goes, and as turns the motor, so ultimately turn the wheels. It's admirably simple.

Yet it strains credulity, all this business with magnets and the flow of electrons, invisible to the naked eye. You can't smell it. You can't hear it. A gasoline engine is noisy and fumish and whirring and blustery, and it's easy to see that stuff is going on in there. By contrast, an electric motor, soundless and subtle, requires something like a leap of faith.

Mr. Miller took some jumper cables and hooked them up to a twelve-volt starter battery and then connected one cable to one of the electric motors he'd been showing around. He put a pair of goggles on a student and said, "Now put this clamp right here on the motor." And zoom, with a little spark that made the kid jump back and laugh, the motor started spinning. It made hardly any noise at all.

They let the motor run for a few minutes, then turned it off, and Mr. Miller made everyone come up and put their hands on it. It wasn't hot. You could hardly even say it was warm. Not anything like a gasoline engine at all.

Fine, so it wasn't loud. So it didn't get hot. So it was a miracle of electromagnetic force. Was it going to make their car go? That's what the kids wanted to know.

It was what Eric Ryan wanted to know too, though he wasn't going to admit any doubts in front of the students.

Formulating an integrated curriculum on the fly for this EV project was making for an interesting challenge for Eric, a second-year teacher who was still working out the best approaches for teaching the primary curriculum. Yet it was the kind of opportunity a teacher dreamed of, a chance to help his students go beyond a textbook definition of inertia or a paragraph on a test to explain amperage. Now inertia was something they'd have to overcome. Now amps wouldn't be an abstraction, they'd be a factor in how far and fast the team's electric car could go.

The easy way to make this EV come together would be to sit the kids down every week and tell them, "Do this, connect that." With the assembled adults on hand, they had the know-how to take charge and give directions, and in a few months no doubt they'd have a car, probably a good one, maybe one that could win, and earn them boasting rights. The kids would get a fun field trip out of it, a couple of adventurous days in Richmond. But that would be that. Soon enough, the whole experience would mean less to the students than next year's prom theme, reduced in their memories to a mildly diverting class project of which the high points were missing a couple of days of school and staying in a hotel.

Eric, Harold, the other teachers, opted for the harder road. They would stand behind their kids as coaches and mentors, give them the tools and the resources they would need, and exercise veto power only when necessary. As much as possible, they would let the students together find their own way, make the choices, learn from their mistakes, and try again.

Harold always insisted that his kids think for themselves, even when they didn't want to; he was one of those teachers who handed you the dictionary when you asked him how to spell a word. Eric was like that too—those questions he regularly posed his students for their journals were meant to make the kids wonder and want to know more.

At the beginning of this EV project, Eric wanted to believe that the students could literally do every single thing—all the research, all the welding, the public relations, the wiring, the fund-raising, and the driving. They would complete every calculation, drill every hole, tighten every bolt, and make every phone call. That was Eric's vision.

Eric had made spreadsheet schedules, task lists, and a timeline and posted them on the wall of Mr. Miller's classroom. Sometimes Harold or Eric might select a particular student and say, "I need you to do this today," and sometimes they asked for volunteers or anyone interested in trying a new challenge. From week to week, everyone could mark the team's progress by items crossed off the list. Every week it didn't seem like the list was getting much shorter, but the timeline was.

Soon enough, Eric's vision ran into the list. Good Lord, but there was a lot to do, and every item took exponentially longer with each teenager you added to the job. Each kid came with a different learning curve and frustration capacity and distraction threshold. Some kids wouldn't give up on a problem until they'd solved it, while others wouldn't last fifteen minutes before they got bored and wandered off looking for something else to do.

Quite a few of the tasks involved a series of smaller, subsidiary tasks, each one of which had to be completed before the next could be started, and sometimes, even with so much to be done, a dozen kids would be sitting around unoccupied because the right tool wasn't in the shop or because they were still looking for some part or other, and Eric realized that a faithful rendition of his vision would mean that the car might be finished in time for the tenth anniversary of the EV Grand Prix, but it wasn't going to be done by March.

Other hands were needed. At first, admitting this was a hard blow for Eric. But in the weeks and months to come, he would glance around the shop and see George Hawkins and George Sr. helping kids practice their welding skills. He would see Katrina's father and Harold and Darrell's Uncle Clyde or Harold Miller's son Doug stepping in wherever they could assist. Or Harold would send lists of parts and equipment they needed to William Hall, the NAPA dealer in Murfreesboro, who would hunt around to find them as cheap as possible for the team. Then Eric realized that in Northampton County, you never did anything all by yourself.

NUMBERS

November had slipped past, Thanksgiving come and gone, and the Escort, still an empty frame, a box with a steering wheel, sat looking skeletal in Harold's shop.

But the latest EV Grand Prix newsletter asked each of the teams to pick a racing number for its car, which reminded everyone in ECORV where they were trying to go, even if they had not yet made much visible progress toward getting there. A big number on the doors of the car served a practical purpose; it was a highly visible shorthand for keeping track of vehicles as they zoomed past in a competition. True, there wouldn't be that many cars competing in the EV Grand Prix. They wouldn't be speeding along at any 150 miles per hour like the NASCAR drivers either. The students wouldn't be operating million-dollar cars, and there wouldn't be seventy-five thousand avid fans packing the stands at Richmond International Raceway. Still, Walt Purdy and the organizers at Virginia Power and the raceway were trying to make this event feel as much as possible like the real thing, racing the way the big boys did it.

Of course, the NASCAR devotees on the team had their opinions on what number should be chosen—Dale Earnhardt's #3 or Jeff Gordon's #24. But Mr. Miller suggested a number with some history, he suggested the number 10. Bill Champion, he said, the next-door neighbor from Mr. Miller's boyhood days growing up in Norfolk, had driven the #10 car at one time. He'd never been one of the famous, big names, but he was a fine man, said Mr. Miller, and now, long retired, he was seriously ill with cancer. Mr. Miller called up Mrs. Champion and told her it would be an honor if his kids could have her blessing to carry the number 10 on their car in the EV Grand Prix.

The students liked that idea, and then when Mr. Ryan added, "Hey, ten was kind of my lucky number when I was a kid—it was my soccer jersey number," it was clear that the fates had spoken. How could they choose anything else? Number 10 it would be.

None of the essential parts that were needed to make the Escort into an EV had yet arrived, though the batteries, those golf cart batteries (the students still rolled their eyes when they said it) were on order. And the higher powers at the EV Grand Prix had passed along word that equipment sponsors would make two of the other major (and most expensive) components—the motor and the power-regulating controller—available to the teams at a discount. This news was greeted happily in the auto shop at Northampton–East, since money the team didn't have to spend was money the team didn't have to find.

However, there wasn't any clear indication of when those sponsored parts would actually arrive. The team couldn't sit about with their disemboweled Escort and do nothing in the meantime.

To solve the paradox of both too much to be done and too many kids with not enough to do at any given time, the teachers had decided to divide the students into task teams. Jennifer and Katrina were assigned to the battery squad, their job to run all the numbers that together would equal the ideal possible placement for their sixteen-count, their eight cubic feet, their thousand pounds worth of batteries.

So, "All right," said Jennifer Robbins, pointing to some of the bigger boys, "you, and you, and you, y'all get in the car." If they didn't have one thousand pounds of batteries yet to arrange this way and that, and so figure out how they would affect the car's balance, then as near as could be assembled to a thousand pounds of boys would have to do.

Erick Vann, Tim Stauffer, Ivory Richardson, and sometimes whoever else was standing idle for a moment, would stuff themselves inside the frame until Erick, hunched over a wheel well, started thinking they must look like a bunch of clowns at the circus climbing in and climbing out of the vehicle. While they were in there, the riding height of the Escort was checked, too, to make sure that when all that added weight went in, the car didn't sag on its wheels like a low-rider cruising the Saturday-night strip.

George Hawkins, with his formulas and calculations and his sharpened pencils always at the handy, sat the girls down to help them analyze their challenge. The batteries would need to remain upright or they would leak acid, and be secured so they wouldn't jostle around or become airborne in case of an accident or a rollover. They ought to be located with not too many in the front or in the back or to one side or the other, to keep the vehicle properly balanced and to optimize handling during acceleration and turning. At the same time, it was important to keep as many of the batteries as close together as possible, and as close to the motor as possible (and the motor would have to be up front where it could be attached to the transmission), because they each would be connected, one to the next, by lengths of cable, and the longer the cable, the more resistance would accumulate, affecting the power that ultimately reached the motor (Ohm's law came into play here—current equals voltage divided by resistance—and the girls repeated it to themselves so many times that after a while it seemed more familiar to them than their own names.) And if the batteries were in the passenger compartment, they'd have to go inside a battery box too. Where would that fit?

"A project like this, it's all about tradeoffs," Mr. Hawkins would remind them equably, as they worked up each new plan and ordered the boys into the car again.

It turned out to be much more complicated than they would have expected—a three-dimensional puzzle that demanded factoring in weight, distance, resistance, balance, available space, and the various ways in which the car would have to perform in the Grand Prix. Jennifer and Katrina would sit with their faces scrunched in concentration, fingers tapping on calculators, scribbling notes and sketches and then balling their papers up in frustration and starting over again. Why was it so hard to stuff sixteen batteries into a car? One setup had them riding too high. Another spread them too far apart. A third put too much weight up front, making it likelier that the tail could spin out in a sharp turn.

Even the teachers, even George Hawkins, didn't know what the answer should be. There was no precedent to follow, no manual outlining Optimal Placement of Sixteen Six-Volt Batteries in a 1985 Ford Escort Hatchback to Win the EV Grand Prix.

"How the heck are we gonna do this?" Harold started wondering. What if it turned out to be logistically impossible, turned out to be their bad luck that they'd gone and gotten the one car that could not be made to do what they wanted it to do?

They built cardboard-scale mock-ups of the batteries, the motor, and the controller (which would be about the size and shape of a couple of shoe boxes side by side) in order to determine where those would go and how much room they would take up so that the team didn't end up with the batteries placed and nowhere to put the motor. Setting all sixteen of the cardboard battery stand-ins on a tabletop made it immediately apparent—in case there had been any doubt on this point—that the power pack was going to take up a large amount of space. The Escort was roomy only in a relative sense—relative to other economy cars. Relative to the batteries, it stopped looking roomy at all.

The kids arranged and rearranged their cardboard parts to measure how much space each configuration would command, then back Jennifer and Katrina would go to the calculators, to the car, to the mock-ups, to the boys, round and round until they were dizzy with numbers. Each time, they came up against the apparently impossible, that the only way to make everything work was to put batteries where they couldn't be put.

Finally, when they were so very and absolutely positive and sure they never would get it right, they got it right. It looked like they had it right, at least: six batteries in the front in the (former) engine compartment, on the left side if you were facing the car, set in a three-level stepped frame to make room for the motor they would install beneath it. Ten batteries in the back, nine to go together in a box where the rear seat had been, and one to go all by itself by the rear wheel behind the driver. The solo rear battery, along with the weight of the driver, was intended to balance the off-center weight of the six front batteries. They had a plan. Or so they hoped.

The time spent working on the puzzle had provided ample opportunity to discuss the pros and cons of battery-powered travel. What at the moment seemed to the students the most obvious draw-back—positioning the batteries—would not be such an issue in a purpose-built EV, Mr. Miller said, where the vehicle could be constructed around the batteries rather than trying to accommodate the batteries to the vehicle, as they were doing with the conversion.

On the other hand, batteries were the focus of most objections to the EV. Their range was too limited, said the critics. They took too long to charge up. It was a technological step backward, a car you had to plug in.

But what was so hard about plugging an extension cord into the wall? It took longer to fill up your tank. And how far do most of us travel in a day? To school, to work, to the store, thirty, forty, fifty miles, distances that easily could be covered by an EV built with existing technology. What if, suggested Mr. Miller, every household with two or three vehicles or more parked out front and in the garage—what if they each traded just one for an EV? One EV for around town, for the local drives, and the gas car still there when you needed it for longer trips. Mr. Miller said he'd bet pretty soon everyone in the family would be fighting to drive the electric.

Because internal combustion vehicles have become so familiar to us, pointed out Mr. Miller, we've gotten accustomed to their shortcomings. We never stop to ask ourselves why we put up with the noise and the stink and the pollution, why we accept sinking money into scheduled maintenance and unscheduled repairs, why we resign ourselves to volatile prices at the pump. We live with all that, said Mr. Miller, because we haven't been offered a chance to choose anything else.

While the battery conundrum had roiled along, other teams of students were organized to take on the remaking of the Escort's battered exterior, to begin fashioning the roll cage, and to run errands and fetch things that needed to be picked up. But the next pressing item to demand attention on that pitiless, bottomless list was the adaptor plate.

The standard procedure in converting from gasoline to EV is to attach the electric motor to the vehicle's existing transmission, and this is what the ECORV team planned to do, having spared the Escort's transmission from the dismantling and left it in the car.

But the transmission wasn't meant to be attached to an electric motor. Putting the two together would require still more figuring and finagling as well as the manufacturing of a precision-machined plate of aluminum, more than a half-inch thick, which would be bolted to the transmission on one side and the motor on the other, thus marrying them securely to each other. An output shaft extending from the spinning armature of the motor would pass through a hole in this plate to be coupled to the transmission shaft; all the power to turn the wheels and accelerate a three-thousand-pound car and move it down the road had to be transferred through this connection, and you definitely didn't want it in any way loose or wobbly or almost-but-not-quite. It had to be perfect.

Only a brief glance around Harold Miller's shop was necessary to conclude that there would be no precision-machining of three-quarter-inch-thick aluminum sheets with the equipment therein. A hacksaw wasn't going to cut it.

It's a wonderful thing when life calls for a professional machine shop, and almost at that precise moment a professional machine shop appears in your life. When Pope Motors delivered the Escort to East, not one but two local newspapers had run stories accompanied by large photos of Jimmy Pope handing over the keys to Anna Collier, one of the dedicated fund-raisers on the team. In Norfolk, in Richmond, in Raleigh, on a slow news day, the story might have rated a paragraph buried somewhere in the community lifestyle pages. In Northampton County, a car dealer handing the keys for a twice-totaled secondhand Escort to a high-schooler got eighteen column-inches in two different papers.

One of the owners of the Machine Shop of Murfreesboro saw one of those stories (how could he miss it?) and called up Harold Miller in his shop. "I see y'all are building yourselves an electric car," said the owner. "If there's anything we can do to help, you let me know."

Now, with the adaptor plate next on the agenda, a couple of the boys from the Machine Shop stopped by Northampton–East one afternoon to take a look at the project and get a picture from Harold Miller about what this plate needed to do. More leaning over the front end of the vehicle, and conferring, and sketching, and referencing a manual—in this case, Michael Brown's *Convert It,* with its photos and illustrations describing the details and function of the adaptor plate.

"We can do that," said the boys from the Machine Shop.

Brown's book talked about accuracy of measurements within thousandths of an inch. But you gotta do what you gotta do with what you have do to it with; a couple of Harold's students took a ball peen hammer and a thin piece of cardboard, placed the latter against the transmission where the plate would need to be affixed, tapped an outline of the shape and the bolt holes into the cardboard with the hammer, and took their template over to the Machine Shop in Murfreesboro. Then everyone crossed their fingers.

The roll cage was a different beast altogether, less precision and more trying to wrestle a drunken elephant into a telephone booth.

The competition rules mandated seamless steel tubing of rather particular diameter and thickness, which the team came by easily enough through a race-car parts supplier. After that, things got trickier. The straight, ten-foot lengths of tubing, which showed a tendency to want to get in the way of everything and rattle suddenly and loudly to the cement floor in the shop and in other manner make a nuisance of themselves, needed to be cut, bent, and welded into a frame that could be fitted inside the Escort and bolted to the body of the car. It was supposed to keep the roof or sides of the vehicle from crushing in on the driver in the event of a crash or rollover and to block the battery pack behind the driver from hurtling forward in an impact.

That such precautions were deemed necessary appeared, at the moment, beyond laughable. The Escort indicated not the slightest evidence that it would ever be going anywhere again under its own power, much less going anywhere fast enough to crash or roll. But the rules were the rules.

Neil Vann, the Parker twins, and Ivory Richardson from Northwest Halifax High School, whose family was of the local Native American Haliwa-Saponi tribe, were tapped to focus on the roll cage for now, though as always with this project, anyone who was interested and not otherwise occupied was welcome to join in.

To get everyone properly started, George Hawkins, Sr., gave Doug Miller a welding lesson. Doug turned around and showed a few of the students. The students started practicing their welding on some scrap metal.

By the time it had passed through these several iterations, the quality of the welding began to deviate considerably from the standard set by Mr. Hawkins, Sr. The practice seams were gobbed and dripped, and one of the girls had given herself a welder's-torch sunburn. Mr.

Hawkins, Jr., stepped in. He couldn't say that he thought much of their potential as future welders, but they were certainly a refreshingly polite and respectful group of young people, who listened attentively to what he said and attempted earnestly to apply it. Except for that Neil Vann kid, the one with all the opinions.

Neil would admit that he and Mr. Hawkins didn't set horses. It wasn't that Neil didn't respect the way Mr. Hawkins did things, all methodical and precise and one-step-at-a-time. It was only that Neil thought in the real world sometimes you just had to get things done, and you couldn't always sweat over whether it was absolutely right to the thousandth of an inch.

Which was not how Mr. Hawkins saw things, recognizing that a small margin of error at Point A can lead to wildly missing the mark by Point Z.

Kelly Daughtry turned out to be just the person for the job of makeover artist for the moonscape of dings and dents to the Escort's doors and frame and body panels. It was slow, methodical, and painstaking work, a matter of applying filler and waiting for it to cure and then hand-sanding it smooth—elbow grease was the only equipment at hand in Mr. Miller's shop for this task—and then more filler, more curing, more sanding, for every divot and ping, large and small.

But Kelly was a meticulous girl. She believed that presentation mattered. When a project was done neatly, with things well-organized and properly detailed, it showed care and commitment; it showed, Kelly believed, that you weren't going to settle for sloppiness and shoddy measures, and in a competition effort sometimes meant as much to the judges as performance. Kelly devoted herself to the filling and sanding with unflagging patience, hour after hour, week after week, until the image of her sanding and sanding and sanding was burned irrevocably into everyone's mind. If someone kidded her about her dedication, she continued unperturbed.

"It has to be right," she would say.

Tim Stauffer was president of the Future Farmers of America club at school; he was the kind of farm kid who had been hefting sacks of this and bales of that almost since he was old enough to walk. Darrell Parker thought Tim must have drunk all his milk when his mother told him to, because if you needed something picked up, shoved aside, or hauled over, Tim was your guy. Tim could lift one end of the Escort like it wasn't any heavier than a bag of groceries; Mr. Miller called Tim the team's "human jack."

Perhaps alone among the students, when Tim heard Mr. Miller first talk about this project, he'd thought, "Yeah, we can do that."

Now that the placement of the batteries and other parts had been decided upon, they could address themselves to building a battery box—boxes, actually, two of them—and Erick Vann and Tim would be part of that team, and Donny Lassiter too, tall and skinny where Tim was strapping and Erick built solid like a linebacker. They were an unlike threesome in appearance, but in manner all of them were quiet, hard-working, steady.

For the batteries that would go in the engine compartment, an open, angle-iron frame strong enough to hold everything securely in place would do. Tim showed up one day hauling an old iron bed frame. Angle iron: check.

The interior box, however, the one that would hold the nine batteries within the passenger compartment, had to be a strong, completely enclosed, and vented unit that was also accessible, so that the batteries could be reached to be maintained. (The kind of batteries they had ordered, "flooded" lead-acids, needed some caring for, particularly if the team wanted to get optimal perform-ance from them.)

The exact shape, dimensions, and placement of this box were ele-ments of the interconnected tangle of calculations that Jennifer and Katrina had been tasked with working out. When all the numbers were put together, it became clear that to keep the weight of the batteries properly positioned, the box would actually have to become part of the car's body, welded in and protruding above the floor and below it. Which meant cutting a large rectangular hole in the bottom of the car.

That would be fine with Mr. Miller. The Escort, as far as he was concerned, tended toward more wobble and give than a car ought to have, particularly a car about to go in for some serious weight gain. A little added stiffness between the rear wheels wouldn't hurt. Properly constructed and installed, the interior battery box ought to add to the vehicle's structural integrity. Properly. Ought to.

Because this box would end up a structural element, and because it would contain the batteries that would pose the greatest poten-tial hazard to the driver in the event of a crash, and because there-fore it would be a safety feature closely examined by the inspection team at the EV Grand Prix before the vehicle would be allowed to compete, it, like the adaptor plate, had to be exactly right. Every-thing would need to fit precisely, the batteries in the box and the box within the car.

The Machine Shop came through for them again; if the team would do up some mechanical drawings, the shop would make the box. Mr. Hawkins, Jr., gave some pointers on making the drawings.

After that, Jennifer and Katrina sketched and labeled and erased and redrew time and again until Mr. Miller was completely satisfied that the box could be faithfully executed from the drawings. It would be spot-welded together from sheet metal and would have a removable lid and a lip running around the entire perimeter, midway up the sides.

Mr. Miller sent some of the kids with the drawings to Murfreesboro, and he arranged with the shop for the students to return and watch the construction of the box when it took place.

"You never know," he said to the students, "you might learn something helpful."

With the plans for the box delivered and the car up on the overhead rack, Mr. Miller, with Mr. Hawkins for reinforcement, pointed out the underside of the floorboard where the cut would be made, in the area where the rear seat was located before it was pulled it out.

"We're gonna have one chance to cut it right." If it was cut wrong, he told them, it would fall in the middle like a collapsed soufflé, and the team would find itself inopportunely in the market for a new used car.

If, however, the cut were done correctly, and if all their measurements and calculations and drawings were right . . . then the box should drop neatly in the hole, with the lip supporting it on all sides, and they would weld the lip to the floor of the car, and there would only be another million things left to do to get them to the Grand Prix.

The car was lowered to the floor. Slowly and carefully, with frequent reference to the plan and the placements and numbers specified therein, the outline of the cut was marked on the inside of the

Escort. Then Erick squeezed inside to take the first turn with the welder.

Erick slipped the goggles down on his face. He took a last look at Mr. Miller watching like a father awaiting the birth of his first child, at the other students who had gathered around to witness this fraught moment, this critical fork in the road of their project. One way led to Richmond. The other led to Oh-my-God-it's-December-and-we-need-a-new-car.

Erick fired up the plasma welder. The temperature inside the vehicle shell went from stuffy to stifling. He lowered the white-blue cone of the flame to the floorboard, and he began to cut.

SHOCKER

With a deafening clatter, a rectangular slab of steel dropped out of the bottom of the Escort and crashed to the floor.

Everyone waited. No one dared to breathe, as if an errant whisper of air might tip the balance to the worse and the whole vehicle suddenly fold itself in half like a clam shell.

Erick and Tim and Donny, soaked in sweat from the heat of the torch and the tension of carrying out the job, one after the other in turn, backed carefully away from the car.

Like a team of surgeons assessing the operating-room work of a promising young resident, Harold and George Jr. peered into the vehicle. They looked at each other. Mr. Miller's eyebrows rose in unspoken query. Mr. Hawkins gave a barely perceptible but definitive nod.

They pronounced it good.

End-of-term exams had crept up on them, the kids pulled away by the demands of studying and the distractions of the approaching holidays. Under the new academic schedule implemented at

Northampton–East in the fall, a year's coursework was now compressed into a single, more intensive semester of longer class periods, so the teachers, too, were focused on wrapping up a subject and the students enrolled in it, and preparing for new classes and a change of faces in January.

Progress on the car idled along through December. The team was still waiting on all the major parts: the motor, the controller, the batteries.

The individual sections to the roll cage were nearly complete, however, and though it wasn't the prettiest piece of work ever to come from the hands of man, it was solid, and it was almost ready to be bolted and welded into the Escort. The battery box coming from the Machine Shop would be finished soon, too, and meanwhile, with angle iron taken in part from that bed frame Tim brought in, the boys had built the second box, an open rack that would go in the front with the motor.

Christmas vacation came, the school emptied, final grades were submitted. Another year gone, another one come, and the Escort sat still and silent through the holidays.

In the late afternoon darkness of an early January Monday, the team assembled again for the first meeting of the new year. How different the mood was now than a few months ago. Instead of discreet clusters of students divided by school, the kids crowded together, talking and laughing, a coherent whole—a team. There was Corey Parker from East, the very youngest among them, a freshman nicknamed "Prez" because in middle school he'd declared it his ambition to run for president of the United States one day. There were the twins, always ready with a quip. There were Katrina and Kelly and Jennifer, giving as good as they got with the boys, and Neil getting everyone mad at him one moment and turning them all to laughing the next, and Ivory, coming week after week all the way from Northwest Halifax with Mrs. Keeter.

A place had been found on the team for everyone who wanted to make the effort; it didn't matter if the kid had two left thumbs on his right hand or if he'd be lucky to stagger out of high school with a D average and a diploma earned by the skin of his teeth. John Parker, who'd been stopping by Harold's shop every so often to see how things were going (who was so happy with how things were going that it was hard for him to stay away, in fact), thought this was really what the project was about. Yes, it mattered if the car got built, if the team went to Richmond, if they performed well in the competition. But to see these students fired up by the challenge they'd been set— to see them making friends and rallying together across the usual lines, school, skin color, socioeconomic, academic-versus-vocational— made those other concerns seem beside the point.

John knew there were plenty of people ready to give up on public education, to call it a disastrously failed experiment, an ideal honored almost entirely in the breach. But John had lived through desegregation in Northampton County. As a teacher, he'd seen a generation of students grow up together for the first time, black and white, from kindergarten through senior high, and while the debates and dissents of their parents raged over their heads, they'd found their own way together simply as kids, trading lunch on the school bus, playing together in the band and on the football team, even falling in love, where such a thing would have been nearly unthinkable ten or twenty years before. So call it an idealist's dream, admit that a rare victory came only at the price of a protracted struggle—John Parker still believed that public education had the power to change the world.

At the moment, however, the ECORV students were preoccupied

with considerably more pragmatic and less grand considerations. They had three months to finish building a car.

Eric Ryan, in his role of Keeper of the Schedule, was particularly concerned about those three months, the time that remained to them if they hoped to finish one month early. For Eric, adapting to a new school schedule completely different from the one he'd more or less gotten the rhythm of in his first nine months at East had been one matter. Giving to all his students in every class an unstintingly dedicated Mr. Ryan was another matter. Then this EV project had come to him suddenly as a wonderful gift but also as something to keep him lying awake at night, staring into the darkness and wondering how he ever was going to pull off his part of the "co" in co-curriculum. He worried he might fail. He was determined he wouldn't.

Because he was the California guy, the one for whom the ZEV mandate and the air problem were less distant abstractions ("California—that's a different continent, isn't it?" the kids would crack) than hometown issues, it had been easy enough to work pollution and energy issues into his classes, discussing the chemical composition of smog with his chemistry students or the inefficiencies of the internal combustion engine with his physics class. But as for making the electric car itself come about, he would admit that so far his contributions had run more to moral support and spreadsheets than getting in there with a socket wrench. Still, he reasoned, someone had to keep things organized and on track, and that someone was not likely to be Harold.

Once he had made the mistake of leaving Harold an important note on a slip of paper.

"Sorry, I must have misplaced it," said Harold when Eric asked him about it.

So for the next important note, Eric wrote on a piece of poster board.

"Can't seem to locate it," Harold said.

The next time, Eric left his note on a length of two-by-four.

"Well," Harold admitted, "I'm sure it's around here somewhere."

It would be found a week later doing duty as a wheel chock for a trailer in front of the shop.

Neil and Donny, Tim and Erick, who had fallen into the role of fetch-and-deliver team, picked up the adaptor plate and the battery box from the Machine Shop of Murfreesboro. The way the students gathered around to admire these items, the way they said, "Wow, it looks so great," and "Man, look at that weld, you can hardly see the seam," you might think they had taken delivery of the latest, slickest, coolest, newest technogadget going, instead of a steel box and a plate of machined aluminum.

Until the motor arrived, they couldn't check to see if the fit was right with the adaptor plate. But the battery box—now they would know if their numbers added up correctly, if the cut had been made properly.

Tim and Erick hefted it, wrestled it in through the back of the car, and eased it into the rectangular hole they'd sliced into the floor of the Escort.

A perfect fit! The rim on the box held it suspended, just as they'd planned. There were elated whoops and high-fives all around. Then with a wire welder—and look, even their welds were starting to come out . . . not so bad—they fused the box to the car. Another step completed.

Now the roll cage team could start bolting into the car the steel-tubing frame they'd built. Safety rules demanded the roll cage, but design rules said the car needed to look as close to "stock," or as near as possible to the original vehicle, as they could make it. How were you going to make a car with a roll cage inside it look like an ordinary vehicle? That made no sense at all.

"We'll put the cage in and then we'll put the headliner back in over it," suggested Mr. Miller.

The cage went in. Or rather, with much sweat and struggle and the kind of maneuvering within the confines of the Escort that would have better suited a team of circus contortionists, it was strong-armed into place. It was the kind of job that seemed to call for having a third hand attached to your forehead. When finally it was installed, "cage" turned out to be an appropriate name for it. It completely surrounded the front driver and passenger area, with bars overhead, around the windshield and door frames and down to the floor, and wrapping behind where the seats would be. It rendered the car suddenly smaller and claustrophobic. Once the seats went in, they were going to need some small drivers.

"Two months!" announced Mr. Ryan.

To the next meeting of the Roanoke Valley Math, Science, and Technology Alliance, Mr. Shields brought Theresa Williams. Although the car was not officially a project of the Alliance, ECORV's participating schools were all members. Mr. Shields thought Theresa could talk about the team's progress.

If Theresa had been coaxed reluctantly into the project by Mr. Shields, she'd caught the spirit since. She and Stephanie were turning out to be the star welders in the shop, and she'd gotten a kick out of learning to use a hacksaw too. She was happy to describe some of what was going on in Mr. Miller's shop at East.

Was there progress, the Alliance members wanted to know? What was happening, exactly? Was this car going to run? Would it be finished on time?

"What have you decided to name the car?" someone asked.

The team had been throwing around ideas. Something snappy and memorable, they wanted, something to give their vehicle personality and character, something to say "this ain't your average Escort."

Everyone looked at Theresa.

"How about 'Shocker'?" she said.

WIZARD OF OH YOU MUST BE JOKING

O h, I don't know," said Mr. Miller hesitantly.

"Is that the image we want?" asked John Parker, who had to keep in mind public opinion and the people who thought this electric car was a crazy waste of time and money and didn't mind saying so whether or not anyone asked.

Did it make the car sound dangerous? Would the judges disapprove?

Too late. The kids were already happily calling the car Shocker, as if they'd been using that name from the first day. Who could get excited about an Escort? An Escort didn't say, "And the winner is the team from northeastern North Carolina!" An Escort said, "Look, grandma's come to visit." An Escort said, "Vanilla pudding, anyone?"

An Escort said, "Forgettable."

But *SHOCKER!* That would get your attention.

The right kind of attention, Harold Miller dearly hoped, a whistle of admiration and a winner's cup, and not the kind that went, "You say you built your battery box out of a *bed frame?*"

They were working in the dark here in Northampton, with no

idea what the other teams might be up to or whether their Escort—all right, "Shocker"—would be laughably outclassed by the competition. They wouldn't know unless and until they got to Richmond.

Harold himself returned to Richmond at the beginning of February, to Virginia Power headquarters in the suburban office park, for the second official all-teams meeting of the EV Grand Prix. Norman Joyner, the electronics teacher from Northampton–West, went along too. This was a safety workshop: battery, electric, mechanical, competition, they were going to cover it all, with speakers from Argonne National Laboratory and a guy from Virginia Power to talk about the setup that would be installed at the raceway for charging the EVs.

It might as well have been an international meeting of nuclear nations. For all the hearty greetings and broad smiles and bonhomie among the teachers, there was plenty of sizing-up going on, a room full of people attempting to ferret out information while revealing none. Everyone was trying to gauge what progress the other teams were making.

First up on the day's agenda were Bob Ferrell and Chuck Greene from York Technical College in South Carolina. They had helped design, on the college level, one of the first electric vehicle curriculums in the country, anticipating that there would be a need soon for EV mechanics. Their portion of the day's presentations was outlined in a handout with a scatter of alarming words like "acid" and "hazards" and "explosion" and "deformation." They had things to say about batteries, their safe and proper care and handling, and getting the best performance out of them, and about vehicle dynamics as well. These topics made them very popular men with the team leaders attending the meeting. The crowd hung on the every utterance of the Messrs. Ferrell and Greene with the kind of riveted attention you'd give your physician following the words "we have the results of your tests."

And yet somehow, when the meeting broke up and everyone boarded a bus for a trip to Richmond International Raceway, arranged to familiarize the team representatives with the layout of the track—somehow, Harold Miller ended up in the seat next to Chuck Greene, having a nice, amiable chat as the bus scooted the perimeter of Richmond. Quite naturally the conversation turned to electric vehicles.

When the two teachers came back from Richmond, Mr. Miller was full of news. "Y'all want to know who was practicing on the track when we went?' he said. "He came over and talked to us too."

Who?

"Ricky Rudd is who. Y'all know what number Ricky Rudd is driving this year, don't you? He's driving number ten."

They chose to decide that meant something, a good omen, a sign that the #10 car had a place at RIR. It could have been any driver on the track, after all, or no driver, on the particular day out of all the possible days that Mr. Miller showed up there.

Mr. Miller and Mr. Joyner had learned many useful things in their day in Richmond, they told the team. Some of the useful and interesting things Mr. Miller had gleaned, at least, appeared not to have been outlined in the official meeting agenda.

Mr. Miller said he'd enjoyed a very agreeable conversation with a nice fellow named Chuck Greene. And while there had been nothing keeping anyone else from having agreeable conversations with Mr. Greene as well, not everyone was quite so gifted in the art of the agreeable conversation as Harold Miller. Mr. Miller asked Mr.

Greene where the trouble spots were—there were always trouble spots in any system—with an EV conversion. What would be most likely to fail, or fail to perform well?

Those GE controllers like to overheat, Chuck Greene advised. Watch for that.

The teams in the EV Grand Prix had been divided between two sponsors providing discounted motors and controllers for the competition; ECORV had drawn General Electric. Daily, the team hoped for delivery of these two essential components.

Mr. Greene didn't say how or in what manner the team ought to correct for this possible overheating problem with the controller—that might have given Mr. Miller's team an unfair advantage. Just, here's an issue you might run into.

Opportunely, not long after Mr. Miller brought home this useful tip, the very objects under discussion, the motor and the controller, finally arrived. And none too soon, either.

The motor wasn't huge—maybe 140 pounds, fifteen inches long and canister-shaped. But it was probably the biggest electric motor any of the students ever had seen.

Donny Lassiter thought, "It's just an overgrown starter motor."

But Erick Vann thought, with some surprise, "We're not just playing around here. We're really building something."

With his first look at the motor, the EV project changed completely for Erick. Until now, it had been an enjoyable something fun to do, a big, hands-on puzzle. The motor made it suddenly real. Erick knew that motor couldn't have come cheap. Somebody—the community? the school board?—had put some serious money and a lot of faith into believing that he and the other students, and Mr. Miller and Mr. Ryan and the other teachers, could build this car.

But could they?

So far, what they had done was eviscerate a vehicle, cut a hole in it, and put a steel box in the hole. Shocker was a car with no doors, no hood, and no seats, with a roll cage crammed inside and an iron frame made from an old bed bolted into the engine compartment. The only thing electrical about it was the original wiring for the lights, the horn, and the wipers, and none of those worked at the moment because there was nothing to power them. For that matter, exciting though it might be to stand about admiring the motor and controller, there was nothing to power them either. Without the batteries, it was impossible even to know if the components worked. ECORV was like a transplant team, all prepped and ready and waiting tensely for the heart that might give this car a new life.

With now less than two months until their March "up and running" deadline, much remained to be done. The batteries to be received. The wiring to be strung. The primary system to be connected together—batteries to the controller to the motor to the transmission. And then a completely separate twelve-volt electrical system with its own small battery had to be wired up in order to run those lights and turn signals and the windshield wipers that weren't working now, and be connected to the main battery pack through an object called a DC/DC converter that would draw a small amount of current to keep the twelve-volt battery continuously charged, serving the same purpose as an alternator in a gasoline car. They had to add in a very small pump motor, also run off the twelve-volt system, to create the vacuum compression for the brakes. They had to install new springs wound to handle the additional weight of the vehicle, to keep the car riding high enough that the part of the battery box hanging below the chassis wouldn't scrape on the ground going over bumps. They called all around the country looking for someone who could wind springs like that for an Escort, until they had found a company in Kansas to do the job. The five-point driver's harness needed to be put in and the safety netting strung across the driver's window.

With April drawing nearer, the teachers began talking quietly among themselves about who would be chosen to go to Richmond. It wouldn't be possible for all the kids who had worked on the car to go as part of the team. Eric and Harold were keeping track of the students who'd put in the extra hours and effort, and now, eyeing the different events that would make up the competition—four behind the wheel (efficiency, range, acceleration and handling, and the race) and two that would demand speaking skills (the design and oral presentations)—the teachers started sorting out which among these kids would do what.

Jennifer Robbins couldn't say when exactly she first understood that Mr. Ryan and Mr. Miller meant for her to be part of the oral presentation team, as though she had missed the first part of the conversation where they had asked her, "Jennifer, are you interested in doing this?" She seemed to have come in to the discussion with that point already established to the affirmative: Jennifer, you are interested in doing this.

Jennifer demanded a lot from herself, and she was the first to find fault and the last to forgive herself for any shortcomings, real or perceived. She would dwell on the one question answered wrong on a test rather than recognizing that she had gotten all the others right. It meant a great deal to her, then, that Mr. Ryan and Mr. Miller had the kind of faith in her to trust her to be one of those speaking on behalf of the whole team. The way Jennifer saw it, the whole school really, and Northampton County.

They would have ten minutes to say their piece in Richmond, ten minutes to tell their story. What could they do to make it interesting?

Mr. Ryan said they needed to think from the judges' point of view. How many oral presentations would those judges have to hear in one day? Fifteen? Twenty? Imagine sitting through group after group of kids coming in, ten minutes at a pop, to mumble about global warming and wiring diagrams. Ho-hum.

What if the ECORV team was tenth or twelfth or, God forbid, last? The judges wouldn't even remember what they looked like two minutes after they walked out of the room.

"You need to stand out," said Mr. Ryan. "Do something that shows creativity, something different from every other team's presentation."

One afternoon, with a gleam in his eye, Mr. Ryan stopped Jennifer to tell her he'd had an idea about the presentation—an inspiration.

Hallucination was more like it, Jennifer might have suggested, when he described it to her.

"I was thinking," he said, "instead of just getting up there and talking, we could do a play, a skit. *The Wizard of Oz*, only it would be *The Wizard of Ohms*, and instead of the Emerald City it would be an Electric City."

He was still working out the idea, he said, but somehow, it would turn out in the end that to get home from Ohms, Dorothy needed an electric vehicle.

"You could be Dorothy," suggested Mr. Ryan, looking dangerously delighted.

Jennifer was seized by an appalling vision of herself skipping along in pigtails and an apron, with a basket and a lapdog in her arms. *There* was something a girl could spend the rest of her high school career trying to live down.

"*Wizard of. . .*?" said Harold Miller when Eric shared the idea with him. "You know, these are *engineers* who are going to be judging this presentation."

"It's very . . . California," said George Hawkins diplomatically.

"Oh, that is so corny," said Kelly, when Jennifer told her. "Even for Mr. Ryan."

But somehow the idea took root. Having pronounced it an eye-roller, almost immediately Kelly found herself thinking about how the skit could go, and it wasn't long before Jennifer and Kelly were hammering out a script together, with Mr. Ryan, in his enthusiasm, giving his best imitation of Mickey Rooney swinging onto a ladder and calling out, "Say, gang, let's put on a show!"

A set! With lights! Lots of lights! Christmas tree lights, in a backdrop that looked like lightning bolts! And Dorothy, she'd be driving a regular car, and on the way to Ohms—with help from the standard-issue Oz crew, of course, the Scarecrow, the Lion, and the Tin Man—she'd learn everything that was wrong with that car. The pollution! The greenhouse gases! The mechanical problems!

Oh, and here was an idea. What if they Velcroed the parts to a cardboard "car", and one by one they could take off all the gas pieces and put on the electric ones, and that way they could show how many fewer parts there were to an electric vehicle, how much simpler it was?

Unlike *The Wizard of Ohms*, which grew progressively more complicated.

Donny Lassiter, so tall and gangly, all arms and legs, was drafted for the Scarecrow. Kelly, not altogether enthusiastically, because she wasn't much for getting up in front of an audience, agreed to take the part of the Tin Man. Katrina was brought on board as the Lion. Neil Ray, Kelly's boyfriend, would be the Wizard. Jennifer bowed to the inevitable. She would be Dorothy. Toto, for the moment, remained uncast.

IF IT GOES

E veryone was starting to feel the pressure. The months—though not enough—that once had stretched in front of them were reduced now to weeks. Weeks before the March ready-to-road-test deadline. Then only a scant four more before the EV Grand Prix itself.

On a warm, late February day, a big truck pulled up at East. The missing piece of their puzzle had come. The batteries were here.

Mr. Ryan drafted some of the bigger boys to unload the sixty-six-pound batteries—seventeen six-volt US2300 golf cart batteries, one extra for insurance—from the delivery truck. It was hot, sweaty work, hefting the batteries down and lugging them into Harold Miller's shop and carefully setting them in neat rows out of the way.

Afterward, when they were taking a breather and drinking cold sodas in the shop, they began noticing small holes in their T-shirts and jeans. Mr. Ryan, puzzled, poked a finger through one in his shirt. That hadn't been there this morning. Then he understood.

"They're acid burns!" he said. "The batteries must have leaked during shipping."

Their US2300s were of the type known as "flooded" batteries; the acid was a free liquid mixed with water inside the case. Twist-off caps in the top of each green-and-white battery case let you add water periodically (because a certain amount gassed off with every recharging) and check the specific gravity of the acid for a roughly accurate determination of the state-of-charge of a given battery—technical stuff they would start getting the hang of in the weeks to come as they learned how to coax the best performance from their lead-acid "fuel tank." Just as easily, however, the acid could slosh out. The burns to their clothes were a mild reminder that there were proper safety procedures to be taken when in the midst of seventeen vats of sulfuric acid; electric shock and acid burns had been covered at the safety meeting in Richmond (the preferred method for neutralizing an acid spill was the charmingly low-tech strategy of throwing baking soda on it).

The arrival of the batteries touched off a frantic flurry of activity. Lead-acid batteries don't like to sit around unused. Ignore them, and they reward you with the petulant gesture of gradually discharging themselves. The longer a battery stays in a discharged state, the more difficult it is to get it fully recharged again, which could mean less speed and less distance for the team's EV.

Not only were the calendar days slipping away, so now was the potential performance of those seventeen batteries. It was time to execute the plan they had figured out with their calculators and cardboard mock-ups. Would it all come together and actually make their EV run? What if they had erred in some fundamental way that would throw everything out of whack and send them back to the beginning when they had so little time left?

Here was how it was supposed to work: Turning the ignition key would close the primary electrical contactor that controlled whether the vehicle's high-voltage circuit was open or closed—metaphorically, if not literally, like lowering the two sides of a drawbridge. Then, the driver would press down on the accelerator, just like in a regular car, the electrons would flow, the motor's armature would spin, the wheels would turn, and Shocker would drive away. In theory.

To make their EV behave like a conventional automobile, however, required the introduction of several intervening gizmos between the accelerator and the motor. The first of these was a "potentiometer," which would translate the mechanical input from the pedal into an electrical signal for the second essential item—the inscrutably microelectronic controller. The controller, in turn, would regulate the speed of the motor.

A motor, you see, unlike an internal combustion engine, has only two modes: on or off, spin or not. An electric motor does not idle. That means it doesn't waste energy while you are sitting at a stop, which is good. But when you want to go, driving demands all kinds of intervals of speed—the highway cruise, the heavy-traffic crawl, the caution-men-at-work creep. An EV needs some way to manage all of those and the in-betweens, and the controller, by smoothly pulsing the power to the motor on and off at dizzyingly high frequencies, makes that possible, the ratio of on- to off-time determining how fast or slow the car goes.

If everything was working correctly in Shocker, the feel ought to be intuitive—push gently on the accelerator and the car would ease forward, floor it and Shocker would shoot off with a whiplashing kick.

That was what Mr. Miller kept promising them. He said they'd be surprised how much power they would get out of their motor. He said they needed to stop thinking "golf cart" and start thinking "drag race."

Mr. Miller said a lot of things, though. He kept saying, for example, that they were going to win in Richmond, so you couldn't be faulted for questioning how faithfully any of his pronouncements mirrored reality. But Mr. Miller was always reminding them about how a motor gives the most torque, the most turning force, when it starts up, whereas an engine has to be revved up to produce its maximum torque. That was why, he pointed out, an internal combustion vehicle needs an electric motor to start it and a transmission with low gears to get it rolling and to pick up speed.

Because an electric motor, on the other hand, gives you all your torque from the get-go, Shocker ought to be able to accelerate briskly from a dead stop in fourth gear, he told them. In fact, one way to drive an EV conversion was simply to put it in the most efficient gear, the one that gave the best balance of range and speed for the situation—highway, city, hills—and leave it in that gear. You might easily go an entire trip without shifting once.

If you don't actually need a clutch to shift, as Harold knew, and they weren't planning on doing much shifting anyway, and if in a conversion the main value of a clutch is to offer a convenient way to couple the motor to the transmission, then what if, thought the Saturday-night racer in Harold Miller, the one always looking for the slightest edge—what if they could connect the motor directly to the transmission and do without the clutch altogether? That would save them a good thirty pounds!

The guys at the Machine Shop of Murfreesboro came up with an idea. They suggested a small steel-and-rubber piece used with industrial motor applications that weighed only a pound: the Lovejoy coupler.

Would it work? They had no idea yet. They would find out soon enough. As soon, they hoped, as they put the batteries in and wired everything, at last, together.

* * *

First, the batteries were cleaned of any residual leaked acid, their twist-off caps tightened down, and then they were numbered and a plan drawn to indicate where each would be placed. If more than one had to be taken out at any point, they would know where to put each back. One by one, then, they were set in their places, in the respective boxes that had been built for them, and distributed throughout the car. Thump. Scrape. The Escort shook a little as the weight, sixty-six pounds at a time, was added. Sixteen batteries went in, and every one fit just as it had been sketched out in the painstakingly drawn and redrawn battery box diagrams. Every something that actually worked the way the way it was supposed to sent a mingled feeling of relief, satisfaction, and pure surprise through the team.

Mr. Joyner, with his expertise as the electrical trades teacher, led the wiring job. Where Harold Miller gave off a broad, animated energy, Norman Joyner was a still, quiet center of patient determination and persistence. He and Mr. Hawkins were as twinned souls in their appreciation of an ordered environment. No clowning around, no horseplay was Mr. Joyner's policy with students—that way nothing got damaged, no one got hurt, and the work was accomplished. For all that, however, Mr. Joyner possessed a wry sense of humor that would slip up on you and set you laughing at unexpected moments.

The batteries would be joined one to the next by lengths of two-aught welding cable donated by a local welding supply company. Nice thick wires, about five-eighths inch in diameter, to carry plenty of current with as little resistance as possible. Each length of cable between the positive terminal of one battery and the negative of another was carefully measured, cut, and crimped with a lug on each end that could be bolted to the posts of the battery terminals. It was slow work, the measuring, the cutting, the crimping, the attaching, and it couldn't be rushed. Every one of the thirty-two individual connections needed to be good and tight; when the car was turned on there would be enough current flowing through the system to melt a battery post, and this, to say the least, would be an undesirable outcome. For one thing, it would ruin the battery, and they only had a single spare. For another, a failure in any single connection would bring the circuit down and the car wouldn't run. Of the many possible outcomes to this project, getting all the way to Richmond only to have the car expire on the first turn was one that at this late date nobody on the team could even bear to think about.

The cast of *The Wizard of Ohms* gave up spring vacation. Instead, they rehearsed.

"I wish there was a better way of getting around North Carolina—I just can't stand all this pollution from gas cars!" Dorothy would lament, with a fuzzy stuffed Toto clutched in her arms. With a swoon (maybe it was the carbon monoxide poisoning), she'd be transported to Ohms, where the Good Witch "Conductra" would advise her to follow the yellow-brick road, "the path of least resistance," to Electric City, where the Wizard would help her get home.

But no, before the Wizard would grant her wish, "You must find and convert the Wicked Witch's 1985 Ford Escort to an electric vehicle for the EV Grand Prix," he commanded.

"Well, how am I gonna do that?" Dorothy would ask, not unreasonably.

With those EV conversion experts, of course—the Scarecrow, the Tin Man, and the Cowardly Lion.

"Let's get started," Dorothy would say, "My aunt's barbecue is waiting for me in North Carolina."

Donny discovered the ham in himself in the role of the Scarecrow, flopping around in a credible interpretation of a guy stuffed with straw, while Jennifer played her Dorothy just tongue-in-cheek enough that her cool quotient might not suffer irreparable harm.

They built a set too. It was about six feet wide by eight tall, made from shower board, the same slick-surfaced pressboard from which Mr. Ryan had fabricated his classroom dry-erase. They cut lightning-bolt patterns into the background and drilled holes around the perimeter and then pushed hundreds of Christmas tree lightbulbs through the holes. That was electric Oz, the land of Ohms.

They made their cut-out car from the same shower board, and all the gasoline and electric components from laminated poster board, with Velcro glued to the backs of the pieces.

In the end, with a promise to keep converting cars in North Carolina, Dorothy would drive her new EV home.

Now if only the real car would go. With less than a month until Richmond, the Escort had yet to move even a single inch under its own power.

"Miller, is this car gonna run?" people were asking Harold. People like a few members of the school board who knew the money that had been funneled into this EV project and worried about the criticism that would arise if it didn't go well. It was evident that many of them were not-so-privately thinking the answer to their question was "no."

The mutterers had kept up their steady thrum of discontent through the winter. There were people who insisted the car would never work, and people who complained that this farfetched plan was as good as guaranteeing another chance for Northampton County to be humiliated and held up to ridicule, and people who hoped for the best but expected a debacle. Their numbers were still small when compared to the members of the community who had rallied behind the students, but their complaints and prognostications nagged at the team's confidence like a steady stream of icy water down the neck.

"Sure it's gonna run," was all Harold ever said, with his big, trust-me smile. "And we'll be bringing home the blue ribbon for you from Richmond."

It definitely sounded good to say that. Most of the time Harold believed it was more than possible. Yet what would happen if the car *didn't* run was a matter of some niggling concern even to an indefatigable optimist like Harold Miller.

It wasn't that any one piece of the system was in doubt so much as that nobody was absolutely confident that the whole would prove greater than, or at least equal to, the sum of the parts. It was all still theoretical—a grand experiment built on more than occasional guesswork.

When the wiring was completed, they connected the circuit to the onboard charger, a small, ten-pound device installed in the vehicle that could be plugged by electric cord into a regular wall outlet to charge the batteries. To be funny, and also because it was the most convenient spot, they placed the plug for the charger behind the flap where the gas cap had been.

If some of the students had imagined that once the wiring was done, they could just turn the key and go, they found they were sadly mistaken. The batteries needed to be charged and the charging tested, because from one to the next, batteries did not necessarily behave consistently. And so far, the charging wasn't going so well.

There was a ground-fault interrupter (GFI for short) within the charger, designed to trip and shut off the charger if it detected any sign that electricity was "leaking" out to the body of the car. But the GFI was so sensitive that even the tiniest drizzle of acid might provide enough of a conduit between battery and battery box for the few milliamps of current that would trip it. So they kept the batteries scrupulously clean. But once they finally managed to stop the GFI from tripping, a couple of the US 2300s in the Escort still didn't want to charge up as thoroughly as the others; if they left things that way, then the consistently undercharged batteries would perform worse and wear out sooner. If they couldn't get all the batteries equally charged, they'd have real problems with range and power.

While the battery-and-electrical team fiddled and experimented and adjusted, March rushed past, the daffodils came up, and Eric Ryan started thinking about a deadline of his own that was looming.

Eric had signed on for two years with Teach for America; when the school year ended in June, so would that commitment. The plan he'd come with was two years in North Carolina, then back to the life he'd left in California, waiting for him like summer things neatly folded away in the closet for a season. Would he leave on a high note, with his EV team succeeding in getting to Richmond to compete? Or would they come so close, as close as they had gotten, only to falter at the last minute?

It was a Saturday morning, early in April, cool and clear. Officially speaking, Monday was supposed to be, finally, Official Test Day, the day they'd check every connection and wire and charge one more time and then put it all together, press the accelerator, and see what happened. It was to be hoped that what would happen would be all the naysayers dining on a hearty meal of crow.

"What do you say we have a little unofficial sneaky test day first?" Harold suggested, quietly, to Eric. Just to see if the car would go, and to be sure nothing could go wrong that would endanger the kids, then back in the shop and no one the wiser.

Eric was game. He was dying to see if the car would go.

Harold thought George Hawkins should be there too. If something didn't work, George, in his methodical, exacting way, would puzzle it out. Only, Harold wasn't sure what George Hawkins would say to the idea of covert operations. George's idea of sneaky, Harold suspected, was rounding off to the third decimal place. George, in Harold's estimation, was as serious as a heart attack.

George said yes.

It was supposed to be the three of them only, but a secret in Northampton County had the approximate life span of a lightning flash and traveled about as fast. Soon enough, John and June Parker were in on the plan, and Doug Miller, and Donny Lassiter and Neil Ray and Erick Vann too, and Mary Keeter said she'd be there. Give it another day and no doubt the entire team would have gotten wind of it, and probably Channel 20 in Roanoke Rapids and the *Daily Herald* too.

As it was, the conspirators convened at East early on Saturday morning.

"If I have to push it, this car is going today," said Harold to no one in particular, unlocking the door to his classroom.

Inside the shop, the fluorescent lights flickered to life over one not altogether promising specimen of automotive industry. Objectively appraised, the Escort looked worse than it ever had, which took some doing. A wreck, a clunker it had been when it came to them, but at least it had given the loose impression of a passably road-worthy vehicle. Between the work to take it apart, though, and the work to put it back together, it had acquired since then a definitely haphazard appearance. It was still missing both doors, the hood, the seats, the carpeting, and the paneling. It was spotted with welding scars and random blotches of tan filler. There were those improbable roll bars sprouting from the dash, and a labyrinth of wiring snaked from end to end, dividing and converging like the branching rivers and tributaries of a circulatory system. There were various fail-safes and system interrupters, too, some automatic and some manually operated, including the main kill-switch mounted on the dash, a big red knob labeled "ON/OFF."

Yet when Donny Lassiter, for one, looked at it this morning, what he saw was the sum of the labors that had gone into it so far, the Saturday afternoons and the long weekday nights, the endless discussions and occasionally heated debates, the guesswork and the precision measurements. There were the batteries, all sixteen of them finally tucked within the frame of the car, after they had shuffled and reshuffled and shuffled again the possible configurations in cardboard mock-up. Donny remembered when they had taken a deep breath, crossed a few fingers, and cut the bottom out of the car for the battery box, knowing that it was a cut-once-and-live-with-the-consequences proposition. That filler sanded so smooth, that was Kelly's handiwork, nothing but determination and sandpaper.

If devotion could make a thing beautiful, that Escort was a Rolls Royce.

It was almost difficult for Donny to remember back to the fall, when Mr. Miller had announced that they would be building an electric car, when probably half the kids on the team, maybe more, all they really knew about electricity was don't stick your finger in a socket. Never mind anything about electric cars. Now, well, Donny could wear your ear off with talk about resistance and amp-hours and why a car with ninety-six volts running through it still needed a twelve-volt battery to work the turn signal. Phrases like "GE nine-inch series-wound motor" and "specific gravity" rolled trippingly off his and the other students' tongues as though these things were the stuff of ordinary conversation—which, at this point, among the team members, they were. It was the language of membership.

They were a bunch of kids, thought Donny, and here they'd gone from thinking an electric car was a joke or a toy or a golf cart to building one themselves, and they'd done it in less than six months. If a group of high-schoolers could do it with a used car and jury-rigged parts and a few grand in cash they'd drummed up themselves, well, you had to wonder, thought Donny, why those big carmakers, with engineering and research departments and all the technology they could dream of at their disposal—why they couldn't do it too.

Assuming, of course, that the car actually ran.

A broad, graveled alley filled the area between the two halves of Northampton–East, bisected by the walkway that joined them. Miller's shop opened onto the alley, and over the years Mr. Miller and his students had assumed something of a proprietary air regarding this space—call it Design and Testing. They pushed the car out of the shop and turned it to face down the alley.

Harold went back inside and came trotting out lugging a battered wooden teacher's chair. He shoved it into the Escort where the driver's seat ought to have been, and then, anxious as parents at a first piano recital, he and George Hawkins bent over the front of the car, checking to make sure everything was screwed in, bolted on, tightened down, hooked up. One thing about Hawkins, he was thorough, and right now Harold was more than happy to have him there. The tricky part about making it up as you went was that it wasn't always easy to think of what you might have forgotten. Was the transmission going to fall out? Was the whole thing going to blow up or short out? Just in case, they told everyone to stand clear. No use electrocuting the lot of them in one swoop. Who would be left to make sure the car got to Richmond?

Everything seemed to be connected, everything seemed to be in order. They'd flip the master power switch to ON, and then all it should take was a turn of the key and a touch to the accelerator. But what a trembling void hung between "should" and "would." Miller felt like a brain surgeon holding the scalpel for the last stroke of a rare and delicate operation.

"Hit the switch," he called out.

"Good God almighty!" cried Harold as a fine bolt of blue light shot up from the motor compartment and the air snapped with a sudden, spitting pop.

In the space of a flash of light a whole parade of thoughts can race through your mind. You can imagine a teacher and a volunteer from the community lying electrocuted dead in a heap on the ground and the tragic accident and the uproar that would follow, all of it played out in your head in the time it takes for a spit of electricity to spark and die, which is no time at all.

Happily, Harold and George were not dead and smoking. At the moment, Harold was laughing.

"Mr. Hawkins here says it was the capacitors arcing," Mr. Miller called out, clapping Hawkins on the shoulder.

Nestled inside the controller, the half-soda-can-sized capacitors held a sizeable electrical charge, releasing it, apparently, when the contactor points closed.

Shocker looked to be earning its name.

"George, would you care to do the honors?" asked Mr. Miller of Mr. Hawkins.

A crash-test dummy would have hesitated to take the wheel, but George Hawkins, undaunted, climbed into the car. It was a mixed honor, given that none of them was really sure the car might not catch fire or spectacularly short-circuit or who knew what. Better George than a student, though. At least the Northampton County schools were not *in loco parentally* responsible for George Hawkins. He went of his own free will. There were witnesses.

George hunched himself in precarious balance on the wooden chair. The roll cage pressed down above his head, but given that there were no doors, no seatbelt, and in fact no real seat, mostly it was just in the way.

Everyone stood back from the car sitting squat and unbeautiful and unmoving as it had been all these months.

"Y'all ready?" George called out.

Of course they were. They could hardly breathe. It seemed like even the birds and the pine trees were waiting. And waiting.

What is Hawkins doing *in there?* Harold Miller thought to himself, grinding his teeth just a bit. George would probably double-check the specs on the Pearly Gates.

Still waiting, Harold prayed silently for the smooth and

uneventful passage of mysterious subatomic particles. "Lord, let's put those electrons through and make it go."

A thousand pounds of lead riding another ton of steel takes a serious shove to get going. Electromagnetic principles aside, anyone looking at the motor, an unprepossessing gray cylinder nearly hidden among the batteries and other components, might have had a hard time really believing it was up to the job. Harold had kept assuring everyone that when the car finally went, they wouldn't be disappointed.

It would be nice, then, if the car did go.

There was a click.

There was a high-pitched whine.

"Oh my Lord, what's *that* now?" thought Harold, his spirits sagging just that little bit that comes with feeling you've been tested quite enough so far, thank you.

Eric Ryan had a reputation for whooping with little provocation. Mr. Excitable. Mr. California. Today, Eric Ryan would be completely drowned out among a chorus of shouts, screams, and hollers. Everyone was jumping up and down like maniacs and shrieking.

Smooth and silent as a summer breeze, Shocker was skimming down the alley.

So startled he almost couldn't believe it, Erick Vann stared stupefied. It was what they had wanted and hoped and worked for all these months yet somehow never absolutely believed could really happen.

Shocker was going under its own power. Shocker was driving.

Everyone was cheering and high-fiving, and Mr. Ryan was

throwing his hat in the air and hugging Doug Miller, and then they were racing after the car turning a broad and lazy circle around the weedy parking lot.

For the first time, Miller's crazy idea suddenly seemed possible. *Maybe we can do this after all,* thought Donny Lassiter.

John Parker hugged June, slapped Doug and Harold and Eric on the back, and drank in the astonished delight on Donny's and Neil's faces. Yes, this was the answer to every critic, every ribbing he'd gotten, everyone who said that these kids couldn't hold their own in the world.

Even George Hawkins broke his customary reserve to crack a downright exuberant grin.

Harold gave it another minute, and then, trying hard to rein in his own jubilance, he called out, "OK, we need to check everything over right now!"

Everyone jogging along beside the car, George drove back to the front of Harold's shop and switched off the power. One by one they ticked off the components—the motor, the controller, the wiring, the batteries. Was the fan they had installed to cool the motor doing its job? Were there any signs of pending shorts, bad connections, wires ready to work loose? By the time they'd finished methodically working their way around the car, they were almost ready to doubt they'd really seen it go before. They were ready to see it go again.

They decided to give it a little trial run down the road. Doug Miller would do the driving this time. Doug was built solid like his father, and he really had to squeeze himself in onto that wobbly teacher's chair, feeling like he was trying to pack an overnight case for a round-the-world vacation.

He looked everything over, turned the key, pressed the pedal.

This car had pick-up!

No matter what his father said, Doug—like everyone else, he

suspected—hadn't quite been able to shake that golf cart notion, that the car would just putter, but it was cooking along, surging forward with the least push on the accelerator. And so quiet, it was weird. Doug could hear the whine from the controller, the hum of the tires, and the rush of the wind through the big open cavity of the car, and that was it.

They were supposed to be breaking it in gently, though, giving it a little shaking out to make sure all the connections connected and that nothing was heating up, so Doug refrained from really letting loose.

Besides, it was a rolling hazard, about as safe as driving a drawer full of kitchen knives down the road. Doug pitched and tilted unsteadily, crouched awkwardly in the wooden chair, trying not to lacerate or impale himself on any jagged or protruding piece of metal or fall out of the car altogether as he steered carefully onto the road that ran past the high school.

He pushed down again cautiously on the pedal. The speedometer's needle crept upward. Ten miles per hour. Twenty. Twenty-five. He'd traveled maybe two hundred feet. Thirty miles per hour.

Back in the parking lot they watched the car go, elated, chattering excitedly, congratulating each other, saying, "I never doubted it for a minute." But then their words died away. Everyone strained their eyes staring at Shocker receding down the road. Was it . . . was that really . . . ?

Oh my Lord. *Smoke.*

"What the heck . . . ?" said Miller, bewildered at the plume of blue-gray smoke roiling up from Shocker's front end and trailing behind the car. "We're burning *oil?*"

What had they done wrong? How could a car with no oil be burning it? Jesus, what if the whole car was about to go up in flames? Everything was in that car. Thousands of dollars in parts. Months of work. All the kids' hopes. Not to mention Doug.

THE ELECTRIC RIDE

In the parking lot, everyone scrambled to jump into cars, peeling out in a short stream of vehicles to tear down the road after the younger Miller.

By the time they'd caught up, Doug had pulled Shocker over by the peanut-weighing station and killed the power. A thin wisp of smoke still furled up from the front of the car, drifting away across the field.

The other cars slammed to a halt by the side of the road, everyone piling out and running over to where Doug stood gazing apprehensively into the former engine compartment. Did anyone bring a fire extinguisher?

At the house in George, John and June waited uneasily. Reluctantly, they'd torn themselves away from the high school that morning after watching that first, triumphant spin around the parking lot. Other obligations called them. Leaving, they couldn't have been more proud or excited if they had built the car themselves. They were so elated by what they'd seen—that Escort, as rough as it looked, going. Really going.

Now, though, hours had passed, the whole afternoon, and the day given way to dusk. Still Eric hadn't come home. Was something wrong? An accident? Someone hurt? Surely Eric would have called if there was anything serious to report, wouldn't he? Or would he? Maybe he hadn't had a chance because something really terrible had taken place.

Just as they were thinking they couldn't wait anymore, that they would head back to the high school, they heard Eric's rattrap truck pull in. A minute later, the kitchen door opened. Eric looked grubby and exhausted. He slumped wearily into a chair.

That morning, they had surrounded the car and frantically looked everything over. There were no flames. No smell of melting wire insulation. Nothing fizzing or spitting out of the batteries. Doug double-checked to make sure he'd thrown the main kill-switch to break the electric circuit, and then Harold stuck a cautious hand on the controller, the motor, the batteries.

Everything felt cool. Everything seemed fine. Where, then, had that smoke been coming from? What could possibly have been burning oil in an electric vehicle? They needed to return the car to the shop and give it a thorough going-over.

They looked from the car, back down the road to the high school, back at the car again.

"We ain't gonna push this," said Miller.

With trepidation all around, Doug turned the Escort on again and pulled out oh-so-slowly, making a gentle U-turn and heading the car back toward the school at a crawl, the others again following behind, watching for any new sign of smoke.

The car made the return trip with no further apparent trouble, but the exuberance of half an hour ago had evaporated. Gloomily, they pushed it into the shop. Had they toasted their car on Sneaky Unofficial Test Day?

By Monday, though, Harold was already making jokes.

"We're the only people ever built an electric car and had it burn oil," he said, laughing.

Once the EV was back in the shop on Saturday, it hadn't taken them long at all to locate and diagnose the problem. Having determined that none of the parts was actually on fire, it was easy to narrow the search to the very limited number of moving parts, which led them quickly in turn to an oil-impregnated piece called a sweat bushing, part of that so evocatively named Lovejoy coupler, their experimental connector between motor and transmission.

The motor put a lot of torque on that coupling system; friction, they guessed, must have heated up the sweat bushing until the oil started to smoke. They uncoupled the motor from the transmission, and after Harold mulled the problem over for a couple of days, he decided to dispense with the sweat bushing altogether and weld a washer in its place, which he did. The drive system was reassembled and everything connected again in less than a week.

A good thing, too, because the car remained so dismal in appearance that getting it to go now looked like hardly half the battle. No one who missed Unofficial Sneaky Test Day even seemed particularly disappointed not to have been there—more like incredulous, and when you stood back and took a good look at the heap of scrap metal and wiring on which the team was pinning its hopes, you could see why. With only weeks remaining until the actual competition, the doors were still off, and the hood and the hatchback as well, the seats had to be put back in and the five-point driver's harness installed, the exterior needed to be painted, various decals and sponsor names applied, and the tires had to be swapped for the new ones Goodyear was donating to all the teams, low-rolling-resistance "Invicta" tires. When all that was done, would the car come in under its gross vehicle weight rating?

It was time to start driving the car too, not just for debugging any problems, but also because both the motor and the batteries needed breaking in. With the batteries, the process was called "cycling"; you could actually get better performance out of batteries that had been charged and discharged ten or twenty times than you could get out of brand new ones. The same was true for the motor—it's efficiency would improve over the first days and weeks of use. Each time they took the car out and drove it around for a while and then brought it back to the shop and plugged it in again, then, in theory they would be gaining themselves a little bit more distance out of the battery pack, a little more efficiency from the motor. They wouldn't expect a quantum leap, but for all they knew the range event could come down to a matter of yards or minutes. Every incremental improvement they could squeeze out of Shocker might make the difference between first place and Other Possibilities Not Open to Consideration When in the Presence of Mr. Miller and Mr. Ryan.

To drive the car, however, would demand at the very least a real seat to replace the wooden teacher's chair, and for anything more than a jaunt around the parking lot, doors and a seatbelt too. Students would be driving, after all. Students who needed the practice, because they'd be driving Shocker in the EV Grand Prix.

And which students would those be? By the time the field was narrowed to the core team members who knew enough about the car, who were not too tall, too heavy, or too busy preparing for other events in the competition, and who were in possession of a driver's license that had not yet been revoked or come perilously close, the decision made itself.

"Katrina, Anna, you're driving in Richmond," said Mr. Miller.

There was a mad scramble now to reassemble the car, and some of the students, not just from East but from the other schools as well, were in Mr. Miller's shop every day after school and long into the evening, and on weekends too, and when they finally left at whatever hour it might be, Mr. Ryan and Mr. Miller would still be there tinkering and talking.

Those two teachers never slacked off, and they made it clear they expected the same from their students. If Katrina wandered half-bleary into physics, Mr. Ryan would say to her, "Got your homework?"

"Mr. Ryan," she'd protest. "Remember me, working on that car all last night?"

"Yes," said Mr. Ryan, implacable. "Do you have your homework?"

She did. She knew better than to think he wouldn't expect her to.

Then she'd drag herself out to track practice after school, and Mr. Ryan would come jogging along next to her, saying, "Katrina, why are you going so slow?"

"Mr. RYAN!" That's all she'd say.

He'd give her a big grin.

And there he'd be after school in the shop, he and Mr. Miller working away, both of them looking as bright and brisk as if they'd just come back from a week's vacation. Did he ever run out of energy?

No matter how much Katrina sometimes wished that just once Mr. Ryan would cut her some slack, it did feel good to have teachers with so much unflagging confidence in her and the other students. Mr. Miller and Mr. Ryan didn't countenance defeatism or discouragement. If you were feeling pessimistic about the team's prospects, you'd best keep it to yourself. "We're going to Richmond to win" was all they ever said.

However, one evening, when work dragged on and on over some niggling little detail, Neil Vann finally ran out of patience. Neil had surprised himself, sticking with the project when in the fall he'd been absolutely convinced the whole idea was crazy. "This is *never* going to work," he'd thought to himself in those first days when Mr. Miller was talking about building an electric car. But curiosity held him long enough that things started coming together.

Then, even though he remained sure it wasn't going to work, each step along the way he'd found himself thinking, "Hmmm. I guess I got to stay around and see what happens next," and one thing led to another and another thing led to a third and somehow here he was still. But poor Neil, when something went wrong in the shop, it always seemed as though he was on the scene. A big, burning blotch of paint dripped in his eye when they were underneath the car painting the bottom of the battery box. He dropped a metal wrench, crossing the terminals of a battery that immediately began to spark and burn and might have exploded in a shower of acid if Mr. Miller hadn't shot over and kicked off the tool.

Suddenly it all struck Neil as foolish; it seemed like he'd spent his whole junior year holed up in this shop with this car, and what for? Sure, they'd gotten the car to run, but so what?

"I don't know why we got to do this when we ain't gonna win," he muttered mutinously.

Mr. Ryan—*Mr. Ryan*—blew up at him. "If you don't want to be part of the team, Neil, you can just get your butt in your truck and go home!"

Everyone else in the shop stopped and stared. Neil fumed. Mr. Ryan fumed. They both fumed for a while. Then they settled down and returned to their work.

With everything going back on, Shocker grew heavier, and heavier, and heavier, like an overindulgent holiday reveler making too free at the buffet tables. Harold Miller stared balefully at the front passenger seat, sitting by the side in the shop, waiting to be reinstalled in the car. Completely useless and extraneous pounds was what that seat represented. The car wasn't required to have a passenger seat, but the rules suggested that the absence of that seat might count against a team in the design competition. For the same reason, they were struggling to reinstall the headliners over the roll bars, along the top of the windshield and doors and on the ceiling, to disguise that steel cage as best they could. The rear seat though, even if they wanted to put it back in, wouldn't fit over the battery box, so they had decided to honor the spirit of the design requirements by making a fake seat of plywood, foam, and auto vinyl, stitched by a local upholsterer who offered to donate the service to the team. It looked pretty good, actually. Better, honestly, than the seat they had taken out.

Pope Motors loaned the team some dealer tags so Shocker could be taken out on the open roads without exciting hot pursuit from the local constabulary. And just to put everything on the up-and-up, when all the requisite parts had been mounted and bolted back in their proper places, Harold ran the car down to Aubrey Whitley's garage in Conway for an inspection.

Aubrey looked it over. He'd never had to pass an electric vehicle before.

"The state says you gotta have a catalytic converter," he ventured.

The state, however, did not say where it had to go. Harold fetched one and tossed it into the backseat.

"We got a catalytic converter," said Harold.

Shocker got its pass.

Now that the car was legal, everyone on the team with a license would be given opportunities to drive it. All these months when Mr. Miller had been promising them that there was no reason an electric car couldn't have all the speed and power of a gasoline-engine vehicle, they'd allowed him the benefit of the doubt, willing to trust him even if in their own thoughts they remained skeptical. But with the chance, finally, to climb behind the wheel, they discovered he was right. Harold Parker was surprised at how fast the car responded when you put the pedal down. For Jennifer, it was an extraordinary feeling of pride and accomplishment to turn the key and drive off in a car she had helped build. And Neil, for all that he'd groused so recently, the first time he hit the accelerator and the car tore off with that electric-motor kick, he thought maybe Mr. Miller's notions weren't so far afield after all. Maybe even the ones about what Shocker might do in Richmond.

Katrina had been chosen to drive in the range event, a contest that would be all about maximizing the distance that could be eked out of the batteries at the speed, between forty and fifty miles per hour, mandated by the event rules. Fortunately, even if you fed Katrina a big dinner, dressed her in heavy clothes and soaked her down with a hose, she wouldn't add meaningfully to the weight of the vehicle. The biggest things about her were her glasses and her smile.

The range competition was scheduled to run for ninety minutes.

Whether the car itself would run that long they did not know yet, but now Katrina was sitting in the newly reinstalled driver's seat in Shocker, Mr. Ryan next to her in the passenger seat, and she was learning to drive the EV for maximum efficiency, maximum mileage.

The driving part wasn't hard—steering wheel, accelerator, nothing new there. They worked a little bit on shifting without the clutch, and that wasn't too bad either. The difficult thing was thinking about driving in terms of amps and volts and kilowatt-hours, and watching the meters on the dash that tracked all these numbers.

A fully charged battery pack is like a well-filled water balloon. Put a pinhole in the balloon, and the pressure forces the water out in a strong stream; the voltage in the pack is the pressure forcing the current to flow. If you squeeze the balloon—which is like stomping down on the accelerator on an EV—the water will come out even faster and stronger, but the balloon will empty sooner. Batteries give the best and most sustained performance if you draw power from them at a steady, moderate rate, so to get the maximum range and efficiency from Shocker, Katrina and the other drivers were learning to accelerate smoothly and keep the vehicle at a constant speed.

With batteries though, unlike the water-filled balloon, the more you demand from them the less they will end up giving you. A battery rated to go 530 minutes at 25 amps will go only 145 minutes—far less than a third of the 25-amp time—at 75 amps. (The same, for that matter, also holds true for a typical gasoline car; more speed or power means worse mileage.) Traveling back and forth over a couple of miles of the road that ran in front of Northampton–East, Katrina would put Shocker in second gear and drive it for a while at forty-five miles per hour, then put it in third gear and drive it for a while at forty-five miles per hour, while Mr. Ryan, or another one of the students, sitting in the passenger seat, would watch the amp meter and chart the numbers so that the team could determine what combination of speed and gear would draw the lowest amps.

The calculations were rough at first; one afternoon, Mr. Ryan, out running with his track team, came across Anna driving Shocker, crawling along a half-mile from school with a nearly empty battery pack. Just as the stream of water—the amount of current—in that balloon slows to a trickle and then a drip as it drains and the pressure decreases, so as an EV's battery pack is drained does the voltage diminish. An electric vehicle won't conk out like a car that has run out of gas. Instead, it slows to a walk, then a crawl, then a creep before finally inching to a halt.

Another day, Shocker's performance made a startlingly dramatic dive for the worse; the acceleration was lousy even while the volt and amp meters were reading too high and the kilowatt-hours too low, until after a discouraging while of this Katrina looked down and mumbled sheepishly, "Oh, I left the parking brake on."

But on the whole, as each day passed and the batteries were cycled through charge and discharge and the motor put through its paces, the careful monitoring of the meters and the speedometer proved that Shocker was getting more distance out of each charge.

What about speed, though? What about power? For the acceleration and handling event, it was never mind efficiency. It would be a one-car drag race over a one-eighth-mile distance, and how fast could they go?

Mr. Miller suggested they send a couple of boys to find a quiet road that could be used for practice runs. Mr. Ryan handed Donny—quiet, polite Donny Lassiter—a can of spray paint.

"Go find a nice straight stretch of road," Mr. Ryan instructed him. "Measure out an eighth of a mile and mark the start and finish."

Eric had in mind a couple of discreet indicators on the roadway, maybe an "X" at the start and one at the finish, big enough for the driver to see but otherwise unobtrusive. When you hand a teenage boy a can of paint and license to use it, though, the results may not be what you anticipate.

"Come on, Neil," said Donny to Neil Vann. Words to strike fear in the heart of any teacher.

The two of them drove to a quiet stretch of Creeksville Road, a public thoroughfare that bisected a chunk of Donny's father's land. No traffic coming in either direction—sometimes there are advantages to living in the middle of nowhere—they carefully measured out the correct distance. Then they painted a broad, bright blue stripe all the way across the road, ditch to ditch. An eighth of a mile away, they painted another.

Nice work, they agreed.

By the time Mr. Ryan arrived in his truck and Tim Stauffer in the car, Northampton County was for the indefinite future one illicit one-eighth-mile drag strip to the good.

Mr. Ryan made a few exasperated noises. "All I wanted you to do was make a couple of little marks!" he said.

He had to say something, didn't he? He was the teacher, whose job it was to champion truth and justice and restraint from the temptation to deface public property.

That obligation having being duly dispensed with, however, there was no use belaboring the point.

"Let's see what this car'll do," said Mr. Ryan.

With less than two weeks to go until Richmond, a representative from the Division of Motor Vehicles arrived with a set of portable scales to weigh the car.

The Escort's gross vehicle weight was 3,135 pounds. Sitting square and squat under its load of batteries, boxes, roll cage, motor, parts, and pieces, would Shocker squeak under the wire? It was going to be close.

Katrina waited in the driver's seat. There were four separate scales, each a low metal platform maybe two feet long and ten inches wide, with a ramp at one end to allow the wheel to roll up onto the scale. Each was adjusted to lie directly in front of one wheel, and then Katrina nudged the car forward into position on top of them, opened the door, and slipped out.

The DMV guy did some checking, jotted a number down, looked up at all of them, watching him anxious and eager and apprehensive all at once, like family members awaiting the surgeon's prognosis following a risky operation. He'd never had quite so attentive an audience for his pronouncements.

"Three thousand, one hundred and thir . . . " time seemed to creep by the nanosecond ". . . ty pounds," he announced firmly.

A rush of relief. A whoop of exhilaration, pumped fists, high-fives. Yes! They'd made it by five pounds. Another hurdle cleared.

"Katrina, don't you eat any more pizza before Richmond," Miller said, smiling. He wouldn't tell them how proud he was of how far they had come, of what they had already done in building this car. Not yet. He'd just tell them to keep their eyes on Richmond.

The DMV guy was jotting more numbers. It wasn't enough to know only how much Shocker weighed. They needed to know also how the car balanced out, whether all their hours of calculations and discussion and playing around with the cardboard mock-ups had paid off, and whether the weight of the batteries was properly proportioned from side to side and front to back.

The weighing was done. The verdict was in. Shocker balanced perfectly on all four wheels.

"What did I tell you?" said Miller, to no one in particular, as though he'd never for a moment expected any other outcome.

With a week to go, the cast of *The Wizard of Ohms* presented their production to an audience of Math, Science, and Technology Alliance members at Halifax Community College. A dress rehearsal of sorts.

The critics were unanimous in their praise but for one caveat. The performance, they suggested, would look more polished and professional if the cast members dispensed with the scripts they were reading from.

"Memorize your lines," they advised.

Memorize? Now?

The students decided that each of them would use the last few words of the line before their own as a prompter to remember when to come in. When, for example, Kelly said, "We need a way to connect the motor to the transmission . . ." and ended with a mention of the Lovejoy coupler, that was Jennifer's cue to say, "Will we need to put the clutch back in?"

Nevertheless, getting the lines down proved maddeningly difficult. They stumbled over words, they flubbed, they fluffed, they stuttered and cracked up and froze mid-sentence. It was like the out-takes episode from a sitcom, except not funny. And every time, with a groan of frustration, they'd start over again from the beginning.

With days to go, the team suddenly found itself short a driver.

When the rules for the EV Grand Prix were first handed out, they stipulated student drivers only. Over the course of the intervening months, this policy had undergone revision as participating schools raised liability and other concerns, and eventually it had been decided that for the final race in particular, adult drivers in possession of a valid license issued by a recognized racing body—NASCAR, for example—would be required.

It hadn't taken too much scratching around the neighborhood of Northampton County to come up with a driver who filled the bill, and the matter had been checked off on the team's to-do list. Unfortunately, it turned out at the last minute that the driver didn't fill the bill after all. The word "valid" in "valid license" was the sticking point. Now, before the week was up, the team needed to add to its ranks someone who did have that valid license—not itself actually a terribly difficult commodity to come by, but on the other hand, not something that every guy on the street would happen to be carrying in his pocket. How often, after all, is it likely to occur that your good friend from high school will call you up at your fertilizer and farm supply business to say, "Hey, would you be interested in driving at the NASCAR track in Richmond next weekend?"

For Keith Edwards, that phone call came on a late April afternoon. The answer was yes.

In the usual fashion, news of the team's latest dilemma had spread fast in all directions. If a town crier could have been found to broadcast word on the hour from the top step of the Northampton County courthouse, Harold Miller would have escorted him there personally.

Fortunately, tidings of the troubles only had to drift as far as the library, where Carol Lowe, the media center coordinator, sprang into action.

"I know someone," she said, and called Keith Edwards.

Keith was a guy who didn't care to sit around the house when he could get out and do things—golf, fly airplanes, whatever gave him a chance for a little fun out and about in the world—and not too long ago he had taken to some amateur auto racing. He'd started on souped-up open go-karts, cranking them up to as much as 85 miles per hour on the local dirt tracks. Then he'd graduated to "mini-stock," single-seater vehicles like scale models of full-sized racing cars, and in one of those he could drive at speeds up to 120 miles per hour, sometimes packed into bumper-to-bumper clusters of other racers all drafting off each other. Recently, when a friend's wife went into labor on a race night, Keith had gotten his first taste of four-cylinder racing with a Mustang. When he was in the thick of it, it didn't feel fast and crazy; he might just as well have been doing 35 on a country road.

"Do you have a NASCAR license?" asked Carol.

"I do," said Keith, game, if mildly bewildered. How was it he was going to get a chance to drive at Richmond Raceway?

Some kids at East had built a car that ran on batteries, and they needed him to drive in a race. That's what Keith gathered from his conversation with Carol. The whole story sounded . . . actually, he had no idea what to make of it. After he got off work, he headed over to Miller's shop at East for his first look at his racing machine.

"An *Escort?*" said Keith.

"This Escort's electric," said Harold. He clapped Keith on the back and welcomed him to the team, happy to observe that Keith was a slight and wiry guy. The last thing they needed was some six-foot hunk of two-hundred-pound brawn stuffed in the car like a dead weight. Ounces counted.

Eric took Keith to give him a crash course in the EV, although "crash" was not a word Eric wanted to hear at the moment in any context associated with the car. He suggested to Keith that they head out for a drive. Keith settled behind the wheel. It was funny, sitting in an Escort with a roll cage over your head. Preposterous, really.

Keith turned the key.

"By the way," said Eric, "there's no clutch. Just put it in third gear and we'll go."

"Okay," Keith thought doubtfully. He pushed the shifter into third and tentatively pressed on the accelerator.

The car surged forward. Keith was so surprised he nearly jerked his foot off the accelerator, but habit and training kept it there. He hadn't expected that much power, that kick. Like so many other people, when he heard "electric car," his next thought was "golf cart." And then, of course, it was an Escort.

It seemed now, however, to be neither golf cart nor Escort. Oh, this could definitely be fun.

Keith let up on the accelerator a little and circled the parking lot, empty at this hour. He could hear a high-pitched whining kind of noise. He glanced over at Eric.

"That's normal," said Eric. "It's the controller. Controls the power going to the motor."

As they made another loop and then headed for the exit onto the roadway in front of East, Eric explained about keeping the amp meter at such-and-such a reading and rattled off something about volts and kilowatts. To Keith all the odd gauges and Eric's talk of current draw and amp-hours meant almost nothing, like the traffic rules of a foreign country. Speedometer, he knew. Accelerator, he knew. For the moment, he'd stick with those familiar features while he got a feel for the car; the rest would have to come later.

When they came to a halt before turning out of the parking lot, the car lapsed into complete silence. No rumble or purr of an engine. It was disconcerting. Had the car stalled? He put the pedal down; off they went again.

Under way, as the Escort picked up speed, it wasn't quiet at all; it rattled and creaked in fifty different ways. The wind rushed through the open windows and the tires hummed against the road. And since a good deal of the car's insulating material apparently had been removed in order to save weight, to Keith it sounded like he was driving a bad road in a steel can filled with loose bolts.

"Is it supposed to make all this noise?" he asked over the racket.

Eric laughed and nodded, and then he urged Keith to ramp up the speed so he could get comfortable with driving it full-out. Shocker could hit a top speed of 75 miles per hour—not quite the 183 that GM had gotten out of its Impact on a test track, but pretty good for a twice-totalled electric Escort. Keith wondered if someone on the team knew someone who'd asked the sheriff's department to look the other way. What was the speed limit on this road, anyway?

Driving along, Keith was parsing out all the different sounds and the way the car handled, establishing "normal" so he'd be able to recognize the clank or the wobble that could tell him something was going wrong with the car. He wouldn't call the Escort nimble; it felt different under his hands than a regular car, heavy without being sluggish. But it steered well and balanced nicely. By the time he and Eric pulled up to the door of Harold's shop, Keith was settling in nicely with this electrified vehicle that decidedly wasn't a golf cart. And anyway, for a chance to have a go on the track at Richmond, he probably would have agreed to do it by tricycle if they'd asked him.

* * *

Ben Moses volunteered his hog trailer to haul the car to Richmond. Moses was a farmer, a tall, imposing man accustomed to wrestling recalcitrant livestock and unwieldy feed sacks where they didn't necessarily want to go, so wrangling an electric car to Richmond seemed a perfectly feasible prospect. Harold Miller thought it would be a fitting thing, pulling up to the competition with their vehicle on a farm trailer.

Ben and his wife, Rhonda, were close friends with John and June Parker, which was how they had gotten caught up in cheering on the EV project. The first time Ben met Eric Ryan, back in Eric's first year, Moses had fixed Eric with a long look before concluding with a laugh, "You are NOT from this zip code."

Rhonda, who was a teacher herself, had put her hand on Eric's shoulder, spun him around appraisingly, and said simply, "You'll do."

Ben rolled up to Northampton–East on Tuesday evening to help Harold load the car on the trailer. The team was supposed to be leaving the next day for Richmond. Harold had shooed all the kids out earlier, sending them home to pack and get a good night's rest.

Because it was built to haul animals, not EVs, Ben's trailer had tall sides, and when Ben and Harold lined up the car with the ramp, they both stood back to give the setup a critical look. Cozy fit, it was going to be. A delicate piece of maneuvering.

Slowly, painstakingly, they eased the car up onto the trailer, with almost no clearance to either side. They'd just make it if they held it steady.

Crunch.

The sound of metal meeting an obstacle and yielding to it was exactly what Harold did not want to hear right now. It was not a particularly bone-jarring, head-snapping impact, but it might just as well have been a direct hit in the London blitz for the way Harold and Ben froze, staring at each other in wordless horror. They did not want to look.

Of course they had to look. Like doctors probing a battlefield wound, they gingerly drew the car back a foot or two, then paused to examine the damage.

The left rear fender. It had a dent, a crease, an indisputably adverse alteration of its planar integrity. This was not good.

"Oh Lord," said Miller, surveying the damage.

Shocker came back off the trailer and returned to Miller's shop, where Miller and Moses passed the better part of the night carefully hammering out the dent. When they had done the best with it they could and added a few dabs of paint, a strategically placed sponsor sticker made up the difference. They decided to give the hog trailer a miss for a second try in favor of using an actual auto trailer.

Now they just needed an actual auto trailer.

For goodness sake, every third boy in this county fancied himself the next star of NASCAR; surely, one of them had a trailer.

It turned out, happily, that Keith Edwards did, and seeing the team's dilemma, he offered it up. By late the following morning, Shocker was safely loaded. The dent was visible only if you knew where to look. The trailer was hitched to Moses's truck. Richmond was two hours away.

ALL ROADS LEAD
TO RICHMOND

Amonth ago, it was a rolling skeleton, raw and rough. Today, on its way to Richmond, piggybacked on the trailer and flying up I-95, Shocker looked sleek and race-car chic, waxed and polished and gleaming, with the big red number 10 on both doors and local sponsor names precisely hand-lettered on the rear panels by a volunteer from the community, and five-star rims on the wheels, donated by Davis Farm Supply.

"Can't touch us," thought Jennifer happily.

The ECORV team was traveling in a small convoy, with the trailer, a school van, private cars with parents and teachers driving, and Mr. Ryan in that ragged red truck of his that he was so unaccountably content with. John and June Parker were with them—as if there were a chance the two would have missed this. The principal from East, Greg Todd, had come along as well, and the Northampton school superintendent, Charles Slemenda, who had supported the EV project unstintingly since John Parker first approached him about it in the fall, would be joining them. The list went on: Katrina's father and other parents, Uncle Clyde, Doug Miller, Carol Lowe, who was a professional photographer as well as a librarian, and Darrell Worley from North Carolina Power, who had served as technology advisor and liaison to the team from the power company. Missing, to everyone's regret, was George Hawkins, and also Randy Shillingburg, who'd championed them at the beginning and cheered them on ever since, now sidelined at the last moment by surgery.

There were others, however, who wouldn't be missed, the naysayers, the ones who'd made a point of telling John Parker that they had no intention of traveling to Richmond just to watch Northampton County embarrass itself.

The kids were nervous and excited at once. They were traveling to another state, missing school for two days, staying in a hotel for three nights, and that alone was reason enough to be feeling pretty flush with life.

But they couldn't forget why they were going to Richmond; now that they were on their way, it was impossible not to wonder how ECORV would measure up against the competition. Almost until this moment, Richmond had seemed so far away—first a crazy idea, later a distant possibility, then someplace that lay at the end of a very long to-do list—that there hardly had been cause to think at any length about the other teams. Time was the only competitor they'd worried about racing against, trying to get the car finished on schedule, with Mr. Ryan and Mr. Miller pushing hard to have it ready for road testing by the end of March. The month since then had passed in an exhausting flurry of a thousand last-minute details.

When the car had come together and they'd put it to the test on the road, and it gave them speed, smooth handling, and good acceleration, for a time the thrill of that victory swept away all doubts, all uncertainties. Shocker kicked amps.

Now, though, with Richmond finally so close, not even two hours away, the suspense suddenly seemed maddening and unbearable. If

Shocker was good, would "good" be good enough? Were they going to find out, after all, that they really were nothing more than a bunch of country kids from one of the poorest counties in North Carolina?

They pulled off I-95 and drove into Richmond through an industrial neighborhood. Not much to look at, but they were all eagerly staring out the windows, watching for any sign of the track. The raceway complex snuck up on them anyway. It was tucked away inside a big fairgrounds and exposition site, so that they turned into an unprepossessing paved drive that ran through a couple of gates and wound around a low hillside, before suddenly there it was just ahead, the back side of the grandstands. They were here. Richmond International Raceway.

In front of them a long line of cars and trucks and car trailers sat. Stopped. Waiting.

Every student, every supporter, every parent and teacher and chaperone of every team who would enter inside the track had to be formally credentialed before they would be admitted to the infield, the Grand Prix's nexus. Although security, safety, and liability issues were at stake, the greater goal behind the credentialing was that it was another way to give the students an authentic experience. Little details like that weren't essential to the success or failure of the EV Grand Prix, but they would help make the kids feel like they were part of something real and exciting.

Virginia Power and the raceway, working together, had kept that goal at the center of their planning.

One by one, the people waiting in the long line of vehicles entered a small outbuilding—not much bigger than a shed, really—

where they were photographed and their names, affiliations, and pictures placed on rectangular cards that would slip into a plastic pocket to be worn around the neck or clipped to a belt or pocket.

It was cool to wear the credentials. It took forever to get them. The line crept forward, vehicle by vehicle.

Finally, though, the procession of ECORV team members completed credentialing and the group was waved on to enter the raceway proper. They rolled forward as the road dipped into a short, narrow, dark, concrete tunnel. Then they emerged into bright sunshine again and found themselves on the infield of Richmond International Raceway, with the long loop of the track sweeping around them.

From the inside it seemed vast, much bigger than it looked from the outside. Mr. Miller had told the students he'd raced here back in the 1950s when there was nothing but a half-mile dirt track and a rowdy Saturday-night crowd to cheer the drivers on. Now the infield, partially paved and partially bare and hard-packed earth, was like the broad, flat bottom of an enormous bowl. The track—sixty feet wide, three-quarters of a mile long, shaped like a "D" and banked fourteen degrees in the turns—rose up all around them to a cement wall, and above the wall the grandstands went up and up still farther, seats for tens of thousands of people. Even the kids who didn't give a rip for NASCAR, and the teachers too, for that matter, and the parents, were looking around in amazement. They'd made it. They were on the infield of a national-caliber racetrack, with a car they had built themselves.

Erick Vann thought how television didn't give you any sense at all of the scale of the place.

Donny Lassiter was thinking, *This is where the professionals, the big boys race. How did we get here?*

Harold Parker found the theme song from the TV sitcom *The Jeffersons* popping into his head: "We're moving on up. . . ."

And the teachers? Seeing their kids standing on the raceway infield, with wide eyes and big grins, seeing Shocker sitting atop Keith's trailer, that was all the victory they needed. However the team placed in the actual competition almost—*almost*—didn't matter.

Each of the teams was assigned one half of a stall in the garage, an infield structure like a very long carport. There were no walls, just steel I-beams for support and heavy, weighted red-vinyl curtains, and a corrugated aluminum roof with skylights overhead. In these same stalls, the real NASCAR vehicles, throaty, road-chewing, precision-made machines, built to the tune of hundreds of thousands of dollars, were ministered to by their crack support crews. Now, lining up underneath the skylights were secondhand economy cars and pickups: a couple of Rabbits, a Dodge Colt, a Honda Civic, several models of Chevrolet.

"I believe this was Ricky Rudd's stall," Harold announced, as the ECORV team backed the Escort carefully off the trailer. Whether this was true or not was beside the point; they'd choose to believe it was so. Ricky Rudd, #10.

Within the enormous, mostly empty bowl of the raceway, the row of garage stalls buzzed with activity as students and teachers swarmed around unloading their vehicles. Of the twenty-five or so schools that had signed on hopefully to the competition, only sixteen had managed to finish a vehicle and make it this far. They came from Virginia, Pennsylvania, West Virginia, Maryland, and Washington, DC. There were several other schools from North Carolina as well, sponsored by Duke Power and Carolina Power & Light. Each school was identified by a big banner hung over its stall, printed with the purple and red EV Grand Prix logo, the school's name, and the utility sponsor. Technically, ECORV represented four different schools, but over Shocker the banner read "Northampton County High School–East." Somehow, the ECORV name had never really stuck to the team nearly as consistently as the more identifying handle "Northampton."

With so many other more pressing demands to the project, the naming had barely registered with the teachers or students of ECORV. Such a minor detail, it never seemed important. Right now, certainly not.

As each new team pulled up, everyone else would pause in their work to see what had arrived. Check out the competition. If in the months they had spent working on their car the kids of ECORV hadn't thought too much about any of the other teams, now they were noticing how many of the banners bore the names of technical and science and mathematics schools, and how spiffy and professional a lot of those other vehicles looked, with expensive paint jobs and bodies plastered with sponsor names.

Erick Vann, a backbone to the team, steady and persevering, felt mixed up with pride, excitement, and self-consciousness. Standing here on the infield of a NASCAR track with so many other people, the ones from the other schools, and the event officials from the power companies and the track and the Department of Energy— that almost seemed reward enough for the work of these past seven months. At the same time, Erick knew that Shocker was performing well; the car could travel more than forty miles on a charge and it could hit seventy-five miles per hour as well. He was eager to see how it would match up against the other vehicles, even while he was wondering if all those other teams were looking at him and the rest of his team and Shocker and thinking they were just a bunch of rednecks with the sorriest car in the field. Shocker had only just missed arriving on a hog trailer.

Jennifer felt a tickle of uneasiness as well. Nothing would shake her confidence that she and the rest of the team had built the best EV it was possible to assemble with the resources within their grasp. They'd brought to the project all the determination and ingenuity they could muster. So many people in the community had pitched in, like Mr. Hawkins and his father; and Jennifer's own father; and the guys at the Machine Shop; and Mr. Hall, the NAPA dealer who had hunted down parts for them; and oh, dozens of people she could name. What if, though, these other teams, with more at their disposal, had done the same? Would the difference tell?

On the other hand, prestigious Thomas Jefferson High School for Science and Technology, from Virginia, up near Washington, D.C., had come with a white Ford Escort almost exactly like Shocker, and it looked like they were still trying to put it together too.

Now the team from Norfolk Technical-Vocational Center was arriving, driving up with a large, enclosed truck. "Like *Knight Rider*," thought Katrina, picturing that goofy TV show with the talking car.

The Norfolk team members hopped out and swarmed around the big truck, opening the rear doors, clambering inside. Then music started coming out, loud: "The Electric Slide." That captured everyone's attention. All up and down the row of garages, people stopped what they were doing and watched.

A pickup was backing out slowly from the truck now, fancy with a pearlized two-tone paint job. There were big speakers mounted on the rear, blasting the music. Every few measures over the music a voice exclaimed, "It's electric!"

Everyone watching gaped.

"Can they do that?" asked Katrina.

"It's got to be against the rules, doesn't it?" someone else said. Those speakers stretched the definition of "stock" appearance, that was for sure.

"Don't worry Mr. Miller," said Harold Parker cheerily, standing by Harold's side. "You know it's always the empty wagon that makes the most noise."

The first afternoon was taken up with unloading, looking around, enjoying the thrill of arriving, but also scoping out the other vehicles and sizing them up. Harold Miller had expected Thomas Jefferson, with that school's reputation, to be the team to beat, but as soon as he cast a mechanic's eye at Jefferson's Escort and the kids still hanging over it with tools in hand, he decided there'd be no trouble from that quarter and moved on.

He'd heard a rumor, too, that the team from Richmond, Hermitage Technical, had lined up a lot of sponsors with money. Hermitage had come with a Dodge Colt wagon—plenty of room, certainly, for batteries in there. He'd be keeping watch on that one.

Nothing that pulled up, however, not even Suitland High School's sporty, new-model Dodge Daytona, could take away from the ECORV kids' excitement and their real pride in their car. Anywhere anyone put a hand on Shocker, Kelly followed behind wiping away fingerprints. If she had anything to do with it, no one was going to be able to spy so much as a speck of dirt or a ghost of a fingerprint on this car.

The vehicles' chargers were being inspected; before the teams left for the hotel, they would plug their cars in to have them ready to begin competing in the morning. Virginia Power had run electric lines to power the charging stations for the vehicles; it was like setting up outlets for twenty hair dryers in the middle of an open field. Overnight, two volunteers, technical people from the power company, would stay to monitor the charging. If any problems arose with one or another of the EVs, they would call the team leader. Norman Joyner and Harold dearly hoped that ground-fault interrupter wasn't going to give them any troubles here.

While Mr. Joyner was supervising his battery-and-electric team checking over everything, one of the teachers from Hermitage Technical Center—the whole team was nattily dressed in matching turquoise polo shirts and crisply pressed khakis—came sauntering up to stand by Joyner's side, giving Shocker an appraising once-over.

"The way I heard it," he observed laconically, "all you people from North Carolina know how to do is bale hay and drive tractors."

Norman Joyner didn't bother to respond, but the granite set of his jaw ossified that little bit more. Donny Lassiter heard the crack, too. Did all these other people think that because Northampton wasn't some big tech school the team must be totally out of its league and without a chance? "We're going to win, now," thought Donny, determined. He was fixing his sights in particular on the maroon-and-turquoise #33 car from Hermitage Technical Center.

THE WIZARD OF WOES

The hotel that night was filled with EV teams, clusters of kids sloping down the hallways to the soda machines, teachers standing in doorways conferring with each other.

Strict rules had been laid down for the ECORV students at the hotel: no boys in the girls' rooms, no girls in the boys' rooms. But the *Wizard of Ohms* cast, what were they going to do? They needed to practice, they were on the day after tomorrow, and they still were trying to get the ten-minute presentation down right. They left the door wide open and all the lights on and piled into Jennifer and Kelly's room. Frazzled and tired, slumped around the room calling out lines back and forth, they suggested all the erotic ambiance of the final day of a tiddly-winks tournament, but nevertheless one of the other students' mothers, who was playing chaperone, popped her head in the open door, saw Neil Ray and Donny in there, and raised hell with them.

What were they doing in that room together? They knew the rules and did they want to mess everything up for everyone and she had half a mind to send all of them right home right this minute! The boys were cleared out. Furiously, Jennifer retreated to the bathroom and climbed, fully dressed, with her script, into the dry bathtub. Everyone would work on their own lines in solitude.

* * *

Thursday, Day 1:

Early the next morning, bleary with sleep lost to excitement and preparations, the team arrived at the track to find the volunteer staff restoring order amid minor chaos. The night before, as they were readying to leave the track, there were dark clouds piling up beyond the edge of the grandstands at turn four. Not long after they left for the hotel, a fierce thunderstorm had blasted through with sheeting rain and powerful winds. The infield was a minor shambles this morning; anything not anchored down had been blown over or tumbled about by the storm. There were puddles everywhere and soggy bits and pieces of paper, and the unpaved portions of the infield were soaked to mud. Big tents that had been set up for the Grand Prix had withstood the wind and rain, but chairs and tables were tumbled about. Fortunately, the cars in the open-sided garage were unharmed, and in spite of the storm the charging seemed to have gone all right. The team set to work carefully drying and cleaning the car anywhere it had been splashed by the driving rains or spattered by grit.

"That rain's a good sign," said Miller. "In my dirt-track days, I always had good luck when it rained."

The teams assembled under the largest of the infield tents for a welcome and orientation and a safety-training session. The trainers emphasized the importance of wearing protective goggles while working around the vehicles in the pits, and they pointed out the eyewash stations (for acid splashes) and the baking soda neutralizer (for acid spills). They stressed the potential unfortunate consequences that could arise when you ran a car into a solid wall at even modest speeds. So don't do that.

After the meeting, passing inspection was the first hurdle of the day. Or to look at it another way, a major hurdle for the whole competition. If it didn't pass inspection, Shocker was going nowhere.

Everything on the car had been checked, double-checked, quadruple-quintuple-checked time and again, every battery connection confirmed, the switches and meters and components gone over, each bolt, joint, and weld reexamined, but just to be sure, John Parker led a final last-minute-detail review.

The inspections were not perfunctory. No one could accuse the technical staff for the EV Grand Prix of anything less than a rigorous enforcement of the safety and design requirements. The technical inspections stretched on for hours. There was a rules check, a safety check, a brake test. Probing questions were asked. A long checklist was duly marked off, item by item. Was there a bleed-down device? Were there any fluid leaks? Did the doors work "flawlessly," as the rules stipulated? How was the tire pressure? Was there a fire extinguisher?

As Shocker was cutting things fine in the matter of weight, the weigh-in proved a particularly fraught few minutes. The car, by the team's estimation, teetered so close to the edge of its gross vehicle weight that Mr. Miller had sent some of the students hunting for the lightest fire extinguisher they could find; the standard five-pounder threatened to push the car over the limit.

The weigh-in concluded. Squeaking under the GVW of 3,135, Shocker sat solidly at 3,130 pounds.

Finally, the inspection team placed small, fluorescent orange stickers on both bottom corners of Shocker's front windshield: "Approved Vehicle."

* * *

A film crew brought on by Virginia Power was making the rounds, shooting the cars and the kids, interviewing teachers and students.

"I don't think I'd like to be the school to compete against us," said one of the teachers from Norfolk Technical Vocational Center.

Harold Miller said only, "I don't care if they come in last, I'm proud of 'em anyway." He said that to the students too—not that he mentioned the possibility of coming in last, but after months of cheering the kids on with the promise that they could go to Richmond and win, now he took the pressure off. "You made it here when a lot of people wanted to bet you couldn't," he told them. "Now have fun."

Anna Collier, though, with the unenviable honor of having to take the wheel for the team first, in the efficiency event, was fighting the jitters. With all the test-driving, the team had put enough miles on the car to be confident that any bugs were shaken out, that no major flaw in the conversion would suddenly reveal itself two laps into the competition. Confident wasn't entirely the same thing as certain, however.

As the name suggested, the efficiency event was designed to determine which of the vehicles used the least amount of energy over a given distance. The judges would monitor vehicle performance with a kilowatt-hour meter installed in the dash of each team's EV, which would measure energy expended. Because the competing vehicles varied so widely in size and type, an inscrutable "weight factor" formula had been worked up by Argonne to bring equity to the scoring.

For the opening act of the EV Grand Prix, the efficiency event was not one that promised to be a real crowd-pleaser. The very word "efficiency," alas, suggested more earnestness than excitement. The vehicles would line up, one behind the other, with a pace car in the lead. They would proceed in this order for ten revolutions around the track at each of three different speeds: twenty-five, forty, and fifty-five miles per hour. At the end of each set of ten circuits, all the vehicles would stop, and the event judges would run out to check all the kilowatt-hour meters.

The event was perfectly exciting enough for Anna. She was in the car, she was on a NASCAR track, she was driving for the team. She wanted to perform her best, she didn't want to let anyone down. She wanted to drive to show "this is what we can do."

When every amp might count, today and in the days to come, the teams would push their vehicles out from the garage stalls to the starting point for each event, which was usually Pit Road, the long paved strip paralleling the track and separated from it by a low wall, where in NASCAR races the cars would dodge in for their lightning-quick tire changes and fuel refills.

Anna sat at the wheel, feeling strung taut as she waited to begin. At last, off they went. Ten times around. Stop. Wait. Ten times again. Stop. Wait. Ten more times. Stop. Finished.

Her jangling nerves settled down after the first few laps, and then it was a matter of holding steady, steering straight, staying calm in the wait between each round of laps. From the practice drives she had made back on the road in front of Northampton–East, it had been determined that she could get best efficiency at twenty-five miles per hour in second gear, at forty in third gear, and at fifty-five in fourth, so Anna had to remember, too, to put the car into the right gear each time. Early on, the car from Thomas Jefferson, the other white Escort hatchback, pulled out for some reason. Seeing it drop out was unnerving for everyone, not least the Thomas Jefferson team, but also the Escort-driving Anna. She kept her focus, though, through the end.

The cars processed off the track. Everyone cheered the drivers in from this first event. As Anna climbed from the car, Erick and Tim, suddenly inspired, hoisted her, laughing, up to their shoulders and paraded her around like a NASCAR champion.

Word was already traveling up and down the row of vehicle bays—Thomas Jefferson had burned out the transmission on their Escort in the first couple of laps, which was why the car had dropped out. Hearing this news, the kids from the other teams, no matter how much they wanted to win, suffered a sharp pang of sympathy for Jefferson's hard luck, peering down at the stall where the Jefferson team members hovered over their ailing car.

Mr. Miller headed over to them to offer his help if they wanted it. Every student and teacher here knew how much work and heart had gone into building these vehicles and how bitterly painful it must feel at the moment to the Jefferson students, wondering if the competition was already over for them. All the other teams knew as well that some similar fate still could strike any of them in the events to come.

In the ECORV stall Anna was relieved, her driving stint successfully completed, though it was impossible to guess how the scores might tally from the efficiency event. Each team could check its own kilowatt-hour meter after the vehicles had come in, but that told you nothing about how the others had performed. The wait stretched on while the judges conferred and points were allocated.

Finally, the scores went up. They generated head-scratching bewilderment all around. The Raleigh County Vocational-Technical Center team from Beckley, West Virginia, driving a Geo Metro Sprint, had taken the initial lead, with twenty points in efficiency. The rest of the field, though, trailed ridiculously far behind, Suitland High from Maryland in a distant second place with only 10.7

points, and the other teams even farther back. ECORV was tied for fifth place with the Central Shenandoah Valley Governor's School from Virginia, with 9.1 points—ironic, considering Shenandoah was driving a 1970s 240-Z, nearly the same car that ECORV had rejected in the fall.

Yesterday the ECORV students were worrying they'd simply be laughed out of the competition and thinking that winning was a far-fetched dream. They were certain they would be thrilled, grateful for a respectable fifth-place finish or something even close to that, most of them still amazed that they had made it to Richmond at all, with a car that actually ran. Sure, Mr. Miller and Mr. Ryan both had spoken of nothing but winning through all the months leading up to this week. But everyone understood that Mr. Miller was just being Mr. Miller; he was the kind of man who, if a flood came through and washed away his home and every one of his belongings, he'd say, "I was thinking of remodeling anyway."

And Mr. Ryan—you couldn't expect any kind of rational perspective from a man who'd willingly, and, if you believed him, even eagerly, packed up and moved from California to Northampton County.

Then, seeing the other EVs as they were unloaded, it had been so hard to estimate how the competition would stack up—some of those vehicles looked seriously intimidating.

But in the wake of the efficiency event, it was hard to know whether they ought to feel happy or disappointed with fifth. No one from any of the teams was really quite sure what to think or expect. Raleigh County's Geo, which, judged by appearance alone, was nothing special to write home about, had trounced everyone else. Then again, Suitland's Dodge Daytona had nabbed second place, and that car, a '93 model in this field of geriatric has-beens, was pretty hot, in electric blue and green with a pink racing stripe, if that really meant anything about the vehicle except a good paint job.

With one event completed, hazarding a guess at how things would stand in twenty-four hours, with the oral, design, and range events all on the schedule for tomorrow, was now, if anything, a less certain business than it had seemed only yesterday. A spectacular performance, a catastrophic failure. Either felt equally possible for any one of the teams.

Friday, Day 2:

Going away for an adventure, three nights in a hotel and all the cable television you could watch, would have been more fun for the kids if they hadn't been completely obsessed with the competition, what had happened today and what might come tomorrow. They hung out in their rooms that evening, going over every detail, talking about the other teams, the way their students behaved, their cars, trying to figure out what Raleigh County's secret had been. The *Wizard of Ohms* cast was still running lines, their last night of rehearsing.

In the morning, Darrell Parker dressed in a tuxedo for the design presentation. He and Ivory had always been happy to put a hand in wherever it was needed as Shocker was being built, but for this morning's event they needed to know everything about the car, every element and feature and its function, why it was chosen and how it had been installed, and sometimes, as in the case of the batteries, why it was installed where it was installed. They might be called upon to explain a few of the odder details, like the boat bilge pump that blew air over the motor to keep it cool, and the flap over the battery vent that was made from a plastic milk jug. These were not conventional EV features, but they made sense, and Darrell and Ivory could say why.

They could speak as well to aerodynamics and design decisions, how the handling was affected by battery placement, how they'd managed the coupling of motor and transmission, and on and on. The design judges might ask them any question at all, down to the selection of paint colors.

Ivory was the quieter of the two of them, but he knew the car inside and out. And Darrell, he could always think on his feet and turn out an answer when it was needed. The tux was just an extra touch.

Bob Zickefoose was one of the design judges, an engineer from an alternative energy company in North Carolina. Zickefoose's company owned an electric car, a red Pontiac Fiero two-seater acquired through a conversion business in California, and it happened that the previous year, well before Walt Purdy dreamed up the EV Grand Prix, Zickefoose had been invited by Northampton High School–East's VICA club to bring the Fiero and talk about his company's work in future technologies.

On that visit, Zickefoose met Harold Miller, and Miller's interest in electric vehicles gave them much to talk about. Harold and Bob put the Fiero up on the lift in Harold's shop so some of Harold's students could get a good look at the parts and how they went together.

Seeing Harold here at the EV Grand Prix with a car and a team of kids gave Bob Zickefoose great pleasure. It did not, however, incline him to be a whit less exacting in his review of the team's work.

Bob understood that while people might think at first that an EV conversion was an electrical problem, in reality it presented a mechanical design challenge. The most laborious and time-consuming part of the process was figuring out where everything should go and how to achieve the best possible balance and weight distribution and handling within the constraints set by the vehicle chosen for the job.

In judging the vehicles at the EV Grand Prix, he looked for how the teams had solved that mechanical challenge, and right off he could tell which teams had solved it by having the teachers make all the decisions. Experience taught him to be suspicious of the car that looked too good. The students would be standing by some beauty of a vehicle, and he would ask them a simple question, "Why did you decide to put the controller here?" or "How did you take the measurements for the adaptor plate?" and the students would stare blankly at him and exchange uncomfortable glances, because they hadn't a clue. In this event, though, the presenters' knowledge was an element being judged, no less than the paint jobs and the battery boxes.

Bob Zickefoose knew the kind of teacher Harold Miller was, and he wasn't surprised when the Shocker design presenters could wax eloquent in reply to any question. That one in the tux in particular.

The categories evaluated by the design judges included presentation, technical content (the thought that had gone into the design and building), actual quality of the conversion, including appearance, and the technical results—how well everything added up to an attractive, efficient EV.

Southern Wayne High School's GMC S-15 pickup, the "Electruck," a very elegant conversion on which the bed hinged up and all the batteries went underneath where you didn't even see them when the bed was down, took first place with twenty points. Reading-Muhlenberg Vocational Technical School, out of Pennsylvania, with a snazzy Fiero GT, nabbed a close second. Raleigh

County took fifth, but with its huge lead following efficiency held on to first place overall. And ECORV?

"We got third place?" said Eric when one of the kids came running to tell him. "We got third place!" he whooped. "We got third place!"

It felt like someone had lit a fuse in the ECORV bay of the garage. To Harold Miller, it was like seeing a light come on in the students' faces. A fifth place, a third place—maybe they did have a real chance here, not just to show up and compete, but like Mr. Miller had said from the first day, to win.

Yesterday, the fifth-place finish in efficiency had left everyone puzzled, but to Harold it said "We're in the competition." After all, the score placed them in the top third. Teams closer to the bottom would have a harder chance turning things around, but Harold knew that with the next couple of scores his kids could have the chance to move up into real contention. The oral event was a hard call—either the judges were going to reward *The Wizard of Ohms* for originality, or they were going to mark it down as too far over the top. Range, he thought, they had a fair chance. Acceleration and handling? Hard to say.

Harold could also see, however, that more pressure was on the oral team now.

Whatever her hesitations might have been when Mr. Ryan proposed the idea of a skit, Jennifer had long since fully embraced her role. She was wearing a girlish, sailor-suit kind of a dress and even glittery red shoes—her dad had glued the glitter on for her, he was so excited and proud of Jennifer. She left a little sparkly trail wherever she walked in them.

Donny was wearing a straw hat and there was hay sticking out of his pockets. Kelly had a funnel-shaped aluminum-foil cap on her head and was wearing a large box wrapped in foil, her head, legs, and arms sticking out openings.

They waited anxiously just outside the media center, a low cinder-block building in the infield, where the oral presentations were being given. On the outside wall of the media center a board tracked the scores as each competition was completed, so people were constantly drifting by, checking out the numbers. There was a tiny little porch, hardly bigger than a dining table, two steps up from the ground, and the *Ohms* cast members perched there, going over everything in their heads. Donny felt as though his innards had sprouted wings and started fluttering between his ribs.

Some of the other teams, their oral presentations weren't anything more than one kid getting up and talking. With note cards. *The Wizard of Ohms* was going to knock those judges for a loop. Please let it be a good one.

Mr. Ryan was saying, "You're going to need to get in there and hustle and get everything set up fast."

"Northampton High School–East?" the door attendant called.

It was time. They rushed in with their set and their cutout car, trying to get everything in place, the lights plugged in, and the Velcroed cardboard components where they needed to be. Mr. Ryan helped them make it go as smoothly as possible. The judges seemed neither impressed nor pleased by the technological embellishments.

"We'll give you a couple of minutes and then you have to start," they said.

At last the cast was set up, but feeling flustered. Mr. Ryan retreated with a final whispered, "You guys are gonna rock!"

After all the rehearsing, Dorothy was finally in the land of Ohms. And look! Here was the scarecrow, the tin man, and the lion to help her convert the Wicked Witch's car to an EV!

A little bit further, a few minutes more . . . the Good Witch Conductra would tell Dorothy she could travel home to North Carolina in her electric car.

Someone dropped a line.

A sudden, horrible silence fell. Whoever had been next, waiting for the cue that didn't come, couldn't remember what to say either.

Under the best of circumstances, they'd been cutting it fine on the time; there was no wiggle room for hemming, hawing, or casting desperate glances at each other while entertaining a sensation like your stomach had boarded the express elevator for the basement. Like a house of cards, the command performance of *The Wizard of Ohms* was coming down.

Jennifer threw out a line and they struggled gamely on, but now everything was out of sorts and the rhythm broken. Had they remembered the bit about replacing the clutch with the Lovejoy coupler? Did anyone mention the belly pan? Time having managed the perverse trick of simultaneously speeding up and slowing to an agonizing crawl, what remained of *The Wizard of Ohms* would feel like the longest too-few minutes any one of the five cast members had ever known.

"Two minutes," a voice from the judges' table called out.

Dorothy and her crew were ad-libbing desperately now, ripping Velcroed "gasoline" components off the car and snatching up the "electric" ones, saying, "We need this and we need to use that," and trying to throw in anything they could remember of the explanations they had meant, a lifetime ago, to carefully interweave with their actions. All they really could think now was that they had to drive the car away to get offstage.

And so they did, and then it was over and they were outside on the little porch in the hot sun again. They couldn't even remember how they'd gotten out the door. Did they say thank-you or just do a bolt? Had anything they'd said in the last five minutes made any sense at all?

They slumped down outside the media building. Jennifer fought back tears. They had worked so, so hard. How could this have happened?

Kelly was angry and upset all at once. They could have used notes—every other team was going in with cards. Why did those people at the Halifax Community College presentation have to fuss about the note cards? If they'd stuck with those cards, everything would have been fine.

They'd gone in thinking that this was their chance, that they could show that just because they were from a little school out in the country, and just because their car wasn't the fanciest one here, didn't mean that they weren't just as smart, just as capable and intellectually sophisticated as the students from the science and tech schools.

"We're supposed to be the 'academics,'" thought Kelly, "and we screw it up."

Eric, who hadn't wanted to put extra pressure on the kids by staying and watching, didn't want to ask them now what had happened. He could read it in their shell-shocked faces; obviously, something had gone wrong. But they started gasping out the story to him forlornly. A mess-up. Not enough time. They'd exceeded the ten minutes. They'd hashed it up. Jennifer was certain they'd be disqualified. What if they'd lost the competition for the whole team?

But Mr. Miller, who'd watched for a few minutes before he, too, ducked out with a case of the nerves, said they were being too hard on themselves. "Y'all were doing fantastic in there!" he said, and he meant it. He beamed; he said they had it all over the other teams for creativity and getting their ideas across, and he couldn't have been prouder.

"But you don't understand," stammered Jennifer. She was devastated.

The time that passed until scores were posted for the oral competition, seemed—though earlier the *Ohms* team would never have believed such a thing possible—to drag even more slowly than the final minutes of the presentation itself. One minute they thought they couldn't bear to see the results, and the next minute they were glancing anxiously at the door of the media center looking for a sign that the judges were coming out.

Finally, the last of the teams finished presenting. The scores were going up. The *Ohms* cast crowded around, first checking their own score. A 19.3! They hadn't been disqualified, and the score wasn't bad, by no means as bad as they had imagined and dreaded it would be. Then they scanned the board for the other teams' numbers. Hermitage was first, with 20 points.

"Suitland got nineteen point six."

"That makes them second? No, wait, third. A. R. Burton got second, nineteen point nine."

They checked the board carefully, and checked it again. No, they had it right. ECORV had placed fourth in the oral competition. They were surprised to have done that well. Tremendously relieved that they hadn't been disqualified. Yet Jennifer Robbins could only think that if they had gotten the presentation right, then they could have taken first place in the event. It might have been the whole team's best chance for a first-place finish. Now it was gone.

Harold looked at the oral score, though, and looked at the team's other scores, then he looked at Eric and said, "Lord almighty, we're in third place."

* * *

You never know what to expect from April in Virginia. Wobbling unsteadily between winter and summer, sometimes it will reward you with textbook spring weather of mild breezes and sweet sunshine. Then it might slip back to raw winds and damp and steely gray skies before turning around and walloping you with a day as enervatingly hot as mid-July.

For the EV Grand Prix, April plumped for hot. Temperatures crept into the nineties, and down in the bowl of the RIR, surrounded by blacktop, with no breeze, it was sweltering. As quickly as the Virginia Power volunteers put bottles of water into a big, ice-filled tub under one of the infield tents, the water disappeared. People took refuge in the shade of the tents and in the garage stalls.

Keith Edwards was oblivious to the heat, to the bright sun bearing down and the blurry ripples radiating up from the black asphalt. He was standing with Harold Miller, looking around at the vehicles and the students milling about, at the broad sweep of the track surrounding them, at the grandstands and the garages, and taking it all in with mild astonishment.

Harold had hoped that Keith could travel with the rest of the team, but spring is a busy season in the fertilizer business, so Keith was only now arriving in Richmond. Coming into the picture so suddenly, and so recently, without benefit of the months of planning and anticipation that everyone else on the team had gone through, Keith was still feeling mildly bewildered by the sudden turn of events in his life. If a fortune-teller had told him a week ago that he would be standing now in the infield at Richmond International Raceway planning his race strategy, he would have demanded his money back for so preposterous a prediction.

He'd missed the session given to the other race drivers the day before to practice on the track, so Keith and Harold were talking about the layout and the turns and the best line to follow, Harold reminding him that with an electric car you wanted to think about how to get the most speed with the least expenditure of energy, and that might mean taking on the track in a different way than you would in a gas-powered car.

"You want to hold your speed as steady as you can, come in high on the turns instead of climbing them," said Harold, then interrupted himself in the middle of that thought to tug Keith forward, saying, "I want you to meet someone here."

"Keith Edwards," said Harold, making introductions, "this is Mr. Elmo Langley. Mr. Langley and I go way back; we knew each other when this place still wasn't nothing but dirt."

"Nice to meet you," said Keith.

"Mr. Langley's driving the pace car for this competition," Harold explained to Keith. He didn't mention that Mr. Langley also was one of the most famous NASCAR pace-car drivers and a former racer himself. Keith wouldn't learn that until later. What neither Keith nor Harold knew was that Elmo Langley had once driven the #10 car too, many a year ago.

"Keith is going to be driving for us in the race," Miller explained to Langley. "Keith couldn't be here for driver's practice yesterday, so we were just talking about how to take the track."

Even that fortune-teller, no matter how clearly she saw it in her crystal ball, might have hesitated to go so far as to suggest that Keith would get to Richmond and almost immediately find himself riding around the track with Elmo Langley. But somehow there Keith was, in the car, Langley driving and cutting through the banked turns and rolling down the straightaways as he told Keith about the Richmond track's quirks and character.

It made all the difference for Keith. Driving would have been good practice, but riding with Elmo Langley made a heck of an alternative and certainly a better story to take back to the local races in the months to come.

Keith studied the track, listening to what Langley said and keeping in mind what Harold had told him about speed and energy. It looked to Keith as though if you held just the right line, you could use the bank of the track to your advantage to avoid having to accelerate out of the turns.

IF IT STOPS

Over in the pits, Katrina was getting ready to drive the range event, and she was looking as petrified as if she'd just seen an armada of ghosts floating through the infield. She was wearing a full-body coverall, Keith's fireproof race driver's suit, that made her tiny frame appear even smaller.

Keith was a soft-spoken, level-headed guy, without a trace of the testosterone-addled hot-dogger in him, and he talked quietly with Katrina about what he'd learned on the track.

"Hold your line in the second groove coming through turns one and two," he told her. "That way, you won't have to climb back up the track coming out of the turns—you'll use less energy that way."

Meanwhile, Mr. Ryan and her father were giving her a running pep talk. Mr. Miller was reminding her about keeping her speed right at fourty-three miles per hour, exactly as she'd practiced on the road in front of East.

"You don't want to brake and speed up; try to keep your speed constant."

"Don't pull over seventy-five amps."

"When you pass the finish line on every lap, we want you to report to us over the walkie-talkie; we'll ask you to give us your readings." A walkie-talkie was strapped to the roll bar above the rearview mirror, so Katrina could reach out and hit the talk button when she needed to.

"Remember to keep drinking your water," Keith told her. "Take a sip every lap or two. It's going to be hot out there, and you're going to sweat a lot in that driver's suit and you don't want to get dehydrated."

Katrina was trying hard to remember everything everyone was telling her, and then suddenly there was a guy standing in front of her with a microphone.

Mark Potter was a seasoned race announcer, another person brought on by the organizers at Virginia Power and the raceway to give the EV Grand Prix all the flavor of a big-time NASCAR event. Potter had seen already that he'd have his work cut out for him; he was accustomed to adding his bit over the bone-rattling roar of a field of supercharged race cars screaming past the stands. In the range event coming up, sixteen soundless vehicles would be going fifty miles per hour, tops. For up to ninety minutes. So he decided to interview all the drivers and find out their strategies, their stories, whatever might give him some material to work with to fill those ninety minutes.

"So," said Potter, holding the microphone up to Katrina, "what's your strategy for this event?"

Katrina was afraid if she opened her mouth, if she said one thing, then everything she was trying to remember would fall out of her head.

"It's a secret," she managed.

Everyone laughed. Good strategy!

Katrina knew there had been snickering from some of the other teams when Anna Collier took the wheel for the efficiency event, a few charges rung on the theme of, "Oh, you've got *girls* driving that trash." Now Katrina would be driving, another girl and, what was more, probably the first black girl ever to drive on this track. *There* was a story for Mark Potter.

The teachers weren't trying to make any kind of point by picking girls to drive; girls were mostly who was available. Besides, Mr. Miller suspected that once you got one of those boys out on a race track, something was going to come over him and that pedal would hit the floor and soon enough there'd be one #10 white Ford Escort hatchback with a depleted battery pack, sitting by the side while the other cars passed by. Girls, thought Harold, would listen. They would stick to the plan.

Zipped into the driving suit, Katrina was feeling woozy already, though whether it was the heat or her nerves she wasn't sure. The track seemed to have grown until it was a thousand miles long. Everyone on the team was counting on her, and she was scared to death.

"Oh, Mr. Ryan," she whispered, "I'm going to cry."

"Don't you cry, Katrina, you're going to do great," he said.

"I think I need to pray," Katrina said, dropping to her knees by the side of the car. She wasn't even sure what she was praying for. Strength? Courage? Fortitude? Maybe all of those.

Unsteadily, she got to her feet again, feeling a little bit better, and then she hitched herself through the window opening and wriggled into Shocker's driver's seat. Though the doors all worked—that had been one of the many elements checked in the safety inspection—the rules allowed the teams to pin the doors with a cotter key for the competition, to eliminate any chance of them coming open. With the doors pinned, however, Katrina had been required in the escape test to prove she could get out of the driver restraints and exit through the window in under five seconds. Fortunately, she was so small and skinny that the worst she'd risked in that exercise was bumping her head, though she'd practiced the escape time after time back in North Carolina, just to make sure she could do it fast.

With the fire suit, driving boots, and a helmet, Katrina just tipped the scales at one hundred pounds. When they strapped her into the five-point harness, she could barely twitch.

"Don't stop until you see the checkered flag," said Mr. Ryan.

Some of the boys started pushing Shocker out to where the cars were lining up. The rest of the team came along as well, carrying buffing cloths to give a final wipe to any stray fingerprints or dust, and jogging along smartly with their ton-and-a-half Escort.

When they came to a halt, Darrell Parker let his hands rest on Shocker just a moment more. Now he was laying on those hands in supplication for the kind of power that a battery pack couldn't give you. They had all come so far together, thought Darrell, it didn't hurt to offer a quick thank-you and to ask God to watch over them just a little longer.

Range wasn't a race, and the drivers were forbidden to draft off other vehicles, so the EVs processed out in a stately line, one behind the other, onto the track, and slowly accelerated up to speed for a lap. Glenvar High School's cheerleaders were the loudest things on the field at the moment. Then the green flag came down, the range event was officially under way, and everyone cheered and hooted the drivers off.

Strapped into Shocker's driver's seat, Katrina understood that her job for the next ninety minutes, or as long as Shocker lasted, was to STICK TO THE PLAN, and the plan was to maintain her speed, in third gear, as closely as possible to a steady forty-three miles per hour.

During the first few laps, all the other instructions she'd been given whirled around in her head in a confusing, panicky blur, although she did remember to find the line Keith had told her about, to stay in the second groove coming through turns one and two.

Intuitively, the plan didn't make sense; right off, Katrina could see that with each lap Shocker was taking a progressively longer route than the other cars that were dropping down to hug the tightest line through the inner edge of those turns. Some of those other cars had already opened up a wide gap in front of Katrina, a half-circuit or more.

Katrina discovered too late that the side mirrors were adjusted at the wrong angle, and with the helmet and the five-point harness she could barely turn her head anyway, so all she could see was the track ahead and the vehicles directly in front of her moving steadily farther away from her. Then something would move into her field of vision—another car pulling even and then surging ahead. She fought the urge to try to keep up, to push the accelerator down just a little more. She wouldn't question Mr. Ryan's and Mr. Miller's wisdom now. "Stick to the plan."

She was coming around the turn in the sixth lap, starting to relax into her job, her heart not beating so wildly as it had been, her breathing not so fast. The instructions were starting to sort themselves out in her mind, and she could remember again when she was supposed to check the meters, when she was supposed to report in to Mr. Miller over the walkie-talkie with her readings. Then, out of the corner of her eye she noticed some kind of motion. Stealing a quick glance over at the passenger seat, Katrina saw her water bottle rolling onto the floor.

"No!" she said, with that feeling you have in a nightmare, when everything unfolds in slow-motion horror.

The bottle had gone irretrievably beyond her reach. Immediately, she felt twice as hot as she had a minute before. A new wave of panic washed over her. The other cars were still swishing past her. She was going to lose *and* she was going to die of dehydration.

"Mr. Miller," she said into the walkie-talkie. "I lost my water bottle!"

"What?"

"I LOST my WATER BOTTLE! It rolled under the seat!"

"Well just keep driving," said Mr. Miller.

"But Mr. Edwards said I need to drink water. I'm hot and I'm already thirsty."

"You'll be OK. Think cool thoughts. Swallow your spit. You're doing great!"

Doing great? Everyone was passing her!

"Everyone's passing me, Mr. Miller," she protested.

"Just stick to the plan, Katrina," he said reassuringly. "Don't you worry about those other cars."

Don't worry—that was easy for him to say. *He* wasn't driving in this hot car, and dying, and getting passed right and left.

Lord, she was hot. The driver's suit was hot. The helmet squashing her hair against her head was hot. The air streaming through the safety netting in the window was hot, and loud too. Think cool thoughts. Think cool thoughts. Thinkcoolthoughtscool thoughtscoolthoughts.

Still, her foot stayed steady on the accelerator. She finished another loop around the track, crossed the start/finish line, and reported her readings: amp meter, speedometer, kilowatt-hour meter. The other vehicles kept passing her.

"You're doing great, fantastic, Katrina!" said Mr. Miller.

Hours, years, entire centuries seemed to be ticking past from where Katrina was sitting. Every lap took longer than forever. The track was a tunnel of roadway in front of her eyes, and her mouth was so dry it felt as though she'd been eating sand, blotting paper, Styrofoam. But still her foot stayed steady, and around and around she went.

In grandstands built for seventy-five thousand, the spectators at the EV Grand Prix—at most, a few hundred—were sprinkled lightly in an area clustered above the start/finish line. It was so quiet, you could hear the metal grandstands creaking as they expanded with the heat. Most of the members of the various teams had remained down on the infield, watching from Pit Road, many of them standing on the low concrete wall, monitoring the progress of their vehicles. For the first few laps, everyone was cheering, but after a while people's attention started to drift.

The rules for the range event required the cars to maintain speeds between forty and fifty miles per hour. Lap after lap the cars rolled along virtually silently, but for the hum of their tires, at roughly suburban thoroughfare speed, and from a spectator's point of view, "This is about as exciting as watching a submarine race," cracked Mark Potter from the announcer's booth. Ninety minutes is a long, long time to watch silent vehicles go around in a circle.

Potter knew that people came to car races to be entertained. They wanted to have fun. They wanted a good show. If an electric car competition wasn't going to give the audience the zoom-and-vroom excitement they'd get at a NASCAR or local dirt-track race, there wasn't any reason, thought Potter, why they still couldn't have a good time. So he filled in with his own sound effects, a "RRRROOOOAARRR" as a car came through a turn, and he cracked jokes, and if one car started easing past another he'd announce it with all the pitched drama of a closely contested last lap of the Daytona 500.

And the cars went around, and around, and around.

Norfolk Technical's pickup dropped out first. Thomas Jefferson's Escort was back on the track again after the team had worked over the transmission, but soon it was out, along with A. R. Burton's Chevy Spectrum.

An electronic lap board rose up over the infield on a towering pole, and it tracked the leader's progress. Eighteen. Nineteen. Twenty. In the infield, John Parker was perched on a lawn chair with a clipboard in his lap, and every time Katrina finished another circuit and reported her readings, Harold or Eric would pass them on to John, who would run calculations to make sure everything was going according to plan, to make sure the readings stayed in synch with the averages they'd pulled driving the roads of Northampton County. From the information collected on those test drives, they had decided they could bet on getting eleven kilowatt-hours out of the batteries, which at fifty miles per hour, should take the car forty-four miles. If Katrina dropped the speed just a little, kept it steady at forty-three, they hoped she could take it even farther.

By now, Katrina was down by three laps from the leading cars; if she slowed by even a fraction, the race officials would probably try to pull her, waving that dreaded black flag at her. But Katrina was doing a remarkable job at keeping the speed at forty-three miles per hour. "Eggfoot Deloatch," Mr. Miller was calling her as Shocker swept through the turns, still holding the line on the track that Keith Edwards had told her about.

Harold had delegated some of the students, teachers, parents, and other supporters as spotters; each was assigned one of the competitor's vehicles, to track its position and speed and how many laps completed—and to announce if it dropped out. More vehicles were starting to show signs of incipient battery depletion, their speeds drifting slower and slower until they sank below the forty-mile-per-hour bottom limit required to continue running in the range event and pulled off the track. The spotters started reporting in. "Jefferson's out." "Shenandoah Valley's out."

In Shocker, Katrina was so busy feeling hot and paying attention to her meters and her speed and her line, and hoping she wouldn't pass out with dehydration, that she'd stopped caring too much about the other vehicles that passed her. When she couldn't see as many cars ahead of her, she figured soon enough they'd be coming up from behind and lapping her again.

In the announcer's booth, Mark Potter was feeling the strain of livening up this event as car after car simply drifted out of contention and pulled off. It was like watching sediment settle in a pond.

In the infield, Harold and Eric and the others waited anxiously as the forty-four-mile mark drew closer and closer. There was no indication that Shocker was losing steam, but they were reaching the theoretical outer limit of the car's range, and there were still a number of vehicles on the track. Forty miles ticked past. Forty-two. Forty-five. Fifty. Shocker kept going.

John Parker was updating the figures with every lap. It looked as though the car definitely was giving better performance on the track than in the rough-and-ready testing they had put it through on the road in front of East. They were getting closer to five miles than four to the kilowatt-hour.

More vehicles were dropping by the wayside, and now everyone on the ECORV team was riveted to Shocker's progress around the track, yelling "Go Katrina!" every time she passed by Pit Road.

For the moment, Jennifer put aside her disappointment in the oral presentation and joined in cheering Katrina. After all, Shocker was truly the product of all their efforts, and maybe it would be best if their victory was one that all of them together could lay claim to, that came like this, in front of the entire field of competitors, with everyone watching.

They hadn't won yet, though.

Harold's walkie-talkie crackled to life.

"Mr. Miller, what's going on?" came Katrina's plaintive voice. "I can't see any other cars anymore."

"Don't worry, Katrina, just hold your pace."

"I really need some water."

"Keep thinking those cool thoughts."

"Mr. Miller, tell Mr. Ryan if I don't die out here I want an A in his class."

Harold turned to Eric, laughing. "She wants an A in your class. Tell her she can have an A."

"Tell her she can keep studying hard!" said Eric.

"And I want a whole pizza too," said Katrina.

"You're part of the team, you get a slice just like everyone else," said Harold.

"OK, I want to talk to my daddy," she said.

Harold handed the walkie-talkie to Pershield Deloatch, who was beaming.

"Just keep talking to her to keep her driving," Harold said. "Tell her anything to keep her in that car."

Katrina's father said the first thing that came to mind. "Baby, if you win, I'm going to buy you a new car."

That had to beat a pizza.

First one then another of the remaining vehicles slowed and peeled off. Even Virginia Power's electric pace car had long since given its last. There were now only two vehicles. Shocker against the

#33 Dodge Colt wagon from Hermitage. Hermitage of the hay-baling crack.

Then there was only one. Hermitage was out. Shocker was alone on the track.

"Go, go, go Katrina!" screamed her teammates, and her father loudest of all.

"This is the first time I've ever announced a race that only had one car on the track," said Mark Potter over the loudspeaker.

By now, people from the other teams were cheering Katrina too, but with the helmet on and the wind racketing through the open window she couldn't hear them, and her eyes were still focused on the track ahead of her. Katrina thought graduation, a couple of birthdays, and the turn of the millennium must have come and gone in the time she'd been out there, and where were all the other cars? They must be right at the opposite corner of the track, she thought, going through the turns at the same pace she was, so she could never see them.

Seventy-nine laps. Eighty. Shocker passed the sixty-mile mark and left it behind.

Eighty-one laps. Eighty-two. Who knows what God thinks of with an entire universe to watch over? But as the car Darrell Parker had laid hands on, with the driver who had prayed for courage she didn't feel went on and on, around and around, steady and measured, Darrell thought, "Just look at the mighty hands of the Lord."

"Yeah, let's go, let's go!" he yelled with Doug Miller every time Katrina went past.

Eighty-three laps. Eighty-four. The ECORV kids were screaming themselves hoarse.

"That car's like the Energizer bunny," said Mark Potter, a little resignedly. "It keeps going and going."

At last, the checkered flag was waving. Ninety minutes was up.

A huge wave of relief washed over Katrina. She had made it. She had done her job. "Oh, thank you, now I can get something to drink."

Tears streamed down John Parker's face. Eric leaped, shrieking maniacally, into a startled Pershield Deloatch's arms—a very Mr. Ryan moment that would be captured on film and printed in the Roanoke Rapids *Daily Herald,* thus subjecting Mr. Deloatch to considerable ribbing from his correctional charges. Harold and his son Doug were waving their hats madly in the air and yelling. Everyone on the ECORV team was running toward where Katrina, still under power, was bringing the car in to Pit Road.

Katrina looked up startled to see the whole team running at her. She stopped the car and unbuckled her harness, wondering what was going on. In a moment everyone surrounded the car, screaming and yelling. Erick Vann grabbed her out of the car, and he and Katrina's father lifted her up on their shoulders.

Katrina, hot and exhausted and so thirsty, thinking only about getting some water, couldn't follow what everyone was yelling about. Then a microphone was thrust in her face and someone was asking her, "So how does it feel to be the winner?"

Katrina looked around, smiling uncertainly. Mr. Ryan was jumping up and down—but he was always jumping up and down—and someone was yelling, "Eighty-five laps! Eighty-five laps!" and someone else was shouting, "You won!"

Finally, she understood. She'd won. Won the event, for the team. Stunned with happiness, smiling jubilantly, still all she could think to say was, "Can I have some water?"

Shocker had traveled nearly sixty-four miles, the final nine laps all alone, and there was charge remaining in the batteries. Shocker had won the range event by miles.

The media covering the Grand Prix descended on the team.

"The jackrabbit," said Harold to the cameras, with a satisfied smile, "don't always win the race."

They asked Katrina how it felt to make a piece of history, to be the first black female ever to win an event on a NASCAR track. She told them what she honestly thought.

"I was just driving for my school," she said.

KICKING AMPS

D riving back to the hotel for the evening, the kids were splayed out in the van, hot and exhausted from the day, drained by the emotional energy they'd poured into their hours at the track. They were still bubbling over their range victory, though, happily rehashing their memories to each other.

"Did you see it when . . . ?" and "You should have heard Mr. Miller . . . ," and "I couldn't believe it when we were the only ones left out there."

They talked over the design judging too, and the *Wizard of Ohms* cast members recounted their travails.

"Y'all don't know, it was just so awful, we were saying anything we could think of," said Jennifer, still mournful.

The rest of the team assured them it couldn't have been *that* bad.

Said Jennifer and Kelly and Donny, "No, it was worse!"

At the track that morning, the oral presentation team members were much too absorbed in preparing for their event to take note of the results of the design competition, while Darrell and Ivory and the boys who'd worked hard on building the car, like Corey and Tim, were too caught up in the design judging to track what was going on with the oral presentation in the media center, and then everyone ended up totally focused on the range event and the team's win there.

With everything going on, somehow most of the students had managed to come away not knowing that they had finished the day in second place. They trailed Raleigh County now by less than a single point.

But Erick Vann, thinking back over the day and putting it all together, realized with happy surprise, "Man, we're killing them."

The teachers knew too. They were keeping tally, but quietly, not wanting to make a big deal of it and add to the pressure on the students. If Raleigh County hadn't taken such a huge lead yesterday with efficiency, ECORV would already have trounced the competition today. On the one hand, their success so far confirmed everything they'd always believed about what their students could do if only they had the opportunity, and on the other hand, frankly they couldn't believe it at all. And they were so happy that they didn't care what happened tomorrow. All right, they did care, they cared a great deal, but the team didn't have to win. If there was anything they needed to prove—to the doubters back in North Carolina, to the people who discounted them just because their schools were poor and didn't have the obvious material resources that some others did—they'd already proved it.

That didn't stop Eric from rolling down his window when they pulled up to a stoplight on the way back to the hotel, and yelling across to the Parkers in their car, stopped next to Eric's truck.

"You know what?" Eric shouted over the noise of the traffic. "I think we could win this thing!"

That evening, the teachers sat the kids down for a team meeting.

All the students looked exhausted and frazzled from nervous energy, from the long, hot day, from the effort they'd been putting in, from blowing everyone else away in the range event. But they hung on every word as Mr. Miller and Mr. Ryan explained their position.

"We came up here wanting to do our best," said Mr. Miller, "and we've done our best."

"And right now," said Mr. Ryan, "We're in second place."

That caused a little buzz—even for the kids who'd figured as much, suddenly, with Mr. Ryan saying it, it seemed real.

Tomorrow they would have Keith, an experienced competitor, behind the wheel. There was a good chance they could hold their position at the top.

Mr. Miller and Mr. Ryan didn't say "win." Tomorrow's final event of the five, acceleration and handling, would favor the leader, Raleigh County, and the little Geo Metro that team was driving. Shocker probably had five hundred pounds on the Metro, which would make it pretty unlikely that the Escort could outdo the smaller car in a drag race or a timed slalom course. Holding on to second place, though, that looked within ECORV's reach.

Mr. Miller said, "We're going to be tough to beat, unless we do something stupid. So let's try not to do something stupid."

Later that night, after the kids had been packed off to their rooms, Eric, sitting on his bed, started calling his friends, the other TFA teachers back in North Carolina.

"Look," he said, "if you're free tomorrow, you should come up here. You're not going to believe this, but we are totally in the thick of this. I don't know that we're going to win—there's a little Geo Metro in first place, and it's going to give us some competition, but I think we're really going to do something."

After hanging up from the last call, he sat for a while longer, feeling strangely unmoored. Change the course of his life, he had thought half-jokingly when he applied to Teach for America. In barely a couple of months his two years would be up; he would go back to California. That was the plan, right? Back to his "real" life? And yet he wondered if anything had ever meant so much to him, so deeply, as the time he'd spent in North Carolina and the way this bunch of kids—the ones he was going to have to go down the hall in a minute to tell to be quiet and go to sleep—looked when the car they built crossed the finish line and won today.

Saturday, Day 3:

Acceleration and handling was scheduled for Saturday morning. The race, the crowd-pleaser, was scheduled for the afternoon as the Grand Prix's grand finale, but the race was just for fun. There was a one-thousand-dollar prize for the winner, which wasn't nothing, but the outcome had no bearing on winning the Grand Prix itself. Acceleration and handling would make that determination.

Keith Edwards was enjoying the warm April morning, getting his head centered, and looking forward to his chance to drive, to have some fun. Racing an Escort, true, but he wasn't going to complain on that point. He was going to be driving at Richmond International Raceway.

Neither Harold nor Eric had mentioned to Keith that the entire competition, win or lose, had come down to one event, the one Keith would be driving in a few minutes. Later, long after Richmond was behind them, it would occur to Keith that this oversight might not have been an accident on the two teachers' parts. In fact, he would suspect that it had been an altogether deliberate strategy, keeping Keith in the dark. Because somehow no one had bothered yet to tell Keith that score was being kept, that there was anything to be won or lost, anything on the line but possibly a trophy and warm feelings all around. He thought everyone was here simply to have fun and see how the electric vehicles performed.

Eric was worried. He knew they had only a slim chance of winning; all Raleigh would have to do was hold its lead, but Shocker would have to outperform the Metro to pull ahead, and that, Eric thought, wasn't very likely. Still, there was that chance, and every little thing would matter in this final event. The slightest misjudgment, a second's hesitation. Hermitage, now in third, would get a shot at first place only if ECORV and Raleigh both blew it.

Eric watched Raleigh's run. He had to know. In time that seemed to stretch for minutes, rather than the few seconds it actually took, the Geo shot forward and ran to the end of the acceleration course, neither a spectacular nor an inadequate performance. Enough, presumably, to hold a lead. Then the driver lined the car up for the handling test, a slalom through orange cones. The Geo dodged and weaved, taking the turns neatly, its compact size serving it well.

The car was nearly through the course.

"He missed a cone!" cried Eric.

The Geo had fishtailed right at the end, not a lot, but enough to throw off the driver and bring the car in at least a couple of seconds off the mark. It wasn't much, but it was enough. The proverbial window of opportunity had just opened for the team from northeastern North Carolina.

"*Oh. My. Lord,*" thought Ryan, feeling at this moment nothing short of completely astonished. "If Keith pulls this off, we're there. We're there."

Keith had no idea.

He was in the car, the boys pushing him to the start. When the officials gave him the signal to go when ready, he eyed his path, took a quick breath, and hit the accelerator.

Shocker whooshed down the makeshift drag strip, straight and true. Aerodynamically speaking, the Escort took its inspiration from cement blocks and Brinks trucks, but Miller and his team had done what they could with what they had. Maybe the plastic shield they'd run down the front and under the belly made that fraction of a difference. Maybe it mattered the way they'd set the hatchback to latch while holding barely open, to let out through the back the air coming in from the open windows. Competition is always about finding that infinitesimal edge.

One-eighth of a mile doesn't last long with the accelerator to the floor, even in a lead-bellied Escort. Keith came to the end and lined himself up to wait for the signal for the second part, the handling test.

Things you learned years ago can come in handy one day in ways you never would have anticipated. In college Keith had roomed with a bunch of athletes, and he'd learned a surprising amount from them about eye-hand coordination. To get through the handling course, Keith knew he was going to need that skill. You couldn't think through each turn: the body had to respond almost automatically to what the eyes observed.

He dove in to the course, working the brake with his left foot and the accelerator with his right, as he was accustomed to doing on the track, steering as much with his feet as his hands to make the vehicle do what he wanted it to do and go where he wanted to make it go. Shocker surprised him; if it was not the most graceful of cars, somehow it hit every turn just right and popped out the end of the slalom without so much as threatening a single cone.

The kids cheered Keith as he climbed out of the car. He grinned at them, traded a couple of high-fives, then let them take over the car to push it back to the garage stall, while he wandered off contentedly to the catering tent for some lunch.

There was minor pandemonium in the ECORV stall in the garage. The kids knew about Raleigh's spin-out now. They knew what that meant.

"Have we won, Mr. Miller? Have we won, Mr. Ryan?"

"We've done our best and that's what counts," said Harold, which wasn't really what the students wanted to hear at that point. "Done our best" was yesterday's plan. But all Mr. Miller would tell them was that they'd have to wait until the officials posted the acceleration and handling final scores.

"Then we'll see," said Mr. Miller.

No one was hungry for lunch. The whole team hung by the scoreboard, waiting.

The numbers were going up. First place for the event, Central Shenandoah (the Z-car!) Second place, a three-way tie between Reading-Muhlenberg, Northern Vance, and A. R. Burton. Where was Raleigh? Where was ECORV?

Raleigh was . . . ninth? 16.9 points. They scanned the board; where was the score for Shocker?

There.

19.3 points.

They had beaten Raleigh.

Everyone on the team looked at each other in silence, as if none of them dared to say it.

"Did we just . . . ?" someone ventured.

"We won. WE WON!"

How could that be? Had they miscounted a score somewhere? Was it possible? They were afraid to believe it. They started adding up all the numbers again. The numbers came out the same. First place in the EV Grand Prix by just under two points.

Keith Edwards was sitting down with his barbecue sandwich in the shade of the tent when a handful of the ECORV students came crowding up around him. Having met most of them only in the last few days, Keith was still vague on all their names, but he motioned to the seats around him in a welcoming gesture.

The kids, however, were on a mission, and it wasn't barbecue.

"Keith," said one, urgently, "if you win this race, we might get to go to Phoenix, Arizona."

"What . . . ?" said Keith, not following.

"We're pretty sure we've won!" said another student.

"*Won?*" thought Keith. "Won what?" he asked.

"The competition," said the first student, not quite impatiently, but with a tone that implied, "What else would we be talking about?" But of course, this was news to Keith, that there *was* a competition.

And now, continued the student, there was a grand prize, "Best of Show," for best overall performance in all events including the race. If Keith won the race, the team would receive the race prize of one thousand dollars and on top of that the Best of Show award, which was a three-thousand-dollar challenge grant to help the team take the car to the APS 500 in Phoenix next spring.

The challenge grant was a detail about the competition the ECORV team had never bothered to pay attention to before, because to win it would require pulling in the highest possible combined rankings both in the overall competition and the race—a scenario that until about twenty minutes ago the team had considered so unlikely that it wasn't worth thinking about, a possibility so far beyond the students' ken that it didn't even register, like the GDP of Botswana.

As for Keith, his head whirled briefly with this sudden input of information. Prizes. Phoenix. Winning. Five minutes ago he'd been thinking this was all a fun and friendly adventure at the track, and now suddenly thousands of dollars and whether or not these kids got a shot at taking their car all the way to Arizona depended on what he did in this race.

It was starting to seem to Keith as though every time he turned around this week there was something else in store for him. If Ricky Rudd drove up now and asked him if he'd like a berth on the real #10's pit crew, Keith would consider it an entirely plausible turn of events.

He'd lost his appetite for barbecue. He walked off to focus his head and keep calm. No point in getting a case of the nerves now— it wasn't as though he hadn't planned on doing his best anyway.

The first goal he would have to accomplish, he knew, would be to place among the top finishers in one of the two fifteen-lap qualifying heats among which all the vehicles had been divided; the higher he placed, the better his positioning would be for the race to come. Then he'd have twenty laps in the final event to take the lead over the other vehicles. All he needed to do was come out ahead at the finish line.

Last night at dinner, Harold had said to him, "Keith, I don't care if you bring me nothing but that steering wheel as long as you cross that finish line first."

Keith didn't take Harold too seriously, but poor Darrell Worley from North Carolina Power absolutely blanched, protesting, "This is supposed to be a friendly race!"

The unknown element in strategizing for this event wasn't how fast he could make the car go but how far he could make it go fast. Eric and Harold had already explained to him that repeated bouts of acceleration would sap the batteries faster; getting that ton-and-a half of lead and steel up to speed demanded relatively more energy than maintaining that speed. Like Katrina, ideally Keith would find a line that would let him hold his speed as steady as possible. Unlike Katrina, though, Keith knew he couldn't win by letting himself get lapped. And unlike Katrina, Keith wouldn't be working with a fully charged battery pack, either. All he'd have to race on was whatever was left over after the morning's acceleration and handling events *and* the qualifying heat. The whole setup felt vaguely like one of those word problems from high school math where you had to solve for *X*, and here *X* was what, dear Lord, was Keith Edwards going to do to win this thing for those kids?

Keith pulled Eric Ryan and Harold Miller aside and said, "What do I need to know to win this race?"

The three of them headed over to Shocker, Keith sat in the driver's seat, and they went over every gauge and every meter. They even made up a cheat sheet in case Keith forgot any details under the pressure of the race.

As soon as Eric and Harold and the other teachers had realized not only that their team was probably going to win the Grand Prix but also that they were now in a position to take the Best of Show award, that "Let's get to Richmond" might be about to turn into "Let's get to Phoenix," immediately, they'd sat down with John Parker and their calculators and tried to figure out what kind of speed they could pull out of Shocker, taking into account that Keith would have to finish well in the fifteen-lap qualifying heat and still have enough left in the batteries to crank it up in the final race. They settled on fifty-five miles per hour in fourth gear for Keith to target. That would pull about 220 amps, which they thought could probably sustain the car through all thirty-five laps. They hoped.

"Whatever you do," said Harold to Keith, "watch that amp meter. You go over four hundred amps and you're going to be out of the race fast."

One of the students standing by said, "Mr. Miller, don't put pressure on him!"

Keith made a couple of adjustments of his own liking to Shocker. He checked the lug nuts on all the wheels. He raised the pressure above the recommended limit on the left-side tires that would be on the "downslope" side on the track, and lowered the pressure on the right, "upslope" side. Raising the pressure might give Keith an advantage in the race. It also might give him a blown tire. Racing meant taking those calculated risks, trying to find your edge.

Keith wouldn't call himself a "car guy." Fiddling around with engines had never particularly captured his interest. What he liked about racing, he'd say, was holding a steering wheel and pushing on an accelerator and seeing how fast he could turn left. No matter how worried or distracted or excited he might be beforehand, the minute he pulled a helmet over his head, buckled himself into a race car, and put his hands on the wheel, he slipped into an intensely focused calm. Some people might think you'd get all nervy and jumpy and hyped up, but Keith was at his most relaxed when he was behind the wheel on a track. He didn't think about work or whether he'd left the iron plugged in at home. He drove intuitively, letting the race reveal itself to him through the feel of the tires on the track and the wheel under his hands and the pull in the turns.

Today, though, he couldn't put out of his mind that he would be on the track at Richmond International Raceway. How many people ever got an opportunity like this? The pros, yes, but regular people like him? Never, except for now, and for Keith, it had all happened so fast, the call from Carol Lowe and meeting Harold and Eric and coming to Richmond, that he had barely managed to register what he was getting himself into.

Now he was facing a once-in-a-lifetime chance to win a race here. But try not to think about that.

For both of the qualifying heats, the vehicles would line up on Pit Road, follow the pace car out onto the track, and then have about two-thirds of a lap to get up to speed before they crossed the starting line and the green flag signaled the official launch of the race.

Keith gave a wave to the kids, then everyone backed off behind the low wall between Pit Road and the infield, and the vehicles rolled off. Edwards heard the cheering behind him as he and the other drivers on the track started accelerating.

Compared to the breakneck speeds and fender-to-fender maneuvering Keith was accustomed to from mini-stock racing, the wide-open RIR track dotted with a handful of competitors could have been a Sunday drive. In any race, for Keith, each lap took forever, time and the world narrowing to the moment he was in. Today, it seemed, forever took even longer. No one was pushing too hard, all the drivers trying to conserve energy for the final race.

Keith cruised easily through the fifteen laps, following the same line Katrina had taken through the turns, keeping an eye on the amp meter and keeping his speed as steady as possible. He passed Raleigh County in the sixth lap and took first place comfortably, to the accompaniment of a sustained chorus of whooping and cheering from the ECORV team, and when Eric checked Shocker's kilowatt meter, it looked as though there was still plenty of juice left in the batteries.

When both qualifying events were done, the field was lined up on the track for the final race. Shocker was sitting on the front row with the first-place finisher from the other heat.

Waiting for the race to start, everyone with ECORV kept suffering moments of doubt. Had they really won the Grand Prix? Did they really have a chance at going to Arizona, of all places? Nothing official had been announced yet.

On the track, Keith had used those fifteen laps in the qualifying heat to get comfortable with all the little variables, like the angle coming through the turns, the way the car handled out there, and how speed and amp draw balanced.

When the green flag went down, though, he was the war horse at the sound of the bugle, tearing off down the track with the rest of the pack. It took him a lap or two to realize he'd better settle down and remember his strategy and watch how he used his energy.

In the driver's meeting that morning, the race officials had cautioned, "We'd prefer you not draft if you're not an experienced race driver."

Keith decided he was an experienced race driver. He'd done speeds twice this fast in far more crowded conditions. He drafted, nestling up close to the lead car.

Every now and then the walkie-talkie would crackle with Harold Miller saying, "Keith, you might be making that other car nervous." Really, Harold had been joking with that crack about crossing the finish line with nothing but the steering wheel. But Keith hung on. That was racing.

The casualties began mounting after only a few laps, as the first of the vehicles burned through their batteries and drifted out of contention.

On the sidelines, the faint, whining swoosh of the cars as they passed by was entirely drowned out by the ever-louder screaming from the spectators, and in particular from the Shocker cheering section. The members of the ECORV team were shouting as much from sheer disbelief as excitement; how had they gotten this far, within a few laps of going to Phoenix, when they'd come hoping simply not to embarrass themselves?

On the track, Keith kept checking the amp meter and the kilo-watt-hour meter. The drafting was paying off, the amp readings were holding within the range Harold had given him and he'd con-served energy well. Closing in on the last couple of laps, Keith was ready to make his move. He pulled out, put the pedal down, and set his sights for the finish.

One lap to go. Half a lap. Keith was holding a three-quarter lap lead. He got cocky. He coasted the last quarter-lap.

The checkered flag came down.

"Northampton High School–East.

And again, "Northampton High School–East."

And again.

The kids felt as though they must have been standing in the winner's circle forever, and that it could never be long enough. Over and over the team was called, the trophies were handed out, pictures were snapped.

And then they were holding it in their hands, the prize, the one Mr. Miller had promised them a lifetime ago, in September.

"We're going to build us an electric car," he'd said, "and we're going to win that competition."

After the scores had come in on Friday, Mr. Joyner made a special trip to K-mart. And after the team stood in the winner's circle and accepted their grand prize and their Best of Show, Mr. Joyner sauntered up to that teacher from Hermitage Technical Center, the one who'd made the crack Wednesday about baling hay. Mr. Joyner handed the Hermitage teacher a newly purchased pair of pliers and a spool of wire.

"This is from the hay-bale and tractor people," said Mr. Joyner.

When Eric finally made it home to the house in George, the lights were on, and there was plenty of food on the table and a big group of Eric's TFA friends were cheering him in the door, celebrating the success of the project.

The kitchen door smacked open. The boisterous Helen Lennon, another TFA, burst into the room, whooping.

"Whoo-hoo," she cried out, giving Eric a high-five. "Guess you know what you're doing next year!"

"I do?" said Eric. "What?"

"Dude," she said, "You're staying. You know you are. You can't leave now."

She was right, of course. As soon as she said it, he knew that he had known it already. He wasn't leaving. He wasn't going back to California. Nothing could tear him away now.

They had a team and a car and three thousand dollars.

They had to get to Phoenix.

EPILOGUE

E lectrifying!" the Roanoke Rapids *Sunday Herald* would trumpet the following day, page one, above the fold, followed by a second page-one story on Monday. "Shocker zaps competition!" the next issue of the *Northampton News* would cheer, with a full page and a half devoted to the story and photos, pictures of Katrina and Keith on the shoulders of their teammates, and the victorious team members together in the winner's circle, each holding up a finger to signal "Number 1!"

In the months that followed, Harold, Eric, the students, and the other teachers enjoyed a ruckus of euphoria and recognitions, an extended victory lap through North Carolina and beyond. The team was celebrated for its determination, for defying the odds and refusing to believe it couldn't succeed.

The kids said they were happy to be known, for once, for something besides coming from one of the poorest counties in North Carolina. Katrina told an interviewer, "This gives us a chance to say, 'Hey, guess what? We're on the map. We're up to date, and we even understand technology.'"

The students took the car to Washington, D.C., where U.S. senators and congressional representatives looked it over. On the way,

Harold and Darrell made up a song about Shocker, to the tune of the popular hit *Lean on Me*, with Anna scribbling down the lyrics. They sang it and sang it until several other students suggested they might strangle the twins on the next refrain. None of them could stop humming it.

Shocker went to the state fair. Shocker went to a Native American pow-wow with Ivory Richardson. Shocker went to the Airmold plant with George Hawkins so everyone could see what he'd been working on all this time, and Shocker went to the Murfreesboro Watermelon Festival. A ride was the prize in a raffle held by June Parker's women's group to raise funds for the team's Phoenix attempt; delightedly, the winner, the venerable senior member of the club, let Eric Ryan scoop her up and slip her through the roll bars and into the passenger seat.

Students at the four high schools who had spent the last school year rolling their eyes and demanding of their ECORV friends, "What y'all want to go wasting your time with some electric car for?" now wanted to know, "How do I get on the team?" And a region long accustomed to shrugging off a reputation defined by statistics of poverty and underperformance suddenly found itself celebrated for the ingenuity and innovation of a group of its own kids.

In addition to the money and grants from the EV Grand Prix, the team won a two-thousand-dollar "Northampton Excellence" award, a two-thousand-dollars grant from Sprint telephone, and a ten-thousand-dollar "Spirit of Kitty Hawk" award from the North Carolina Technological Development Authority—half of that sum a challenge grant the team earned through raising an additional ten-thousand-dollars toward Phoenix.

There was never any question about whether they would go to Phoenix, or even if. Anything seemed possible after Richmond. But if in the first year it had been enough to build a car and get it to the competition, Phoenix would demand much more. In the EV Grand Prix all the teams were first-timers. In Phoenix the kids from North Carolina would go up against a field more than twice as large as the one they had faced in Richmond, schools from around the country and from Canada too, most of which had a lot more experience building electric vehicles. Richmond was two hours to the north. Phoenix was a long way across the country, which meant plane fares and shipping the EV thousands of miles out and back. And then Mr. Ryan decided they needed a second car too, because the scoring system in Phoenix, they learned, would favor a smaller, more nimble car. How about a Metro?

With Shocker, everything had been first-time guesswork. Could they build on what they'd learned with the Escort and at the EV Grand Prix to make a more elegant job of that second vehicle? Why not? The way the members of the ECORV team saw it, they had a reputation, a standard of performance to live up to, and that meant pushing the technology as far as a group of high-schoolers and the community behind them could make it go.

When the team arrived in Arizona, at the now-renamed APS Electrics, it came in the company of two vehicles, two different ECORV entries in the competition: Shocker I, the Escort, moderately fine-tuned, and Shocker II, a 1989 Geo Metro donated by Don Bullock Chevrolet in Rocky Mount and built for quick acceleration and reponsive handling. Shocker II ran on new-generation lead-acid batteries (that turned out to be unreliable and a pain), had a regenerative braking system that was supposed to route recharging power to the battery pack while the car was slowed (but they burned it out just before leaving for Arizona), and an electronic battery-monitoring system (that worked fine, at least).

In Phoenix, Harold and Darrell Parker sang the national anthem for the start of the events. Keith Edwards was there to drive again. Kelly Daughtry took on the oral presentation, dressing up like a farmer and delivering a can of Northampton County peanuts to each of the judges. Norman Joyner stayed up all night before the first day of competition, with Donny Lassiter and a technician from the Electrosource battery company, disassembling Shocker II and its battery pack and putting both back together, persuading the hotel kitchen manager to let them plug the car into one of the industrial stove 220-volt outlets.

When the final scores were tallied in Phoenix, the team from North Carolina proved that its victory at the inaugural EV Grand Prix was no fluke. Competing against thirty-seven other vehicles, Shocker II won the APS Electrics. They returned in triumph to North Carolina, to a state-police-escorted parade through the streets of Raleigh, ending up at the capital, where the governor rode in Shocker II, with Corey Powell, "The Prez," in the passenger seat, giving instructions. And then, a month later the team returned to Richmond for the second EV Grand Prix and won that too.

In the following year, Harold Miller and Eric Ryan launched a for-credit, integrated-curriculum Electric Vehicle Technologies class at East that students clamored to enroll in. The four-school consortium was dissolved and the team renamed Northampton Electric Auto Team (NEAT). In the spring, NEAT took first for design and third place overall at the APS Electrics, won in Richmond yet again, Mr. Ryan was named teacher of the year for Northampton County, and when fall came the team hosted the first Northampton Electric Vehicle Rally. Shocker III was built, a 1985 Ford Escort, and more top finishes followed in a growing number of electric vehicle competitions, including one launched by Carolina Power & Light called the EV Challenge. With technology grants, a solar charger for the vehicles, which doubled as an outdoor classroom for the study of solar-electric technologies, was built in front of Northampton–East. When the legendary "King of NASCAR," Richard Petty, stopped through Northampton County, even he took Shocker for a driver, memorably opining, "It don't make no racket." There were no more jokes around Northampton County, either about extension cords and golf carts; now when people saw Harold Miller they asked, "Can y'all build me one of those cars?"

Harold finally retired from teaching at Northampton–East in 1999. Almost immediately thereafter he accepted an invitation to help lead the EV Challenge. The Challenge had started as a small electric vehicle competition for schools within CP&L's North Carolina territory, but with the EV Grand Prix now unfortunately defunct— Virginia Power had taken over the event at just the moment when deregulation came in to shift the company's financial priorities to matters with a more immediate and discernible effect on the bottom line—schools that had caught the EV program bug were eager for something to take its place. The Challenge might fill the spot.

Harold joined the EV Challenge as assistant director; "Remember, I'm retired," he would say. But he would partner with a director he felt pretty confident he could work closely with—Eric Ryan.

After five years teaching at Northampton–East, Eric left to take up a fellowship at the Wright Center for Science Education at Tufts University in Boston, where, in a sense, the EV adventure began for Eric and Harold. Following his year at Tufts, Eric at last returned home to California and made plans to develop a practice as an educational consultant. But North Carolina wasn't ready to let go of him altogether yet. Soon enough, he was barnstorming around the South and beyond with Harold Miller, driving a natural gas-powered pickup and towing the EV Challenge mobile education trailer, with an electric Triumph Spitfire conversion loaded on board, seeking out high schools interested in participating in the program.

Over the next few years, until Harold really, really retired and Eric finally took up that life in California he'd been intending to return to for a decade, the two helped grow the EV Challenge to include more than forty schools, adding a middle-school program for which teams built miniature solar racers. For high school students, the Challenge awarded points toward victory not only for the design and performance of the EVs themselves, but also for raising the public and political profile of electric vehicles: take your congressional representative for a ride; get an article in the newspaper; show off your EV in the Christmas parade. Every year, the teams lined up at the start of the EV Challenge with increasingly sophisticated conversions, Porsches and pickups, Escorts and Accords, and Shenandoah Valley Governor's School still running that 1971 Datsun 240-Z it had driven at the first EV Grand Prix.

In the meantime, however, EVs were not faring well on the national scene. The battle against California's ZEV mandate had succeeded in eroding it piece by piece, and GM, whose electric Impact, renamed the EV-1, had never been made available beyond a very limited leasing market, continued to lead the fight.

In 1999 the U.S. government predicted that world oil demand would increase by 50 percent over the next two decades, driven largely by transportation needs. The number of vehicles and miles driven continued to increase. By 2003 there were more registered vehicles than licensed drivers in the United States, but thanks to the runaway popularity of SUVs, light trucks, and minivans, average new-vehicle fuel mileage had declined to about twenty miles per gallon, the lowest since 1980.

By 2004 the United States also was importing well over half of its oil supply. With five percent of the world's population, the nation was responsible for about one-quarter of world annual energy consumption.

As vehicles and miles driven continued going up, air quality was going down in places like North Carolina's rapidly growing Raleigh-Durham area. In the four-year period between 1998 and 2002, the average number of unhealthy ozone days there had increased by almost 50 percent over the previous four years' average. Nearly half of all Americans were breathing air considered unhealthy by the government's own standards, and the United States was pumping out roughly a quarter of the world's annual emissions of carbon, the leading suspect in global warming.

In the summer of 2003 the ZEV mandate was finally scrapped altogether. In lieu of the tens of thousands of zero-emission battery-electrics that had never materialized (thanks to the opponents' campaign of negative PR, lawsuits, and delay) the state would settle for cleaner-burning internal combustion vehicles, more gas-electric hybrids (innovated by Japanese automakers), and a push to develop hydrogen-fuel-cell electrics—a technology that even its promoters admitted was probably years, and quite possibly decades, from any possibility of broad, practical implementation.

In that same summer of 2003 GM demanded that all its EV-1s be returned, over the bitter protests of a loyal and vocal group of EV-1 drivers who didn't want to give up their cars. No matter, said GM. What little was left of the program was being ended. The vehicles would no longer be supported. GM's sustained disdain for its own product and the auto industry's continued insistence that no one wanted electrics, that they were too expensive, that the technology was hopeless, had assured that most Americans were never given an opportunity to decide for themselves, even to see an EV, much less take one for a drive.

In 2002, in the EV Challenge the Northampton–East team, driving Shocker III, a seventeen-year-old secondhand Escort conversion built by teenagers in a high school shop on a shoestring budget, traveled more than 110 miles. Harold Miller is still wondering why a bunch of high-school students can manage what the big car companies insist can't be done.

Harold Miller is still shaking his head, still saying, "It don't make sense."

In researching this book, I found these resources particularly helpful and informative:

The Web site Howstuffworks.com.

Build Your Own Electric Vehicle by Bob Brant (McGraw-Hill/TAB Books, 1994).

Convert It by Michael P. Brown with Shari Prange (Electro Automotive, 1993).

Taken for a Ride: Detroit's Big Three and the Politics of Pollution by Jack Doyle (Four Walls Eight Windows, 2000).

Taking Charge, The Electric Automobile in America by Michael Brian Schiffer (Smithsonian Institution Press, 1994).